Buttry, Daniel L.

Blessed Are the Peacemakers

To Linda!

You shared in some of this story, particularly the chapters on International Ministry.

Peace,

Read The Spirit Books

an imprint of
David Crumm Media, LLC
Canton, Michigan

For more information and further discussion, visit
www.BlessedAreThePeacemakers.info

Cover art and design by
Rick Nease
www.RickNease.com

Published By
Read The Spirit Books
an imprint of
David Crumm Media, LLC
42015 Ford Rd., Suite 234
Canton, Michigan, USA

For information about customized editions, bulk purchases or permissions, contact David Crumm Media, LLC at info@David-CrummMedia.com

Contents

Dedicated to

Ken Sehested, Wati Aier and Daniel Hunter

You have been wonderful friends and companions
on the journey of peace.
You have taught me many things
and challenged me to excellence.
Together we've engaged in some special
peacemaking mischief!

Introduction to the International Ministries Edition

Seeking Peace For Two Centuries
— A Great Cloud Of Witnesses

By Daniel Buttry and Reid Trulson

"I repent of whatever expressions or acts of my past life may have cherished the war spirit, in myself or others. I repent that I have so long delayed to enter my protest against the practice of war, by some overt act—a measure, which appears to be, in the present state of things, the indispensible duty of every Christian, and I resolve, that hereafter I will endeavor to diffuse the sentiments of peace, as far as lies in my power."

—Adoniram Judson to Massachu-setts Peace Society, May 9, 1821

The Judsons: Pioneer Peacemaking Missionaries

Adoniram and Ann Judson sail out of Salem Harbor

On July 13, 1813 Adoniram and Ann Judson arrived in Burma, having sailed from Salem, Massachusetts as Congregationalist missionaries. Anticipating meeting the British Baptist missionaries William Carey, Joshua Marshman and William Ward in India, the Judsons studied scripture concerning baptism during their four-month ocean journey. In the process, their understanding of baptism changed, leading them to be immersed as believers by Ward. Suddenly the Baptists in the United States discovered they had missionaries in Asia.

In 1814, Baptist delegates from eleven states and Washington, D.C. met in Philadelphia and organized the "Triennial Convention" (now known as American Baptist International Ministries) to support the Judsons and other missionaries who would follow in their footsteps. The following year, clergy and laypeople from a variety of denominations formed the Massachusetts Peace Society in Boston. After receiving several issues of the Society's journal, *Friend of Peace*, Adoniram Judson sent a letter from Burma in 1821 to become a member. He wrote, "Since war has been universally advocated and applauded by nearly all classes of men, it appears to me (without intending to reflect on those whose views may be different) that it is not optional with any to remain neutral or silent on this great question." He expressed the conviction that peace, Bible and missionary societies were "forming that threefold cord, which will ultimately bind all the families of man in universal peace and love."

Judson may have been acquainted with William Carey's peace views published in an earlier issue of *Friend of Peace*. Carey had written, "The great things which God, by His Spirit, is doing in the

United States, are truly astonishing, and call at once for the most grateful praises, and the most entire confidence in all His gracious promises. Among these things must be reckoned the missionary exertions now making; and the Peace Society lately established at New York, and other places; a society with whose object my heart most cordially coincides, and which must, through the Divine assistance, which will assuredly be granted, be finally successful in the accomplishment of its ultimate object." Soon both Carey and Judson would have their convictions tested.

Adoniram Judson

War broke out in 1824 between England and Burma leading the Burmese government to view all white foreigners with suspicion. Although they were Americans, Judson and fellow missionary Jonathan Price were seized as prisoners along with two Englishmen, a Scotsman, a Greek, two Armenians, and a Spaniard. Together they were thrown into the notorious "death-prison" in the capital Ava where they were fettered with heavy leg irons during twenty-one long months of captivity. At times the prisoners were hung upside down with their shoulders touching the floor. Ann had to bring the food to sustain Judson and others amid their deplorable conditions.

When the British army captured Rangoon and advanced up the Irrawaddy River, the Ava prisoners were marched twelve miles to another prison outside of Aungbinle. The spouses of the imprisoned missionaries feared the men would be executed or even sacrificed for the hopes of a Burmese victory. Soon, however, the Burmese king realized he needed interpreters to negotiate a peace agreement. Judson was released from prison under guard and became one of the interpreters, helping to negotiate and draft the treaty that ended the war in February, 1826. With the ending of the war, Adoniram and Ann Judson continued their pioneering mission work.

Peacemaking in the Early Years of Baptist Missions

Judson was not alone in understanding peacemaking and nonviolence to be part of the overall witness for Jesus Christ. In 1782, thirty years before the Judsons departed from Salem, former slave George Liele had indentured himself to a British colonel to buy passage on a sailing ship to Jamaica. Thirty-two years before Baptists in the United States would organize to support mission, George Liele had independently become the first American Baptist foreign missionary. The Baptist movement that Liele launched in Jamaica would, by the 1840s, send more than 40 missionaries to Cameroon. In his missionary service, Liele sought to "live as nigh the Scriptures as we possibly can." The covenant that Liele prepared for the first Baptist church in Jamaica included the provision, "We hold not to the shedding of blood..."

George Liele

Other early Baptist missionaries and mission leaders held similar views. Born into a free black family in Exeter, NH, Thomas Paul became pastor of Boston's Joy Street African Baptist Church and helped start New York City's Abyssinian Baptist Church. In 1823, Paul sailed to Haiti where, for six months, he gave pioneer missionary service under appointment from the Massachusetts Baptist Missionary Society. Paul had joined the Massachusetts Peace Society at least three years before Judson became a member.

Henry Holcombe, the pastor of Philadelphia's First Baptist Church was the first vice-president of the Baptist Board of Foreign Mission (the Board that the Triennial Convention established to oversee the daily work of the mission.) The year after Judson joined the Massachusetts Peace Society, Holcombe founded the Pennsylvania Peace Society. That same year Holcombe's published sermons on peacemaking sparked the organization of two auxiliary peace societies, one in Georgia and an African-American peace society in Philadelphia. Holcombe expanded his ideas in his 1823 book, *The Martial Christian's Manual*, which held that followers of Jesus must abandon all violence.

Howard Malcolm, a member of the Board, was a founder and later president of the American Peace Society (1828) which was formed from a merger of the Massachusetts, New York and other local peace societies. Malcom, the first person deputized by the Board to visit the Judsons and other missionaries in their work on location, sought to embody nonviolence in his personal actions. Traveling over 53,000 miles for two and a half years (1835-37), Malcom refused to carry weapons for self-defense. Seeing widespread lawlessness during his travels he observed, "We have scarcely a missionary family that has not been robbed." His one exception to traveling unarmed was made for the sake of others. "So much was said," he wrote, "by some my English friends in Rangoon, of the folly and danger of going unarmed, as I had hitherto done, and of the imputations that would be cast on *them*, if they suffered me to go in this manner, that I consented to borrow a pair of pistols and a bag of cartridges." Only once—when approaching some alligators—did he take out the pistols, only to discover that he had no bullets to fit the pistols.

Francis Wayland, a leading pastor, mission leader, president of Brown University and of the Triennial Convention, preached a sermon in 1823 entitled "The Moral Dignity of the Missionary Enterprise." The sermon, a strong defense of mission at a time of growing anti-mission sentiment, was published, went through several printings, and became widely circulated in the United States and England. Wayland set forth a holistic understanding of mission. "Our design is radically to affect the temporal and eternal interests of the whole race of man," he said. And among those "temporal interests" he included war. For Wayland, the issue was clear. "In practice," he said, "the precepts of the gospel may be summed up in the single command, thou shalt love the Lord thy God with all thy heart, and thy neighbor as thyself." The work of mission must address the social realities of war and peace. "Our object will not have been accomplished till the tomahawk shall be buried forever, and the tree of peace spread its broad branches...." Twelve years later, Wayland published *The Elements of Moral Science* (1835) that became the leading ethics textbook in American universities and brought pacifism to the attention of readers around the world through its wide distribution and translation into numerous languages.

French-born Jean Casimir Rostan served his country in diplomatic service in Cuba from 1825-27. He then came to the United States for theological study after which he was appointed as the first American Baptist missionary to Europe (1832). Returning to Paris, Rostan resumed activity in the Society for Christian Morals which he co-founded in 1821. Rostan worked with others in the Society for the abolition of war and capital punishment, for prison reform and against the slave trade. Rostan's mission service came to an abrupt end with his death from cholera in 1833.

Missionaries pursued the making of peace in varieties of ways. For instance, in North East India in 1876, Rev. E. W. Clark and fifteen Ao Naga families from the Dekha Haimong village moved a three-hour walk away to a nearby mountain crest to establish the new village of Molung. This village sought to order its life as followers of the Prince of Peace in several ways: the believers did not give offerings to propitiate the demons before building the village; the village abandoned warfare and committed itself to nonviolence; slavery was prohibited in the village; and religious liberty was established with "no law to make Christians."

Peacemaking marked the work of missionaries with "just war" convictions as well as those that rejected all wars. Rev. Washington Irving Price was a Civil War veteran who had served in the Ohio Volunteer Infantry. As an American Baptist missionary among the Sgaw Karens in Burma, he wrote, "I believe that it was just as much my duty to aid and encourage the Karens to be loyal to the Government to which they and we are so deeply indebted, as it was my duty and privilege to give myself to the defense of my own loved native land at the time when her life was threatened." Price reported in 1887 that he and other missionaries "have been forced to occupy the position of 'go-between' for their people and the Government. This brought to us a vast amount of labour and responsibility that does not, at first sight, seem to be germane to our legitimate work. But, not only was the peace and prosperity of the country at stake, but the lives and homes of the people for whom we labour, as well as our own lives and the property of the Mission were in peril. Under these circumstances we dared not refuse to do what we could."

Missionaries also were "go-between" peacemakers between villages and within people groups. James S. Dennis' book *Christian Missions and Social Progress* (1899) quoted Price's report that "sectional feuds have almost entirely disappeared, and the brotherhood of the Karen race is recognized." Fellow Burma missionary Josiah N. Cushing gave a similar report: "Blood-feuds have been very prevalent and deadly in the mountain communities. Villages that have become Christian have refused to keep up such feuds, and heathen villages with which they were at enmity have felt the influence, and allowed the feuds to lapse."

Missionaries that worked locally to mediate between disputing parties found their actions mirrored by mission leaders such as "missionary kid" George Dana Boardman who advocated and worked for mediation between nations. Boardman was born in Burma and was the only surviving child of the Judsons' missionary colleagues George Dana Boardman and his wife Sarah Hall Boardman. After George Boardman died in 1831, Sarah stayed in Burma, preaching in Karen jungle villages and supervising mission schools, taking young George into the jungle with her on these mission journeys. In 1834 she married Adoniram Judson who had been widowed since 1826. George "the Younger," now Judson's stepson, would become the noted thirty-year pastor of Philadelphia's First Baptist Church and a four-term President of the American Baptist Missionary Union

Boardman was a member of several peace societies and served as President of the Christian Arbitration and Peace Society. He advocated the establishment of a Peace Department to stand alongside the U.S. Army and Navy departments and sought to convince leaders that arbitration was a feasible option. "Within our own century," he noted, "there have been seventy-six cases of successful international arbitration; to nearly one-half of which, I am proud to say, the United States has been a party." In 1984 the idea advocated by Boardman in the 19th Century became a reality in the founding of the U.S. Institute of Peace by an act of the U.S. Congress.

Representing the Society in 1890, Boardman spoke about disarmament in Washington, D.C. before a gathering that included the Secretary of State, members of the Cabinet and Congress. He made his case in an 1890 pamphlet entitled *The Disarmament of Nations or Mankind One Body* that was distributed internationally. He was a participant in the 1899 Hague Convention called by Russian Tsar Nicholas II that attempted to ban bombing from the air, chemical warfare and the use of certain types of modern technology in war. The Convention successfully established the Permanent Court of Arbitration, the first global mechanism for the settlement of disputes between states. As of 2011, the United States and 112 other nations are members.

In 1922 following World War I, the Northern Baptist Convention (now American Baptist Churches/USA) adopted a "Resolution on the Abolition of War." The Resolution, reaffirmed by the ABC General Board in 1987 and 1998, states:

> We record our conviction that war as a method
> of settling international disputes is barbarous,
> wasteful and manifestly contrary to every Chris-
> tian ideal and teaching. We reaffirm our belief
> that our country should have its part in an asso-
> ciation of nations for expressing our common
> humanity, adjusting difficulties and outlawing
> any nation that resorts to arms to further its own
> interests.

We earnestly petition our national government to participate with other nations in the International Court of Justice and to take whatever other steps may be necessary to secure such cooperation on the part of the peoples of the earth as will bring about a stabilizing of world conditions and permanently banish war.

During the 1940 Northern Baptist Convention annual meeting in Atlantic City, NJ, a number of delegates held a Peace Breakfast at the Hotel Madison where they formed the Baptist Pacifist Fellowship. Membership was open to those who would sign the following statement:

As I view my loyalty to the Person, Spirit and Teachings of Jesus Christ, my conscience commits me to His way of redemptive love; and compels me to refuse to participate in or give moral support to any war.

The Fellowship included the prominent mission leader, Dr. Kenneth Scott Latourette, noted Yale University historian of World Christian Mission and an American Baptist Foreign Mission Society (ABFMS) Board member for more than twenty years. By the 1950s at least 15 American Baptist missionaries were also members.

World War II and Japan

One was Thomasine Allen who began her nearly 45 years of mission service in Japan in 1915. By 1938, "Tommy" Allen's call to particularly serve the poor led her deep into rural Japanese life at Kuji, a community of farmers, fisherman and miners on Japan's northeast coast. Christians were unknown in the community, and the house available for her was considered to be haunted. Nevertheless Allen settled in and started a kindergarten to minister to families. When World War II began she chose to remain in ministry on location. She endured two years of internment in four different camps before she was released to the States in a 1943 exchange of prisoners. Her commitment to "be Christ" and to make peace in service to the Japanese people remained constant. In the U.S. she served the Japanese-Americans at the Tule Lake Relocation Center until her return to Japan in 1947 where her ministry at Kuji flourished. She started a Sunday School that met *daily* and became accredited as the Kuji Christian Center School. She started a clinic and a Baptist church that reached into nearby towns and villages by starting agricultural schools. After retirement in 1958 she remained active in the work of the center and in founding a junior college in 1970. She was twice given high awards by the Japanese government.

When the Japanese invaded the Philippines in December, 1941, twenty-one American Baptist missionaries were serving there. Ten missionaries and their children were taken prisoner and interned for the rest of the war in appallingly harsh conditions. They all survived the war. Eleven missionaries fled to the mountains in the interior of the island of Panay. They were sheltered by Filipino Baptist friends who risked their lives to provide refuge and hospitality in an isolated forest glen the missionaries called Hopevale. For 20 months they survived in their hiding place thanks to the courageous care of the Filipinos.

However, in December, 1943, a Japanese sweep of the area to discover foreigners resulted in their capture. The day after they were seized, the order was given to execute them all. The missionaries asked their captors for a time to pray, which was permitted. They formed a circle and prayed, sang a hymn and presented themselves to their executioners. One by one the adults were beheaded and the child was stabbed: Jennie Clare Adams, James and Charma Moore Covell, Dorothy Antionette Dowell, Signe Amelia Erickson, Frederick and Ruth Meyer, Francis and Gertrude Rose, Erle and Louise Rounds and their son Erle Douglas Rounds. Their bodies were put into a bamboo house that was then burned.

Jennie Adams had written many poems about the life at Hopevale. One of the more powerful poems is "I am weary of war and the fighting." The final verse of the poem reads:

I am weary of war and the fighting,
The sound of the cannon and guns,
The droning of heavy bombers
Searching for mothers' sons.
There must be a better method,
A path we have failed to take
That would lead us out of chaos
Could we from our lethargy wake,
The pathway of love among nations,
Dispelling all hatred and pride,
The way that the Master taught us,
A way that has never been tried.

The Covells had been missionaries in Japan in the 1930s. Jimmy Covell believed that participation in war in any circumstances was incompatible with the Christian faith. He engaged in a symbolic protest of wearing funeral black when students at the Kanto Gakuin school where he taught were required to participate in military maneuvers. He also refused to attend the ceremony when the Emperor's picture was hung at the school. His actions led to him being labeled an anti-war dissenter and dangerous. As the political situation between the U.S. and Japan deteriorated, the Covells were reassigned to the Philippines.

Peggy Covell, eldest daughter of Jimmy and Charma, was shocked and grieved as the news of the deaths of the missionaries reached the U.S. But she also knew her parents' love for the Japanese people and their rejection of war. With her skills in speaking Japanese she served as a social worker at a relocation center in Colorado where Japanese-Americans had been forcibly interned. There she shared about her parents' story even as she sought to meet the needs of people who had lost everything out of American war hysteria and prejudice. The Japanese-Americans interned were deeply moved by her story and passed it along.

The story of Peggy Covell's loving service, despite her parents' martyrdom, reached the ears of a Japanese prisoner-of-war. After the war he returned and shared the story with Captain Mitsuo

Fuchida who had led the Japanese attack on Pearl Harbor. That testimony prompted a quest by Fuchida to seek the source of such love and forgiveness in the pages of the Bible. Fuchida eventually became a Christian and an evangelist, completing an amazing circle of reconciliation.

On December 8, 1941, the day following the Pearl Harbor attack, William and Lucinda Axling, American Baptist missionaries who had served in Japan for 41 years, were placed under house arrest. They were confined to their second story apartment on the campus of Waseda University in Tokyo for nine months. After the American government moved the Japanese from the west coast of the United States into detention camps, Japan began reprisals on its resident foreigners. At this time the Japanese government moved the Axlings out of house arrest and placed them in separate men's and women's camps where they remained for almost two years. Throughout their confinement, the Axlings maintained a clear witness to Jesus and sought peace between Japan and the United States.

In 1954, nine years after the war ended between the United States and Japan, William and Lucinda Axling were granted an audience with the Emperor and Empress of Japan. The traditional court formality was set aside and the Axlings were able to talk openly with the royal couple about their faith and their desire for peace and reconciliation between Japan and the nations against which it had fought during World War II. The Emperor awarded William Axling the Second Order of Merit. This was the first time that this high honor was given to a non-Japanese person.

William and Nadine Hinchman went to Japan as missionaries shortly after World War II ended. Among his many missionary efforts Bill Hinchman planted the Tokyo Peace Church near Waseda University. He envisioned a congregation that had peacemaking at the core of its Christian witness. When the church was fully established as a congregation their first acts were to establish sister congregations that spoke about reconciliation through Christ. One partnership was with a Baptist Church in the Soviet Union, bridging the divide of the Cold War. The other partnership was with a Korean Presbyterian church, humbly confronting the racism of Japanese toward Koreans as well as the damage Japanese militarism inflicted on Korea during the War. The Tokyo Peace Church also wanted to bear ecumenical witness through partnering with a Presbyterian congregation rather than relating only to other Baptists.

With a large student population, an elderly Japanese deacon stood strongly with Hinchman in making the peace witness for the church. As a young man the deacon had survived the fire

Bill Hinchman

bombing of Tokyo during the war. He described walking through the charred ruins of the city and being unable to help the dying who were pleading for water. As he walked those streets he committed himself to God to work for the rest of his life for peace and an end to war. That commitment was expressed in part through his leadership at the Tokyo Peace Church, training the rising generation for their own peace witness.

The Tokyo Peace Church now has long had a Japanese pastor. It has become a haven for immigrants to Japan fleeing violence from their homelands. They have supported global Baptist peace conferences and provided scholarships for participants coming from poor countries. The seed Bill Hinchman planted is bearing a rich harvest for peace far beyond his time of ministry.

Dr. LeRoy R. Allen and his wife Elsie, though not related to "Tommy" Allen, were members with her in the Baptist Pacifist Fellowship. Though appointed as American Baptist missionaries in 1942, their departure for active missionary service was delayed by the war. As a conscientious objector, LeRoy performed noncombatant service under appointment by the Medical Assignment and Procurement Board. He was posted in several U.S. locations and worked in part as a tuberculosis control officer. Within the U.S. Public Health Service he had gained rank equivalent to the military rank of Colonel. Elsie had been born in India to missionary parents and grandparents. From 1950-52 Dr. Allen was Medical Director of the U.S. government's Special Technical and Economic Mission to Burma. They began their active mission service at Vellore Christian Medical Center in 1953. Whether under appointment of the government or the mission society, the Allens sought to live out Jesus' mission call that combined proclaiming peace and curing the sick (Luke 10:5,9).

William T. Randall was a teenager during World War II but traveled as a missionary to Okinawa to minister among the Japanese people. Dealing with his own earlier hatred of the Japanese during the war years he said, "I learned very acutely that to harbor revenge would only divide and separate." After ten years as a missionary, Randall became the pastor of the Futenma Baptist Church in Okinawa. In 2000 he published *Social Justice through Nonviolence in the 20th Century*, a book about Mahatma Gandhi and Martin Luther King, Jr.

Connections at Home and Afar

Martin and Mabel England served as missionaries among the Kachin people of northern Burma, beginning in 1933. When the Japanese invaded Burma in the early days of World War II, the Englands escaped in a harrowing journey under Japanese attack. The riverboat they were on was sunk. They lost all their belongings but made it safely out of the country.

Back in the U.S. the Englands settled in Louisville, Kentucky where they met Clarence and Florence Jordan. As the two couples shared their vision of a lived-out faith, together they conceived a dream for an intentional agricultural community in the U.S. South that was committed to racial reconciliation. They bought land outside Americus, Georgia and formed Koinonia Farm. When the Japanese retreated from Burma, the Englands returned to their mission work among the Kachins. Koinonia went on to have a huge impact for racial justice, inspiring people such as Jimmy Carter and Millard Fuller, the founder of Habitat for Humanity.

In Burma, both before and after the war, the Englands bore witness to the need for peace and economic justice. Martin England challenged people to the choice between "Jesus or the Chief," the "Chief" representing the authority of earthly figures and the tendency to be loyal to one's tribe while hating other tribes. England expanded this globally, challenging the tribalism of race and nation, especially as expressed in the domination of the wealthier countries such as his own United States. He wrote of the connection between peace and justice, "Whatever else may need doing, there can be no peace between a world half starved, half glutted, between a world that puzzles how to get enough to keep alive and a world in constant danger of suffocation from its surpluses."

In 1953 Mabel's failing health forced the Englands to return to the U.S. Martin joined the staff of the Ministers and Missionaries Benefit Board (MMBB). Besides his formal job to care for retired ministers and missionaries in the South, he was given the covert assignment of caring for people whose work in the civil rights movement put their lives and well-being at risk. He visited civil rights activists in jail and cared for people who were economically afflicted by the risks they took. One of those visits in 1963 was to Dr. Martin Luther King, Jr. after he had been arrested in Birmingham, Alabama (See Chapter 3). During the visit, King passed a written statement to England who immediately sent it to Dean Wright, MMBB's Executive Director in New York. Wright had the statement published, and the world soon came to know it as the famous "Letter from a Birmingham Jail." England also secured life insurance benefits for Dr. King through the MMBB. King was viewed as a high insurance risk and could obtain no coverage through regular providers, so this support proved to be an especially vital blessing to the King family following Dr. King's assassination.

C. Conrad Browne was another early Baptist Pacifist Fellowship member and conscientious objector. From 1941-46 Browne did alternative civilian service in lieu of combat duty, working first in a forest service camp and then in 1945 as director of Baptist conscientious objector units under the American Baptist Home Mission Society. After three and a half years with the YMCA in Chicago, Con and his wife Ora became part of the Koinonia Farm in Americus, GA. Con's service as Koinonia's "Work Coordinator" from 1949-63 gave him a curious range of tasks. He taught at the Interdenominational Theological Center, was a bookkeeper, oversaw the farm's chicken flock, designed several new buildings, ran the egg route, directed youth camps and preached. With fellow Koinonia residents, Con and Ora endured attacks by the Ku Klux Klan and others that included "bullets, bombs, beatings, burnings and a boycott." From 1963-71 Browne was president/director of Highlander Folk School in eastern Tennessee (see Chapter 25 about Myles Horton and Highlander Folk School). Fannie Lou Hamer, voting rights activist and civil rights leader in Mississippi, received training in Browne's first Highlander workshop.

Following service with Highlander, Con Browne was introduced to ABFMS by Jitsuo Morikawa as well suited to give missionary service in leadership development among poor rural minorities through grass-roots education and action. Browne believed that the resources for people's education and liberation lie within themselves. He noted that the educational philosophy of Paulo Freier as expressed in his book, Pedagogy of the Oppressed (See Chapter 14 about Paulo Freier) had been put into action years before at Koinonia Farm and Highlander Folk School. During his missionary service in the Philippines (1973-79), Browne led "problem-solving workshops" that helped local people discover empowerment to confront their challenges. Homesteaders organized to save their land from encroachers. Women organized to visit young people imprisoned in a stockade. Rural youth formed "modules" to visit churches and encourage other youth. Negrito families learned how to successfully petition the government for the preservation of their land and culture. And people came to faith in the process, one workshop resulting in the baptism of eighteen young men.

Misión por la Paz

The wars in Central America saw other ABFMS/IM missionaries rise to the fore in peacemaking witness. Gustavo Parajón and his wife Joan were missionaries in Nicaragua where Gustavo had been born. Gustavo was a medical doctor and in that capacity founded PROVADENIC, a system of health clinics throughout the country, especially in the under-served rural areas. He also served as the Pastor of the First Baptist Church of Managua. When a catastrophic earthquake devastated Managua in 1972 leaving over 10,000 dead, Parajón founded CEPAD as an ecumenical relief and development agency.

Following the fall of the Samoza dictatorship and the success of the Sandinista revolution in Nicaragua, civil war broke out. Various "Contra" insurgent groups, assisted by the United States, sought to overthrow the Sandinista government. Because of his willingness to work with the Sandinistas in meeting the needs of the Nicaraugan populace, Parajón was criticized by Christian conservatives in the U.S., and CEPAD was accused of being a Communist organization. CEPAD clinics were attacked by the Contras, and health workers were assassinated.

Parajón joined with a group of Nicaraguan Moravian Church leaders and the Mennonite John Paul Lederach (featured in Chapter 18) to form a group that mediated between the Sandinista government and indigenous Contra groups in eastern Nicaragua. After an extensive process of going back and forth between the two sides and hosting a series of direct talks, they succeeded in establishing the first cease-fire that eventually led to the comprehensive settlement of the wars in Central America.

Gustavo Parajón

Following the establishment of the Presidents' Peace Plan mediated by Oscar Arias (see Chapter 42) Parajón was selected as a person-at-large trusted by all sides to be on the Nicaraguan National Reconciliation Commission. He worked to establish local reconciliation commissions that aided in the demobilization of soldiers from both sides. The local commissions helped ex-combatants return to their home communities where they sometimes lived next to their former enemies. Parajón established the training procedures to equip the local reconciliation commissions for their work, often using the Bible as their only resource for how to find the ways to peace on the ground. His peacemaking work resulted in honors from the American Baptist Churches, the Baptist World Alliance and the Central American Parliament, among others. When Parajón received the distinguished Francisco Morazán medallion from the Central American Parliament both Sandinistas and former Contras gathered to honor him for his reconciliation work.

Ruth Mooney was a missionary in El Salvador while the civil war raged in that country. Her peacemaking work focused on grassroots education to empower people in the churches. Like Con Browne, she and her team based their teaching on the philosophy of Paulo Freire, developing Christian education materials that encouraged participation, critical thinking, and transformation. After the war they wrote Bible studies focusing on reconciliation, reconstruction, and conflict transformation. She continued her Christian education work in Cuba and then in Costa Rica where her team developed a peace curriculum of Bible studies, Building a Culture of Peace in our Church, Neighborhood, Family, and Personal Life, that was used in congregations throughout Latin America.

Ruth Mooney

African Peacemaking

In 1997, shortly after the official apartheid regime ended, Charles and Sarah West went to South Africa to engage in missionary service that included extensive reconciliation work. The Wests were invited by the Baptist Convention of South Africa, a predominantly Black South African body. The South African Baptists were primarily divided along racial and cultural lines reflecting the divisions of the larger society. The decades of hurt, injustice, distance and anger from the apartheid years created a huge challenge to healing. For Charles West this was his call to get engaged in the name of Christ. As he wrote, "Striving to be a peacemaker, working towards binding the broken heart and setting captives free from hatred and pain is hard work, but it is very much the mission of the church."

After much delicate and difficult preliminary work a gathering was held in Colesberg, South Africa with disparate Baptist groups present. There was talking that sometimes erupted into shouting. Accusations were made. People cried. Eventually participants turned to soul-searching. Attitudes shifted, and apologies were extended. West was a participator and facilitator at the meetings. At one point all the scarring incidents of the past were recalled and written down on large sheets of paper hung around the meeting hall. Then the papers were rolled up and placed under the communion table. As the participants approached the table to partake of the Lord's Supper they were asked to remove their shoes and step into someone else's. As West recalls, "The cliché 'walking a mile in someone else's shoes' is an age-old adage that touches on the power of looking at life through another's view. The metaphor conjures images of shifting one's perspective and allowing for a deeper understanding of even one's enemies." The foundations of reconciliation worked out at Colesberg eventually led to the formation of a unified Baptist witness in the country called The South Africa Baptist Association. The SABA included Black, mixed-race Colored, India-cultured, and both British and Dutch-cultured White South Africans.

West's reconciliation work took him further afield as he was invited along with the Mennonite peacemaker Ron Kraybill to work in northeast India. Northeast India has been the scene of many different ethnic and political insurgencies. West and Kraybill led workshops and trained church leaders and community activists in Bible studies for how to deal in nonviolent creative ways with the violence throughout the region. West particularly focused on the story of Jacob and Esau, a story from Genesis of lies and deceit, unkind and unthinkable favoritism shown between brothers, and the unfair and unlawful taking and distribution of resources. It's a story of murderous intent and long exile. Yet this ancient story climaxes with restitution offered for wrongs done. Forgiveness was extended despite the bitter conflict, making reconciliation and embrace possible. In 2006 Charles and Sarah West moved to Zambia continuing their mission work with a strong passion for the ministry of reconciliation.

Many missionaries have been involved in theological education around the world. From 1999 to 2008 Virgil and Lynn Nelson taught at the Pastoral School in Kikongo in the Democratic Republic of Congo. In his various courses Virgil would work in teachings about dealing positively with conflict. As he approached the study on Acts 6, a conflict story in the early church over the uneven distribution of food, Virgil tackled a perennial conflict at the Pastoral School. Every year at Christmas a gift of bags of rice were provided for faculty, staff and students. The students always felt they were short-changed. Nelson got permission from the school director to turn this into a teaching moment and give the students the responsibility of handling the distribution. The result was a long, in-depth discussion about determining and meeting need. Through this and other teaching experiences Nelson enabled leaders to go back to their home communities and deal positively with family, church and clan disputes.

After retiring from International Ministries Virgil and Lynn Nelson joined with Evelyn Hanemann of the Baptist Peace Fellowship of North America to do a series of church-based trainings in Liberia in the fall of 2011. They conducted workshops on

nonviolence, on responding to trauma in ways that bring healing, and on empowering people for action. The focus for these
programs was on Liberia holding a presidential election free of
violence, a major step in rebuilding the country after two decades
of civil war. The Liberian Council of Churches and their international peacemaking friends rejoiced when the election was
relatively trouble-free.

Peacemaking into the 21st Century

International Ministries entered the 21st Century with its
Board adopting a "Go Global"strategic plan that identified "working toward God's Reign of justice, peace and abundant life" as
integral to its mission. The Board declared that Christ-like mission
included a commitment to "pursue peace, justice and reconciliation through ministries of conflict transformation and education,
as well as standing with and serving the victims of conflict." International Ministries is continuing a ministry focus of "seeking
peace and providing refuge."

As part of the "Go Global" plan, International Ministries called
"global consultants" to work around the world in short-term projects in various areas of mission expertise. In 1986, Lauran Bethell
was preparing to teach English in a Christian school in Thailand
and was studying the Thai language when her calling took a major
change in direction. She had to pass through a large, notorious
red light district in Bangkok where she saw women working in
the degradation of the sex trades. She joined with Paul and Elaine
Lewis to establish the New Life Center for girls at risk of labor
and sexual exploitation. Lauran became the first Director of this
residential program to provide literacy, vocational training, and
Christian education for the girls. She also facilitated rescues of
numerous girls from prostitution and other forms of exploitative
labor. The program drew international attention for its excellent
impact, including from the TV program "60 Minutes," and visits
from U.S. First Lady Hillary Clinton and Secretary of State Mad-
elaine Albright, among many other prominent officials. The New

Life Center was also given an award for its exemplary service by the Prime Minister of Thailand.

As Bethell responded to calls from other countries to share what she was doing, she learned more about the growing global problem of human trafficking. In 2001 she became one of IM's first global consultants and moved to Prague, Czech Republic. Three years later she initiated "Project Hope" in Prague, working with Bulgarian Roma women involved in prostitution, many of whom had been trafficked. Gradually she developed an international network to support anti-trafficking activists and ministries to the victims of prostitution. Bethell has been like a 21st Century Thomas Clarkson (see Chapter 31) in her efforts to end this scourge of modern slavery. Eventually she moved to Amsterdam, from where she continues to travel around the world supporting the development of local initiatives for freedom and healing as well as coordinating the international anti-trafficking network. In 2005 Lauran Bethell received the Baptist World Alliance's Congress Human Rights Award, presented by former U.S. President Jimmy Carter, for her advocacy for the victims of human trafficking. IM now has many missionaries who work in various countries with ministries to people in prostitution and to victims of human trafficking in varied settings of abusive labor.

Dan Buttry was commissioned in 2003 to be a global consultant for peace and justice after years of peacemaking work as a pastor, with National Ministries (now the American Baptist Home Mission Societies), and the Baptist Peace Fellowship of North

Jimmy and Rosalyn Carter present BWA Human Rights Award to Lauran Bethell

America. He has travelled to many conflicted countries to provide training in conflict transformation, equipping peacemakers with Bible-based tools for their reconciling work. One of the areas where he has worked most extensively has been northeast India. Buttry teamed up with Wati Aier and other peacemakers to facilitate the Naga reconciliation project (see Chapter 44). During many of those talks, John Sundquist also participated in the mediation team, both when he was Executive Director of International Ministries and later during his retirement when he continued his mission service as a volunteer. Buttry has had a special emphasis in inter-religious peacemaking, whether in situations of religious persecution or inter-communal violence that erupts along religious lines. This inter-religious peacemaking has taken him to India, the Philippines, Indonesia, Lebanon, the Republic of Georgia, Liberia, Kenya and other countries to help Christians live out Jesus' command to love one's enemies and pray for those who persecute them.

Two hundred years after the Judsons sailed to Burma, missionaries with International Ministries continue their work for peace, justice, freedom and human rights as part of their calling to serve God as the "hands and feet" of Jesus as the Spirit continues to transform the world. There are many stories yet untold. There are many stories of peacemaking creativity and courage by the people in the national churches with which IM partners. There are new missionaries stepping forth who are carrying out various peace ministries as Christ's ambassadors for reconciliation. Echoing the scriptural recognition that "all of us make many mistakes" (James 3:2), "Go Global" renounced the temptation towards mission triumphalism: "We confess that we have not always lived up to our ideals but daily recommit ourselves to them." So International Ministries enters its third century of mission aware that its efforts to seek peace have been, and continue to be, imperfect and incomplete but believing that the future of peacemaking is, as in the words of Adoniram Judson, "as bright as the promises of God."

Sources:

Reid Trulson, "Baptist Pacifism: A Heritage of Nonviolence," *American Baptist Quarterly*, September, 1991

Friend of Peace, Volume 1, No. 9 (1817), Volume 2, No. 7, Volume 3, No. 4, (April, 1822), and Vol. 3, No. 7 (January 1823)

Edward Judson, *The Life of Adoniram Judson*, American Baptist Publication Society, 1883.

Rosalie Hall Hunt, *Bless God and Take Courage. The Judson History and Legacy* (Valley Forge: Judson Press, 2005)

Edward A. Holmes, "George Liele; Negro Slavery's Prophet of Deliverance," in *Baptist Quarterly*, 20 (1964) London, Baptist Historical Society

Ivah T. Heneise, *Pioneers of Light. Stories of the Baptist Witness in Haiti: 1823-1998* (Penny Farms, FL: International Christian Education Fund, 1999)

"Henry Holcombe, A Southern Baptist Reformer in the Age of Jefferson," in *The Georgia Historical Quarterly*, Vol. 54, No. 3, (Fall, 1970)

Henry Holcombe, *Martial Christian's Manual* (Philadelphia, 1823)

Howard Malcom, "War Inconsistent With Chistianity," and "Criminality of War," in *The Book of Peace: A Collection of Essays on War and Peace* (Boston: George C. Beckwith, 1845)

Howard Malcom, *Travels in South-Eastern Asia Embracing Hindustan, Malaya, Siam, and China: with notices of numerous stations and a full account of the Burman empire* (Boston: Gould, Kendal and Lincoln, 1844)

Francis Wayland, "The Moral Dignity of the Missionary Enterprise." A Sermon Delivered Before The Boston Baptist Foreign Mission Society On the Evening of October 26, And Before The Salem Bible Translation Society On the Evening of November 4, 1823.

Francis Wayland, *The Elements of Moral Science* (Boston: Gould, Kendall and Lincoln, 1835)

"Memoir of Mr. Rostan," in *The American Baptist Magazine* Vol. 14, No. 7, (July 1834)

Source: "Casimir Rostan," in *The Calumet*, Vol. 2, No. 4, (November and December, 1834)

Mary Mead Clark, *A Corner of India* (Philadelphia: American Baptist Publication Society, 1907)

James S. Dennis, *Christian Missions and Social Progress*, (New York: Fleming H. Revell Company, 1899), Vol. 2.

Janet Kerr Morchaine, "George Dana Boardman: Propagandist for Peace," *Foundations*, Vol. IX, No. 2, April-June, 1966.

Joan Jacobs Brumberg, *Mission for Life: The Story of the Family of Adoniram Judson, the Dramatic Events of the First American Foreign Mission, and the Course of Evangelical Religion in the Nineteenth Century*, (New York: The Free Press, 1980).

American Baptist Policy Statements and Resolutions, http://www.abc-usa.org/LinkClick.aspx?fileticket=ny0%2fyIDB55U%3d&tabid=199

Baptist Pacifist Fellowship file at Swarthmore College Peace Collection

Beyond the Ranges; an autobiography by Kenneth Scott Latourette, (Grand Rapids: Wm. B. Eerdmans Publishing Company, 1967)

Jennie Clare Adams, "The Hills Did Not Imprison Her," American Baptist Foreign Mission Society (2nd edition, 1991).

Through Shining Archway, American Baptist Foreign Mission Society, 1945.

Roberta Stevens and Ann Borquist, "From Suffering and Sacrifice Comes Joy: The Story of the Covell Family," *American Baptists In Mission*, Summer 2000.

David Stricklin, *A Geneology of Dissent. Southern Baptist Protest in the Twentieth Century* (Lexington, KY: The University Press of Kentucky, 1999)

David Stricklin, "Martin England and the 'Chief': On the Far Frontiers of Baptist Ethics," (Baptist History and Heritage Society, 2003) http://www.thefreelibrary.com/Frontier+in+Baptist+ethics+history%3a+a+panel.-a0111014965

David Stricklin, "Martin England and the 'Chief': On the Far Frontiers of Baptist Ethics"

"Letter From a Birmingham Jail" source is: Everett C. Goodwin, "MMBB's Support for Fair Compensation and Human Rights" in

Tomorrow. A Newsletter of the Ministers and Missionaries Benefit Board, 4th quarter, 2011.

"Life and Service of Gustavo Parajón Remembered," American Baptist News Service, March 21, 2011

"Gustavo Parajón: The Doctor Who Practices Peace," The CEPAD Report, 2010, Issue 2.

Baptist World Alliance: www.bwanet.org

Missionary files of American Baptist International Ministries, Valley Forge, PA

Person experiences and conversations of the authors with Gustavo Parajón, Conrad Browne, Bill Hinchman, Charles West, Virgil Nelson, Lauran Bethell, Ruth Mooney and John Paul Lederach.

IIntroduction: What Is a Peacemaker?

IN THESE PAGES, YOU will meet heroes.

The world is troubled now and has been troubled in many earlier eras. In these pages, you will meet men and women who were not afraid of the worst that humans can unleash through ignorance or ill will. Like all of us, the people in this book agonized over the tragedies they encountered in the world. Sometimes they were terrified, too, but ultimately their faith in a wide range of religious and ethical traditions won out in their lives. They summoned the courage to make peace. Depending on your own spiritual tradition, you might call many of these men and women saints.

What you will discover in this book is that their heroism did not depend on the qualities our popular culture celebrates in heroes. As a group, they were not exceptional in muscle, martial arts, great beauty or wealth. Their gifts lay in the way they communicated their love, hope and wisdom—through teaching, preaching, organizing, mediating and protesting. Some shared their great visions to move millions. Some communicated through music and the arts. Some gave their lives and were martyred in the pathway toward peace.

This book will inspire you to evaluate your own life, your own response to the world's troubles. But inspiration is not all you will experience.

In these pages, you will find world-famous names, including Gandhi, King, Tutu and Bono. You will rub shoulders with Nobel Peace Prize winners. But in most cases, you will be meeting men and women unknown to the larger world. Flip through the chapters. You won't recognize most names. For each King we celebrate standing on a mountaintop, there are thousands of nameless peacemakers changing the world. In reading this book, you will learn that generations of peace activists—each building on the work of others—have been circling the globe for many years. This book makes visible for the first time networks of peacemaking that are invisible to most people in our needy world. By reading their stories, you become a carrier of those stories and spread their light. You become a part of the unfolding network. As you read, you will find ideas in these pages about acting on your new wisdom.

These ideas are potent! In 2007 on the island of Trinidad, a 13-year-old girl had been reading about the life of Gandhi and decided to act on his teachings. Choc'late Allen was concerned about the high levels of urban violence around her, so she began 12-hour-a-day fasts at local libraries, reading books about peace aloud to children. Her actions drew widespread attention and soon she was traveling around the Caribbean, especially to urban centers such as Kingston, Jamaica, where her message reached thousands. Choc'late declared: "We have the power of making the right choices! We have the power of accepting responsibility for our action! We have the power of doing anything!"

So, brace yourself! Join me in these true stories—and this true journey. The world needs us.

The world needs you.

What is a peacemaker?

A peacemaker is not necessarily a "peacekeeper." Peacekeepers (except for the U.N. Peacekeepers) try to stay out of trouble. They keep the peace by not making any waves and not causing any disruptions. The white clergy in Birmingham urged the Rev. Dr. Martin Luther King Jr. to be a peacekeeper—to stay out of trouble. King responded in his *Letter from Birmingham Jail* that the trouble was already there in the society, not something created by those engaged in civil disobedience. Through entering nonviolently into a confrontation with a violent and unjust system, "We merely bring to the surface the hidden tension that is already alive. We bring it out in the open where it can be seen and dealt with." A peacemaker is willing to wade into the trouble, into the conflict, even into the violence to transform the situation. The peacemaker goes into the war to forge peace rather than staying safely at the fringes hoping things get better someday.

What does a peacemaker need?

Two words: Inner strength. In the violent struggles viewers see every night on television, people need to be physically strong, but in nonviolent struggle, an inner strength is needed. And here is the good news: Anyone of any age, size or gender may find that inner strength.

King described the nonviolent army as open to anyone: "In the nonviolent army, there is room for everyone who wants to join up. There is no color distinction. There is no examination, no pledge, except that, as a soldier in the armies of violence one is expected to inspect his carbine and keep it clean, nonviolent soldiers are called upon to examine and burnish their greatest weapons—their heart, their conscience, their courage and their sense of justice."

Gandhi said, "In nonviolence the masses have a weapon which enables a child, a woman, or even a decrepit old man to resist the mightiest government successfully. If your spirit is strong, mere lack of physical strength ceases to be a handicap."

Where can peacemakers be found?

Peacemakers work at the highest levels of government—and deep in the almost-invisible grassroots. They are people who strive to overcome violence, bitterness and division wherever they live and work. Any one of us can become a peacemaker.

One such person is Joseph Githuku who lives in Kiambaa village in Kenya. His wife and four-year old son were killed in a massacre during ethnic and political violence in 2008. The church in which they sought refuge was burned down on top of them. Githuku says, "I can forgive, but I cannot forget that they did bad things to me." Githuku, an ethnic Kikuyu, lives in a predominately Kalenjin area. In spite of his own profound personal losses, he seeks to forge reconciliation doing what he can do. He packs a drum of anti-mosquito spray on his back and travels to his neighbors to help in malaria eradication. "We are trying to show them how to live together to make peace between the Kikuyus and the Kalenjins." Joseph Githuku is a great example of someone who takes what he has at hand to make a substantive contribution to building peace.

Most peacemakers don't begin with a grand vision. Like Joseph Githuku we each can see conflict around us in the world—and we are each marked by those conflicts. We can each act transformatively, taking what we have at hand, just as Mr. Githuku used his anti-mosquito spray for reconciliation. Each of us can act for good, for justice, for healing, for hope, for peace. It's as simple as that.

Will you like all of these peacemakers?

No. Truth be told, some peacemakers can be obnoxious people to live with. Personality traits that make some people bold enough to stand up to repressive powers can intimidate the average person. Some prophets have clusters of traits that are hard to live with and work with if you are a family member or colleague.

Not all peacemakers are saints—and not all saints are saintly every day. Humans are frail and flawed. If you've read about the lives of recognized saints—perhaps St. Francis—then you know that even the greatest of saints don't always have sweet personalities. The same is true of peacemakers. Sometimes grit, stubbornness and even anger motivate people to take on the entrenched forces that spawn violence. Peacemakers can force us to deal with conflicts we would rather avoid, problems we would prefer to sweep under the rug. They try hard to speak the truth and that can make us squirm under their challenge to make us act better than we often do.

I don't agree with everything that was done by every peace-maker in this book. Some of them made political decisions I don't like. Others shifted in their politics throughout their careers, per-haps because they changed, or their context changed, or both. Some people acted in one way while they were leaders in non-violent opposition movements, but then when they came into political power their values seemed to shift. I had to wrestle with whether to include some people in this listing, but in spite of my reservations there was something that nagged at me about how they worked for peace. If I was nagged about their witness, then I knew there was something in their life and work that was a chal-lenge to me, something stretching me in my thinking and action.

At some point in their lives, each peacemaker in this book did something that simply will not let us go. Once we've encountered their stories, we must remember those great moments.

How are the peacemakers organized in this book?

The true stories of more than 60 peacemakers are organized in sections, based on one aspect of their genius, a particular gift or emphasis in their work that is relevant to us today. Most of these men and women cross categories.

King's story appears in a section on prophets and visionaries—but, of course, he was far more than that. He was a nonviolent activist, a theoretician and a martyr. The theoreticians are also practitioners. Most of the organizers are also nonviolent activists. As you read this book, you will see how these lives connect across all of the sections, but clustering these peacemakers around one aspect of their gifts helps us to see more clearly the wide range of ways people can engage in making peace.

The list of individuals in each category is not a ranking, rather a representation. Outstanding peacemakers have not been included in this book for a variety of reasons: Someone similar is already in the book; I've told the person's story in one of my other books; or I selected a story for the sake of balancing the range of examples. The range runs from household names to people you will meet for the first time in these pages. The range includes men and women, young and old, people from around the world, people from different religious traditions.

Our popular culture is a terrible window into the real world. Judging by TV ratings and best sellers, our heroes are comic-book crusaders and contest winners, athletes and movie stars, crime-fighting cops and gun-toting warriors. By reading this book, you're entering a world of heroes who live by a different code. The good news is: You may never become a super hero or the star of a TV series, but anyone can follow the path toward peacemaking.

Helen Keller said, "Although the world is very full of suffering, it is also full of the overcoming of it." Peacemakers know the suffering of the world well, and sometimes they pay the price for their work with their own lives. But these peacemakers have found ways to overcome and transform conflict, violence and war. They have not limited themselves to the rules of the troubled world as they found it—but through courage and creativity they brought into being new kinds of communities, outposts of a new kind of world.

Wherever there is bad news there are people of good news, even if their stories are seldom told. As you read, start retelling these stories to family, friends, co-workers, neighbors. You'll be spreading this light and, even in those first steps, you'll be strengthening all of us for the work of making peace.

One Name Left Off the List

A Preface By Ken Sehested

MAYBE YOU'VE SEEN THE cartoon. Two monks meet in a darkened monastery hallway, one of them holding a candle. The other one says, "Frankly, I find it more emotionally satisfying to curse the darkness."

Don't we all, at least some of the time? If you've never been so tempted, chances are you haven't done any serious wrestling with the temptation of despair.

This new book by Dan Buttry assembles a global range of individuals whose lives bear witness to the kind of hope that, as the writer of Hebrews notes, is the "evidence of things not seen." Between faith, hope and love, love may be the greatest, but hope is surely the hardest. Building on the collection of his two previous bundles of stories, *Interfaith Heroes* (volumes 1 and 2), Dan has gathered for us a fresh set of vignettes, narrative snapshots from every part of the world. These stories span the last century—some still are unfolding—and a variety of religious traditions. Dan presents them in concise, highly readable prose. Some are well known: the Mahatma Gandhis and Desmond Tutus, the Dorothy Days and the Anne Franks. But a good number are less known or not known at all by the general public.

This isn't hagiography, those whitewashed tales of the saints. Dan acknowledges that passionate people can also be prickly. Nor are all of these men and women pacifists. What they share is a commitment to peace building, a willingness to struggle against enormous odds, with abiding commitments to reduce violence and the injustice that gives rise to bloodshed.

While some of these characters engaged in serious intellectual work, none did so in isolation from the brutal dramas of their times. These are not mere dreamers of peace and accountants of justice but incarnate brawlers for an end to enmity. Each illustrates William Blake's insight that "He who would do good to another must do it in Minute Particulars." And the collective effect of these snapshots is to make hope infectious and courage contagious. You will, I think, find good company and food for the journey in these pages.

One Name Left Off the List

One name missing from the table of contents is that of the author himself. That's the trouble with being a good photographer—you rarely show up in your own photos. It's my welcomed task to correct that omission.

Dan Buttry (b. 1952), son of an Air Force chaplain, hoped as a young man to be a combat pilot. After failing the rigorous eyesight requirement for that career, he joined the Army ROTC program at Wheaton College. It wasn't until these college years that he made the conscientious choice to be a follower of Jesus. But no sooner had he begun nurturing an evangelical piety than a classmate challenged him on how he could square his warrior hopes with the straightforward teachings of Jesus. That challenge began a process—heightened by the deadline to register for the draft—which led to what is now referred to as a "crystallization of conscience." The result was another conscientious choice—declaring himself an objector to war.

Soon after came the decision to enter seminary to prepare for pastoral ministry. It coincided with the period of the mid-1970s when the world was becoming aware of the great famine afflicting the Sahel region of Africa. That awakening to the pain of the world (he and I share a common history in this regard) was epochal. The awareness impacted the way he read the Bible, reframed his baptismal identity and refined his vocational plans. As careful readers of Paul's letter to the church at Corinth know, the Apostle's teaching about being "in Christ" results not in a solitary "new creature" (as the King James version has it) but a "new creation" *2 Corinthians 5:17*. It's not our hungry little ego that is bolstered by this transformation. What is transformed is the lens by which we encounter and engage the world. As has been eloquently said by an African church leader, "There are things that can be seen only with eyes that have cried."

One of the scandalous things Dan discovered in learning about famine was that such massive starvation could happen in a region that was a net exporter of food. How could that be? What economic and political logic could drive such an outrage? Questions about structural justice began to emerge in Dan's mind, along with the connection these structures had with the eruption of war.

Prior to exploring the large questions of conflict between nation states, Dan first became acquainted with small-scale war, as the pastor of Dorchester Temple Baptist Church in a crime-ridden neighborhood of Boston. These were the years he began to put wheels under his faith and shape to his vision. He began searching for creative ways to confront the root causes of war amid the structural violence of urban poverty and racism. For instance, when black families were moved into an all-white neighborhood by the housing authority—and were met with a firebomb—Dan's congregation and the neighborhood around his church began around-the-clock vigils near those endangered families. His commitment to nonviolence did not make him a pacifist. He understood instinctively that peace, like war, is to be waged, actively pursued, likely with conflictive results.

Dan's analysis of racism, and its connection with poverty, blossomed during these years. These were also the years when he found ways to align himself with the movement for nuclear disarmament and with resistance to U.S. policy in Central America.

Concern about the latter prompted his arrest during a Pledge of Resistance campaign aimed at stopping U.S. backing of the Contra war in Nicaragua. Exposure to police violence deepened both his political awareness and his commitment to nonviolence.

Reconnecting Faith and Action

Not surprisingly, the connection between Bible study and practical action strengthened in Dan's life. Spiritual formation and prophetic action, so often segregated in church life, were integrating in Dan's. As frequently happens when you learn more about the expanse of injustice and violence in the world, along with the massive structures that feed and foster such brutality, keeping hope alive became a pressing issue.

Dan credits a local Catholic priest—an ally who had become a friend and mentor—with leading him toward the grounding conviction that faithful persistence, despite overwhelming odds, is the mark of mature faith.

In 1987 American Baptist Churches (ABC) leaders tapped Dan to staff the national body's "peace concerns" office. It was a natural progression in the scope of his work. Among his duties was serving on the board of directors of the Baptist Peace Fellowship of North America (BPFNA), which is where he and I first met. Founded to create a network of justice-seekers and peacemakers within various Baptist bodies, the BPFNA was at that time on the verge of escalating its connection with Baptist-flavored peacemakers outside of North America. These global relations led to the first-ever International Baptist Peace Conference, held in Sweden in 1988, followed later by a similar conference in Nicaragua in 1992.

Late one evening in Nicaragua, after most had retired, Dan and a few others sat up most of the night dreaming about the need for a new missions paradigm. They envisioned supporting adviser-trainers with practical mediation skills and pastoral wisdom to help Christian communities practice "the things that make for peace" amid serious social conflicts. Soon the BPFNA began actively collaborating to make space for Dan to do this work, initially as part of his ABC duties, then later, when he returned to the pastorate, as a part-time BPFNA employee.

Eventually International Ministries of the ABC caught the vision and hired Dan as a full-time Global Consultant for Peace and Justice, specifically to respond to invitations from around the world for training in conflict transformation theory and skills. To my knowledge, Dan was the first person in the history of mainline Protestant missions whose job description was explicitly for this purpose. One way to gauge the usefulness of his work is the fact that his Bible Study Manual on Conflict Transformation, an experiential learning tool, has been translated into eight other languages. Though much of his work is, by necessity, out of the limelight, the Central Baptist Theological Seminary in Kansas awarded him an Honorary Doctorate in recognition of his ministry in 2010.

"This is new for us."

Even with a heavy schedule of international travel, Dan has been involved in the Detroit area, where he lives, with a variety of justice initiatives, especially in regard to Christian-Muslim dialogue. He and his wife Sharon, a community minister and pastor, have been key organizers of such initiatives.

Dan is both a skilled trainer and insightful street-level theologian. Regarding the former, I've seen him at work—most recently just before writing this preface, when he spent a morning with 20 pastors of the Ahka people of northern Thailand. Even with the complications of translation, Dan had the group fully animated, talking with him, with each other, doing simple role-plays, and unearthing overlooked insights from Scripture.

A few days earlier, in mediation work with leaders of the Naga people in northeast India, Dan reminded the group of Paul's advice to the early church in Rome:" Do not be overcome by evil, but overcome evil with good" *Romans 12:21*. When one factional leader began insisting that their party couldn't stand idly by after a provocation from another group, Dan quickly listed a wide variety of alternative responses—practical, even militant ways, each requiring the courage of a warrior, to respond to insults in nonviolent ways. The leader responded, "This is new for us."

Peace, like war, is waged. "But Christ has turned it all around," says a poem by Walker Knight that President Jimmy Carter quoted in part after the1978 Camp David Accords leading to a peace treaty between Israel and Egypt. "The weapons of peace are love, joy, goodness, longsuffering; the arms of peace are justice, truth, patience, prayer; the strategy of peace brings safety, welfare, happiness; the forces of peace are the sons and daughters of God."

Preface

By the Rev. Kenneth James Flowers

DR. MARTIN LUTHER KING, Jr. said that "anybody can be great because anybody can serve. You don't have to know Einstein's Theory of Relativity to serve. You don't have to know about Plato or Aristotle to serve. You just need a heart generated by grace and a heart full of love to serve." That's what you'll see in these blessed peacemakers.

I saw that heart generated by grace and full of love in two people featured in this book: Bernard Lafayette and James Lawson. These men were ordinary pastors like me. They were ordinary people who did extraordinary things because they believed what King taught, which is what Jesus taught. It was the nonviolent love ethic worked out in some of the most difficult situations imaginable. But the love ethic of King, while rooted deeply in Jesus, was something that connected to all people, whatever the race, religion or nationality. King specifically referred to the "soul force" he learned from Gandhi, and he spoke of the "world house" of the beloved community. King envisioned all of us coming together as the diverse people of humanity, human beings coming together for good. In that beloved community, freedom and justice are the "Order of the Day." Love is the binding principle, and nonviolence is the thread that guides us.

I first met Bernard Lafayette in 1979 when I was an 18-year-old student at Morehouse College, Dr. King's alma mater. Lafayette, along with Coretta Scott King, Andrew Young and Dr. Hugh M. Gloster, President of Morehouse College, founded the National Black Christian Student Leadership Consultation (NBCSLC) to mobilize African-American student leaders from colleges and universities to pick up the work of the original Student Nonviolent Coordinating Committee (SNCC). "Black" eventually was dropped from the name to encourage a broader base to the organization. Then after going through extensive training in nonviolence they formed the action arm of the NCSLC called the Association of Christian Student Leaders (ACSL), of which I became the president.

Moreover, Dr. King inspired me to be a freedom fighter, and Coretta Scott King helped shape my vision, but it was Bernard Lafayette who put flesh to my peace activism. He used to tease me that I was short like Dr. King, that I looked like him and sounded like him. So Lafayette put me on the front lines, even though I was a youth. During the 1981 terrible crisis in Atlanta when so many children were missing and killed, he challenged us to march for peace to end the violence. He told us, "Leaders lead, and this is your time to lead." I wanted him to lead the march and thought nobody would listen to us students. But Lafayette told us that during the civil rights movement the students didn't wait for Dr. King to come before they acted. They got involved, and the leaders emerged. So we marched.

Likewise, in the early 1980s when the Klan planned to march in downtown Atlanta, Lafayette challenged us to march against the Klan right there in the downtown area. So we marched under the NCSLC/ACSL banner. Lafayette provided the impetus for the action, but then he pushed us to do the work of organizing. That gave us all a great learning experience. Even in doing the Martin Luther King, Jr. Center's Summer Institute on Nonviolence, using the manual he wrote, he had me help him with the training. I learned by doing alongside this veteran peacemaker.

I met Jim Lawson when I lived in Los Angeles from 1987 to 1995. Lawson was the Pastor of the Holman United Methodist Church. He also served as the President of the Los Angeles Chapter of the Southern Christian Leadership Conference(SCLC). The SCLC was the leading civil rights organization in Los Angeles, and that Los Angeles chapter was more prominent nationally than any other except Atlanta's. This was because of Jim Lawson's leadership, who he was and what he had done.

Moreover, I worked as Director of the Ecumenical Black Campus Ministry Program at UCLA, and every year we had a big scholarship luncheon on Martin Luther King Day. One year we had Lawson as the keynote speaker. He was such a deep thinker. He wasn't the kind of speaker to just pump you up; he made you think. By the end, you were on your feet not because of the emotion but because of how profound he was as he challenged you.

When I got to know Lawson in the late 1980s, his hair was white, framing his smooth brown face, and he was an icon for Los Angeles. You could look to him and see what Dr. King was all about. Lawson, like King, stood for freedom, justice, equality and peace. He had been a friend and co-laborer with Dr. King in Memphis, and he kept refreshing the vision for us in the call to action in contemporary Los Angeles.

Peacemaking heroes connect us to the challenges we face today. They can connect us to other peace-loving people around the world. All of us have intrinsic worth as human beings. We are all somebody of infinite value because we've all been created in the image of the divine. So as peacemakers we are given the challenge to lead the way in the choice before us, as Dr. King put it, to "live together as brothers or perish together as fools."

For me as an African-American, I see the election of Barack Obama as President of the United States as a partial fulfillment of Dr. King's dream. It's certainly not a total fulfillment, only partial, but we are a step closer to that color-blind society King envisioned. The majority who put him into office were white voters. But Obama was more than just a black person elected President. He talked about how Dr. King influenced his life as a community organizer. President Obama is a Harvard-trained lawyer. He could have gone anywhere for a premium job. But something deep down inside (I believe, God Almighty) drove him out of the elite classrooms to the streets of Chicago. Then it drove him to the State Senate, then to the U.S. Senate, and then to the U.S. Presidency. It was that same force that earlier drove Dr. King from the security of an elite university to a humble pastorate in Montgomery, Alabama, then on to Atlanta, to Birmingham, to Selma, and to Memphis. President Obama came to the presidency not by the route of the military but as a community organizer, inspired by the peaceful ethic of Dr. King. Though he is the Commander-in-Chief who has to deal with war, President Obama has exhibited a primary concern for peace, being willing to talk to enemies even when it is diplomatically unpopular. That's the influence of King's vision touching the highest places of the land.

As you read this book, I have to tell you that I know Dan Buttry first hand. I've known him for about fourteen years, first as pastor, then as a missionary. We have demonstrated together about racist practices at corporate headquarters. We've enjoyed the streets of Rome together at a global peace conference. But above all that he is a peacemaker, one who specializes in conflict resolution and one who believes beyond a shadow of a doubt in peace and love. He is a Christian minister who holds fast to the principle of loving your enemies and praying for those who persecute you, as Jesus taught and as King echoed.

Dan Buttry has given us this rich album full of peacemakers' portraits. You'll meet Dr. King, Bernard Lafayette, James Lawson and so many others. Dan has created this album in the hope that these peacemakers' examples will shape our lives—and together we can contribute to world peace. I know Dan dreams of the day when we won't have to worry about troops in Iraq or in Afghanistan, when we won't have to worry about what's happening at the DMZ on the Korean peninsula, when we won't have to worry about the conflict between Israel and Palestine. I know it would be a joy for Dan if he could see historic enemies sit down and find a path to peace. When we continue to use violence, instead of realizing King's Beloved Community, we tumble into a Broken Community. We need to recognize that now is the time to live the dream of Dr. King, of Dan Buttry, of the peacemakers in this book, even of Jesus of Nazareth, and of God Almighty who created us all equal.

I'm honored that my friend has asked me to be part of this ground-breaking book. Of course, it's more than a book, more than an album. You're holding in your hands a major piece on peace. Now, it's up to you to realize how to use this piece in your life—and in our world.

The Reverend Kenneth James Flowers is the Pastor of the Greater New Mt. Moriah Missionary Baptist Church in Detroit, Michigan, and President of the Michigan Progressive Baptist Convention, Inc. He has also been a community leader, an interfaith leader, a non-violent activist and a teacher of Kingian nonviolence across the U.S. and around the world.

PART 1

Prophets and Visionaries

"I Have a Dream"

THE ISAIAH WALL STANDS near the United Nations, proclaiming the ancient words of the Hebrew prophet:

They shall beat their swords into plowshares,
Their spears into pruning hooks,
Nation shall not lift up sword against nation,
Neither shall they learn war anymore.

For diplomats working in New York City, the prophet's vision echoes the United Nations Charter to "save succeeding generations from the scourge of war." We all need voices like that of Isaiah, calling us to a better way of living together. Prophets arise within religious traditions, calling people to live in peace and justice according to divine dictates. Prophets also can be secular, speaking from values shared by all humanity or within a particular culture or nation. Prophets speak truth about our world—and call us to our higher standards.

History is rich with prophets. No movement for justice or peace was ever launched without someone taking the prophet's mantle and giving direction to the longings among hurting people. Before the Europeans came to North America, a Huron prophet named Deganawida challenged warring tribes to come together in peace. He traveled across the eastern Great Lakes region with a vision deeply rooted in the religious traditions of the tribes. His call to peace inspired a weary Mohawk warrior named Hiawatha to put political form to the prophetic vision. Deganawida's dream took shape in the formation of the Iroquois Confederacy. Five tribes came together to form the confederation: The Senecas, the Mohawks, the Oneidas, the Cayugas, and the Onondagas. Later the Tuscaroras joined and the confederacy was renamed the Six Nations. They buried weapons in a pit and then planted a pine tree on top as a symbol of the life growing out of their peace compact. That peace agreement bound the tribes together for at least two centuries. The Iroquois Confederacy also created a democratic structure for decision-making that was adopted in large part by the young United States government, enabling large societies to make major decisions through peaceful means.

In Latin America, Bartolomé de Las Casas stands as a prophetic giant over the centuries since the European invasion of the Americas. He saw Columbus return from his first voyage to the "New World" and sailed there himself in 1502. At first he was a priest within the system that enslaved the indigenous Americans. But in 1514 the genocidal cruelty of the Spanish colonization drove him to a dramatic conversion. He became a courageous defender of the Indians, traveling between Spain and the New World to denounce not just the excesses of cruelty but the whole unjust system. Las Casas came to see Christ in the suffering of the Indians, "crucified not once, but thousands of times." Las Casas' concern as a priest became, not the salvation of the Indians, but the salvation of the Spanish themselves. He saw the Spanish system persecuting Christ in the persons of the poor Indians. Las Casas seemed a lone voice at the time, but his voice still echoes hundreds of years later in lands where poor and indigenous peoples continue to suffer exploitation and the denial of basic human rights.

Another prophet contemporary with Las Casas was the Dutch Christian humanist Desiderius Erasmus. He passionately urged peace at a time when religious conflicts were rapidly moving toward the Reformation split of the Catholic Church and the subsequent proliferation of religious warfare throughout Europe. He wrote an essay titled, "War Is Sweet to Those Who Have Not Tried It," a caution that rings as relevant today as in the early 16th Century. He challenged Church teaching about participating in just wars. Instead, he called for reconciliation in the spirit of Christ: "How can you say Our Father if you plunge steel into the guts of your brother? Christ compared himself to a hen: Christians behave like hawks. Christ was a shepherd of sheep: Christians tear each other like wolves." Erasmus practiced what he preached at great risk in those volatile times. He disagreed with Martin Luther and would engage in rigorous debate, but he refused to condemn the Reformer as a heretic, bringing harsh criticism upon himself from Catholic leaders. Erasmus believed talking through the conflicts and disagreeing was far preferable to going to war.

Joanna Macy is a Buddhist scholar and teacher who bridges the worldviews of the East and West. She has facilitated workshops around the world to help people do deep emotional thinking that lays the foundation for peace-building. For Macy, "The most remarkable feature of this historical moment on Earth is not that we are on the way to destroying the world—we've actually been on the way for quite a while. It is that we are beginning to wake up, as from a millennia-long sleep, to a whole new relationship with our world, with ourselves and each other." Macy helps workshop participants explore what a life-sustaining society would be like, something that cannot be done individually but must be a shared project with others. She has been especially powerful in helping people unpack the deep barriers of grief, fear, numbness and despair that prevent our action for peace and sustainability.

Prophets can sometimes arise from surprising sources. One person who most pointedly addressed the matrix of relationships forging modern war was Dwight D. Eisenhower. He had been the commander of the Allied forces in Europe in World War II and then President of the U.S. as a global superpower during the Cold War—not positions from which one would expect prophetic words of peace. Yet he spoke about the "grave implications" of a new threat within the U.S.: "In the councils of government, we must guard against the acquisition of unwarranted influence, whether sought or unsought, by the military-industrial complex. The potential for the disastrous rise of misplaced power exists and will persist." He also critiqued the economic implications of militarism: "Every gun that is made, every warship launched, every rocket fired signifies, in the final sense, a theft from those who hunger and are not fed, those who are cold and are not clothed." No religious prophet could have spoken as pointedly as this military man.

Prophets give shape and direction to our hopes. When Martin Luther King said "I have a dream," he was articulating the dream millions of people had but could not express so eloquently. The prophet's words are embraced, repeated, set to melodies, chiseled into stone and passed on from generation to generation. They keep the flame burning bright to light our path toward peace and justice.

CHAPTER 1

Mohandas "Mahatma" Gandhi
(1869-1948)

Our motto must ever be conversion by gentle persuasion and a constant appeal to the head and heart. We must therefore be ever courteous and patient with those who do not see eye to eye with us.

—Mohandas Gandhi

The day I stood where Gandhi was assassinated in Delhi, India, I thought how powerless that assassin's bullet was in stopping him. History's verdict on Gandhi is still in the balance. I enjoy Michael Hart's book, **The 100: A Ranking of the Most Influential Persons in History**—*except that Gandhi only makes Hart's honorable mention list. I think Hart got that wrong, considering what has unfolded over the last 25 years with nonviolent people power. Movements on every continent now point to Gandhi as a guiding light. So he is first in this book.*

A TINY WIRY MAN, clad only in a loincloth, shoulder shawl and sandals, strode with his walking stick mile after mile on a journey to the sea. Day after day he trekked through the villages of India. Hundreds, then thousands of people followed him. He finally arrived at the beach and proceeded to distill salt from the ocean water. This simple act was the most vivid blow against the mightiest empire on the globe at that time. It ignited imaginations and actions that would eventually loose the empire's largest colony. The nonviolent campaigns for freedom led by this man would ripple around the world and become the model in similar struggles for justice and peace.

Mohandas K. Gandhi led the movement in India for independence from British colonial rule. He utilized a nonviolent methodology he called *satyagraha*, a Sanskrit word that Gandhi explained in this way: "Its root meaning is 'holding on to the truth,' hence 'force of righteousness.' I have also called it love force or soul force." He called his efforts "experiments with truth." Through his experiments he shaped a philosophy and methodology of resistance that has spawned similar movements on every continent.

Gandhi initially developed his nonviolent philosophy and practice during the twenty years he lived in South Africa following his legal training in London. His first major campaign was against the Asiatic Registration Act of 1907, which required every Indian in South Africa to register with the government and to produce a certificate whenever a police officer demanded it. Gandhi led a campaign to refuse to obtain the certificate. Government offices were picketed, and certificates were burned in public events. The police arrested those involved in the protest actions. At one point, out of 13,000 Indians living in the Transvaal, 2,500 were in jail as registration certificate protesters!

When the Indian Relief Bill that overturned the registration act was passed, Gandhi returned to India to join the movement to expel the British and help his homeland obtain independence. Gandhi was given the honorific title *Mahatma*, the Great One, first by the Indian poet Rabindranath Tagore, then by a public appreciative of his leadership. Sometimes he was simply called *Bapu*, father.

To strike at the heart of the economic ties that supported the colonial system, Gandhi organized campaigns of non-cooperation with British political and economic power. In an effort to undercut the British dominance of textile manufacturing, he began spinning his own cloth every day and urged all Indians to do the same. Meanwhile British textiles were boycotted. The spinning wheel became a symbol for the struggle, and the *khadi* homespun cloth became the uniform of the independence movement. When violence erupted, Gandhi called off the campaign. He was arrested and served two years in prison.

The second economic campaign struck at the salt tax, which was the second leading source of income from India for the British. Gandhi used his "Salt March" across India to the sea to strike a blow at the British monopoly on salt and also to arouse the Indian public for nonviolent resistance. After his 400-kilometer journey and making salt at the seashore, Gandhi was arrested along with more than 60,000 Indians who joined the anti-salt tax campaign. The British officials began negotiating with Gandhi; but nothing much came of the talks, and Gandhi was imprisoned yet again.

For Gandhi, a key to *satyagraha* is understanding the relationship of ends and means. If one hoped for a peaceful and just end in a struggle, then the means used in pursuit of the struggle needed to be consistent with that end. "If one takes care of the means, the end will take care of itself," he wrote. "We have always control over the means and never of the ends." Gandhi taught that refusing to cooperate with exploitation and injustice made a person free. Acts of non-cooperation, however, could bring down the weight of repression, so willingness to sacrifice oneself nonviolently was to be the great means in the struggle. As Gandhi said, "I am prepared to die, but there is no cause for which I am prepared to kill."

Nonviolence was not a tactic of weakness for Gandhi, but a far more powerful force than violence. "Practice nonviolence not because of weakness," he said. "Practice nonviolence being conscious of strength and power." Even more courage was necessary in nonviolent struggle than the courage to engage in battle with arms. If the choice was between being violent and being cowardly, Gandhi would opt for violence. But that was not the choice since nonviolent resistance presented another option. Besides having courage, the practitioner of *satyagraha* must be courteous:

"Disobedience to be civil, must be sincere, respectful, restrained, never defiant, must be based upon some well-understood principle, must not be capricious, and above all, must have no ill-will or hatred behind it." Gandhi set a high standard for the activists in his campaigns, but he modeled that standard in his own behavior, always courageous, polite, self-sacrificing, gentle and unbowed.

Besides the struggles against British colonialism, Gandhi strove for justice within Hindu society, especially in his appeal for raising the status of the "untouchables," the *Dalits*. Gandhi called them *Harijans*, "children of God." Though he was from an upper caste, he advocated an end to the social and economic injustices of the caste system. He engaged in a series of fasts about the ill-treatment of the *Dalits*, including one "fast to the death" from prison that successfully eased a particular restriction.

During World War II Gandhi refused to participate in the British war effort, claiming that Indians could not fight in a war for democratic freedom when they were denied freedom themselves. The "Quit India" campaign for independence stirred up much turmoil in the country, to which the British responded with mass arrests. Gandhi again spent two years in prison. Finally he was released, and the British agreed that power should be transferred to Indian leadership. After the war, the negotiations for the British to leave culminated with the independence of India on August 16, 1947.

But independence was born amid horrific bloodshed. Throughout the struggle against British rule there had been division among many of the Hindus and Muslims—in spite of the vision of Gandhi and the Muslim leader Abdul Ghaffar Khan for a multi-religious nation. As the British colonial rule was ending, the inter-communal violence became massive. To halt one outbreak Gandhi began another "fast to the death," finally winning agreement from key leaders to try to halt the killing. But his dream for India crumbled as the former colony broke up into the nations of India and Pakistan.

Gandhi was assassinated in New Delhi on January 30, 1948, as he walked on the grounds of the guesthouse he frequented.

Among the well-wishers who came to meet him was the assassin, a Hindu militant who despised Gandhi for his conciliatory approach to Muslims and to newly formed Pakistan. Gandhi's victory in achieving freedom fell short of his hopes, because of the deep religious and political divisions between the Hindu and Muslim communities, but Gandhi's nonviolent philosophy and methodology was embraced by many other freedom struggles. Other peacemaking giants have arisen who point to him as their inspiration and guide. Gandhi said, "You must be the change you wish to see in the world." He was that change to a degree few others have achieved.

CHAPTER 2

Dorothy Day
(1897-1980)

**We will not be drilled into fear.
We do not have faith in God if we
depend upon the Atom Bomb.**

—Dorothy Day

*Dorothy Day is a godmother in
my activist family tree. I learned of
her through **Sojourners** magazine.
Again and again, so many people
I respected were referring to her.
I wish I'd been able to know her and sit at her feet. But
then she would have been too busy serving the poor,
challenging the powers and stirring up the pot for me to
even sit down! The challenge is to follow in her footsteps.*

DOROTHY DAY WAS ONCE a Communist who became a leading
voice for radical nonviolent Christianity in the United States. She
lived a life of voluntary poverty, cared for the homeless, published
The Catholic Worker newspaper and founded a movement by the
same name that continues to this day.

Day's early adulthood was spent as a muckraking leftist journalist, joining herself with various protest movements while living
as part of the sexual revolution of the 1920s. Faced with her second pregnancy, she was spurred onto a religious quest that ended
with converting to Catholicism, abandoning her lover and keeping
her baby. She also kept the passion for the poor and the struggles
for justice that had marked her earlier years, but now that passion
was wedded to a deep spirituality.

In 1933 she met Peter Maurin, and they co-founded *The Catholic Worker* to address concerns of war and poverty from a radical Catholic perspective. Only 2,500 copies of the first issue were printed, but by the end of the year they were publishing 100,000 papers per issue. They sold papers for a penny apiece so that anyone could buy one—and they still gave away thousands of copies. The paper didn't just criticize what was going on; it challenged readers to make a personal response. Most of the initial writing came directly from Dorothy Day herself.

Beginning in 1935, through the pages of *The Catholic Worker*, Day propounded a philosophy of neutral pacifism based on the teaching of Jesus. Few paid attention to what she said at first, but when the Spanish Civil War broke out, critics from both sides were alienated by her position. The Catholic Church supported the Fascist Franco (as did Hitler and Mussolini). Meanwhile the American left, which identified with many of Day's social positions, supported the Republican side, which included Communists, socialists, anarchists and many American leftist volunteers. Day wrote, "We are not, of course, pro-Franco, but pacifists, followers of Gandhi in our struggle to build a spirit of nonviolence. But in those days we got it from both sides; it was a holy war to most Catholics, just as world revolution is a holy war to Communists." About two-thirds of the readers abandoned *The Catholic Worker* because of the pacifism espoused in its pages.

Day and *The Catholic Worker* continued to hold to the pacifist position during World War II. "Our manifesto is the Sermon on the Mount," Day wrote. "We love our country... We have been the only country in the world where men and women of all nations have taken refuge from oppression." But for Day, action in the face of violence was expressed through doing acts of mercy, not by going to war. Many of the faithful readers of *The Catholic Worker* went to prison or spent the war years laboring in rural work camps.

Dorothy Day was a strong voice against anti-Semitism as Hitler was rising to power in Europe. *The Catholic Worker* was certainly the first Catholic journal, maybe one of the first non-Jewish papers in the U.S., to decry the growing persecution of the Jews under the Nazis. She was one of the founders of Catholics to Fight Anti-Semitism. She became a staunch critic of Father Charles Coughlin, the fiery priest who used his radio programs to promote anti-Semitic ideas and who published the spurious *Protocols of the Elders of Zion* in his journal *Social Justice*. Day could be pointedly acerbic in her critiques of such hate speech, especially when the hate came from a religious source.

Day and Maurin founded the House of Hospitality to feed the hungry and shelter the homeless in New York City, a ministry that began with Day's willingness to open her own apartment to needy people during the winter. The House of Hospitality was the first in what grew to be many Catholic Worker Houses across the country. Before Mother Teresa picked up the dying in Calcutta, Dorothy Day was welcoming the poorest of the poor, the destitute, addicted and dying into the Catholic Worker Houses. She said, "Once they are taken in, they become members of the family. Or rather they always were members of the family. They are our brothers and sisters in Christ." Religion or background did not matter, only that a person was in need.

During the Cold War missile attack scares of the 1950s and 1960s she was jailed three times for refusing to participate in civil defense drills in New York City. She viewed the drills as an attempt to promote nuclear war by getting people to think it was survivable. For her, participation in the drills was complicity in the entire nuclear war preparation enterprise with its waste of billions of dollars in military spending. When the alarms went off, she and a handful of others sat in protest on the steps of City Hall. "We will not be drilled into fear," she said. "We do not have faith in God if we depend on the Atom Bomb." She was arrested each year when the civil defense drill was held—until such drills were suspended after 2,000 people refused to participate in 1961.

Day was nearly hit by rifle fire from the Ku Klux Klan while visiting the racially integrated community of Koinonia Farms in Georgia in 1957. The Klan bullets smashed into the steering column of the car she was driving. By the time of the Vietnam War she was called "the grand old lady of pacifism" and had a strong influence on a rising generation of peace activists. She protested the draft and the war in Vietnam. Day was last jailed in 1973 at the age of 75. She was jailed for taking part in a banned picket in support of striking farm workers and their leader Cesar Chavez.

Day was given many honors. Mother Teresa was one of the people who came to visit her as her health was failing, but she brushed off such attention, "Don't call me a saint. I don't want to be dismissed so easily." Theodore Hesburgh of Notre Dame University said Day was known for "comforting the afflicted and afflicting the comfortable". He presented her the Laetare Medal from Notre Dame for her social witness.

Dorothy Day challenged people to act in love. There was always some sort of action that could be taken in the face of the challenges of poverty and war. She wrote, "Young people say: What good can one person do? What is the sense of our small effort? They cannot see that we must lay one brick at a time, take one step at a time, we can be responsible only for the action of the present moment. But we can beg for an increase of love in our hearts that will vitalize and transform all our individual actions, and know that God will take them and multiply them, as Jesus multiplied the loaves and fishes." The impact of Day's loving actions for justice and peace continue to multiply through those whose lives were changed by her witness.

CHAPTER 3

Martin Luther King, Jr.

(1929-1968)

Our nonviolent direct action program has as its objective not the creation of tensions, but the surfacing of tensions already present. We set out to precipitate a crisis situation that must open the door to negotiation. I am not afraid of the words 'crisis' and 'tension.' I deeply oppose violence, but constructive crisis and tension are necessary for growth.

—Martin Luther King, Jr.

I stood among thousands of Latvian young people who dared to demonstrate for independence from the powerful Soviet Union. It was the second such demonstration, and I'd just come to the Soviet Union for a Baptist friendship tour following an international Baptist peace conference that summer of 1988. We had produced booklets for the conference containing three of Dr. King's greatest texts. As we passed out King's prophetic words—there in what was then the Soviet Union—we talked openly together about the power of nonviolent action in a struggle for freedom. To see the Baltic Republics win their independence with the loss of only four lives was a powerful illustration of King's belief: "Darkness cannot drive out darkness; only light can do that."

KING RUSHED FROM THE church to his house as soon as he heard the news. A crowd of angry African-Americans were gathered there, armed with knives and guns. The front of the house was damaged from a bomb hurled at it. King pushed through the crowd to the back of the house where he found his wife Coretta and their 10-week-old baby safe. What would this young pastor, who was preaching nonviolence, do now that his own family had been attacked? King stood before the crowd and spoke with deliberate calm to quiet their rage: "Don't do anything panicky. Don't get your weapons. If you have weapons, take them home. He who lives by the sword will perish by the sword. Remember that is what Jesus said. We are not advocating violence. We want to love our enemies. I want you to love our enemies. Be good to them. This is what we must live by. We must meet hate with love."

Few preachers have practiced what they preached in as difficult circumstances as those Martin Luther King, Jr. faced. He was a leader in the movement that challenged the structures of racism in the form of segregation in the American South. Then he expanded his visionary protest to the more complex structures of oppression—what he called the "giant triplets of racism, extreme materialism and militarism." Through it all he maintained a deep commitment to the philosophy and practice of nonviolence, rooted in the teachings of Jesus in the Sermon on the Mount and shaped through the methodology of Mahatma Gandhi.

Martin Luther King, Jr. was born into the family of a Baptist preacher from Atlanta, Georgia. He received his theological training at Morehouse College, Crozer Seminary and Boston University. In 1954 he was called to pastor the Dexter Avenue Baptist Church in Montgomery, Alabama, not knowing that a year later it would become the center of a historic struggle. On December 1, 1955, Rosa Parks refused to give up her seat on a bus, striking a nonviolent blow to the segregated system in public transportation. The Montgomery Improvement Association (MIA) was formed to organize and mobilize African-Americans for a concerted campaign of protest, including a boycott of the buses. King was chosen as president of the association. Through his stirring sermons and preaching about nonviolence and love of enemies, Dexter Avenue Baptist Church became the gathering point for the mass meetings that stoked the fires of protest. Thousands of black workers and shoppers walked downtown or rode in the carpools the MIA organized.

The bombing of Dr. King's house was one of the crisis points for the struggle, but King and the others in the movement were undeterred. Arrests, physical intimidation by the police and the Ku Klux Klan, bombings and job losses did not stop the bus boycott, which continued for over a year. When the U.S. Supreme Court ordered the desegregation of the buses, King and other movement leaders boarded a bus at the stop in front of his home to celebrate their victory.

King and some of the other activist pastors founded the Southern Christian Leadership Conference (SCLC) to provide leadership to local struggles from Selma to Memphis. SCLC also became a national voice advocating for civil rights legislation in Congress and appealing to the nation's conscience through marches and speeches. King and his staff would speak around the country, then focus on particular cities in strategic campaigns for various civil rights.

The cornerstone of Dr. King's nonviolence was love. He wrote, "We shall meet your physical force with soul force. Do to us what you will, and we will continue to love you."

King's vision was put to the test again in the 1963 campaign against segregated businesses in Birmingham, Alabama. Waves of protests were met with arrests, with King and his colleague Ralph Abernathy both arrested in a climactic protest. While King was incarcerated, some of the time in solitary confinement, he wrote *Letter from Birmingham Jail* in response to a published statement from white clergy urging African Americans to be patient and wait. In the letter, King spelled out the core of his nonviolent philosophy. He saw nonviolent direct action as a tool to create a crisis that would challenge an unjust system. It did not create the conflict but rather brought it to the surface, King said. He opposed violence. "We see the need for nonviolent gadflies to create the kind of tension in society that will help men rise from the dark depths of prejudice and racism to the majestic heights of understanding and brotherhood."

As many continued to be held in the Birmingham jail, King gave permission to allow children to march. Six hundred young people were arrested, and many were battered by fire hoses or attacked by police dogs. National public pressure, from the Federal government included, built up in response to the police violence used against nonviolent and often praying protesters. Sheriff "Bull" Connor was eventually forced to resign, and many public accommodations were desegregated. King shifted the campaign from Birmingham to Washington, D.C.

The massive March on Washington for Jobs and Freedom was organized. The marchers called for many advances in civil rights including passage of a basic civil rights bill. From the steps of the Lincoln Memorial before over 200,000 people King electrified the crowd with his *I Have a Dream* speech. He talked about the returned check of promise given to African Americans marked "insufficient funds" and the demand of the current generation for justice and freedom. He talked about not being satisfied as long as injustice and brutality continued. Then he lifted up the vision: "I have a dream" he almost chanted. He proclaimed a vision of the beloved community, one of his favorite themes. He dreamed of a time "when all God's children—black men and white men, Jews and Gentiles, Catholics and Protestants—will be able to join hands and to sing in the words of the old Negro spiritual, 'Free at last, free at last, thank God Almighty, we are free at last.'"

For King the beloved community would not come easily. It required courageous nonviolent action, namely means that were consistent with the peaceful and just end envisioned by the dreamer but also sufficiently powerful to deal with the long-entrenched structures of bigotry and racist privilege. He said, "Wars are poor chisels for carving out peaceful tomorrows. We must pursue peaceful ends through peaceful means." As angry victims of injustice wanted to respond with violence, he warned: "Returning violence for violence multiplies violence, adding deeper darkness to a night already devoid of stars. Darkness cannot drive out darkness; only light can do that." For King nonviolence was a powerful weapon, but "a sword that heals."

The beloved community could not be achieved just through trying to live peacefully together. Justice was necessary—whether it was the economic justice that addressed the grinding poverty that so many lived under or the racial justice that undid the legalized structures of discrimination. King taught, "Injustice anywhere is a threat to justice everywhere. We are caught in an inescapable network of mutuality, tied in a single garment of destiny." So his campaigns broadened to deal more with the issues of poverty, which cut across the racial lines. He tried, in an unsuccessful campaign, to confront the structures of slums in Chicago. In 1968, prior to the national Poor People's Campaign scheduled for Washington, D.C. , he went to Memphis to help striking garbage workers. While in Memphis Dr. King was assassinated as he stood on the balcony of his hotel room. The visionary of nonviolence and the beloved community would get to the mountaintop and see into the Promised Land—but even as he foretold on the night before his death, he would not make it himself.

The legacy of Martin Luther King, Jr. is beyond measure. He was the youngest recipient of the Nobel Peace Prize, receiving it in 1964. He rose up as a leader within the civil rights movement, but his vision caused him to question the structures of poverty and the war in Vietnam. His fame spread around the world, coupled with Gandhi as the two apostles of peace and nonviolence. King centers for the study of nonviolence are found in many countries, far transcending African-American and U.S. cultural contexts. In many U.S. cities riots broke out following his death, but on the other hand many milestones in civil rights were achieved and social and political opportunities opened up for African-Americans that can be traced directly to the movement in which he played such a central role.

With a national holiday in the U.S. and frequent remembrances of "The Dream," it is easy to let Dr. King's story and all of his talk about love fade into the static of popular culture. King's love was real and profound, but also intensely focused and able to shake strongholds of power. King's nonviolence was a means of struggle against injustice, which was viewed as a grave threat by those in power. He was imprisoned many times, targeted by bombs, wire-tapped by the FBI and eventually gunned down. He was harassed and hunted because he was not a tame dreamer.

The hope he ignited in many hearts was a death-knell to a system of dominance that had exploited black people for centuries. That hope resonates today in the hearts of many other oppressed peoples around the world.

When King thought of his own legacy, he put it very simply: "Say I was a drum major for justice; I was a drum major for peace; I was a drum major for righteousness.... I just want to leave a committed life behind."

We are still trying to march to his beat.

Masahisa Goi
(1916-1980)

May Peace Prevail on Earth.

—Masahisa Goi

I can't recall when I saw my first peace pole, but I've been moved by the simple concrete testimony of this prayerful expression. I initiated the planting of a Peace Pole at my denomination's mission center with 13 prayer translations, including 3 that had never been placed on poles before. As I travel the world, I take pictures of Peace Poles I've found in delightfully surprising places—surprising to me, but not to the visionaries who planted them.

A SIMPLE, FIVE-WORD PRAYER has been "planted" in many languages on more than 200,000 Peace Poles around the world: "May Peace Prevail on Earth." The prayer bridges religious and linguistic divisions, bringing people together in a common expression of prayer and hope for peace.

The visionary behind the World Peace Prayer was the Japanese philosopher and spiritual leader Masahisa Goi. As a child Goi was very frail, so to deal with his poor health he began to explore the disciplines of yoga, spiritual healing and the martial arts. He engaged in long periods of meditation. During World War II he worked in a factory, but outside of his work he organized various cultural events including a choir. The war was a traumatic spiritual experience for him, and he began to yearn desperately for peace, not only for Japan but also for the world.

Goi founded Byakko Shinko Kai, an organization to promote spirituality and spiritual practices dedicated to world peace. He studied teachings of various religions including the Chinese philosopher Lao Tsu and the Bible. Through his books and lectures he encouraged people to seek inner peace as well as world peace.

In a long journey of prayer in which he asked to be of service to humanity, Goi believed the prayer "May Peace Prevail On Earth" was given to him. He believed that if people put their efforts into this prayer for peace it would have a uniting effect for all humanity. In 1955 he founded the Movement of Prayer for World Peace, which eventually became The World Peace Prayer Society. The group was established to transcend all religious, social, ethnic and political barriers through the promotion of the prayer. Peace Poles were designed to be inscribed with the prayer in various languages. These poles would then be set into the ground as constant reminders and witnesses to the hope for peace.

Peace Poles have been planted in every country, in ordinary places such as houses of worship and homes and in places of special conflict. Many religious leaders have planted Peace Poles, including Pope John Paul II, Mother Teresa and the Dalai Lama. Masahisa Goi's simple prayer has become an inspiration to millions of people around the world who have never heard his name but have shared his passion and hope.

To obtain information about Peace Poles in the United States, contact Shop Peace of The World Peace Prayer Society at www.-shoppeace.org (26 Benton Road, Amenia, NY 12592, phone: 845-877-6093). For other sources around the world contact: http://www.worldpeace.org/

CHAPTER 5

Helen Caldicott

(b. 1938)

As a doctor, as well as a mother and a world citizen, I wish to practice the ultimate form of preventive medicine by ridding the earth of these technologies that propagate disease, suffering, and death.

—Helen Caldicott

While working on the nuclear weapons freeze campaign in Boston, I remember Helen Caldicott coming to speak. Her gripping narration of the impact of a nuclear detonation over our city brought home the reality of our Cold War peril. I found myself incorporating much of what she said into my own presentations as we sought to make sure such a calamity would never happen.

A 10-MEGATON NUCLEAR BOMB is detonated above the center of your city. In the first circle of destruction people and buildings are vaporized. In the next circle buildings are flattened and people killed instantly. In the next circle massive fires are ignited, quickly killing anyone who survived the blast. You see the map of your city and the growing span of utter destruction. You place your own home on the map and feel the chill of what might happen. Survivors of the blast and fires will likely die from radiation poisoning in the weeks to follow. In the farthest reaches, many miles from the center of the blast, survivors face a strong likelihood of death from cancer or leukemia in the years ahead, assuming the nuclear war did not trigger a "nuclear winter" wiping out most life on the planet.

Such was the standard opening of a presentation by Dr. Helen Caldicott at the height of the Cold War between the United States and the Soviet Union. She brought the reality of nuclear destruction to communities across the United States. She helped crystallize the understanding of the threat faced in the United States, and the threat that the United States, with its massive arsenal and first-strike capability, posed to others. Caldicott was one of the visionaries who helped turn the nuclear arms race into a freeze which eventually led to the ending of the Cold War and to the first steps of nuclear disarmament.

Born Helen Mary Broinowski in Australia, Helen Caldicott became a physician. She eventually taught pediatrics at Harvard Medical School. In 1980 she resigned her medical appointments at Harvard and a children's hospital to dedicate herself full-time to the over-riding health crisis she saw in the growing threat of nuclear war.

As a teenager she read Neville Shute's *On the Beach*, which depicts an accidental nuclear war that ends human life. The story is set in Melbourne where the young Caldicott lived. "This scenario branded my soul," she said. The vision haunted and inspired her life passion. In Australia Dr. Caldicott had provided leadership in opposition to the atmospheric nuclear testing carried out by France in the Pacific. She used documents that showed Australian water systems had been contaminated by nuclear fallout from the French tests to mobilize a campaign to demand a halt to the atmospheric tests—a campaign that eventually forced French nuclear tests underground. Caldicott also educated trade unions about the medical dangers related to nuclear power and the mining of uranium, a concern that has continued throughout her life.

When Caldicott came to the United States she joined Physicians for Social Responsibility (PSR), giving renewed energy and focus to the organization. Soon she was the head of PSR and its chief voice about the nuclear arms race, growing the membership to around 23,000 physicians. As she traveled to other countries she stimulated the formation of similar physicians' organizations. These groups were eventually connected into the International Physicians for the Prevention of Nuclear War, which received the Nobel Peace Prize in 1985. The international body represented 145,000 physicians in 40 countries.

Caldicott also founded the Women's Action for Nuclear Disarmament in 1982, a group now known as Women's Action for New Directions (WAND). It remains one of the most prominent grassroots groups in the efforts to halt the spread of nuclear arms. Caldicott traveled extensively across the U.S. organizing women to be advocates for a nuclear freeze and against the new weapons systems proposed by the Reagan Administration. WAND organized a Political Action Committee to support women as pro-peace candidates for Congress. By focusing on physicians and women, Caldicott mobilized two key constituencies that helped delegitimize the madness of "mutually assured destruction", the doctrine that provided the rationale for the building of tens of thousands of nuclear weapons on each side.

For Caldicott, education was the antidote to the psychological numbing that is produced by an overwhelming issue like the nuclear arms race. She sought as many platforms as possible to educate people about what could happen if a bomb was dropped, the issues that must be faced and alternative approaches to the policies that were being pursued. In her presentations, Caldicott was both very detailed and chilling in her scholarly presentation of the facts of a potential nuclear exchange. She could also be cuttingly funny as she talked about the "missile envy" that drove the superpower competition. Ultimately, however, these were deeply passionate matters for Caldicott. She said, "To be unemotional about the end of the earth approaching, is mentally sick. To feel no feelings about it, to be uninvolved is inappropriate, to be psychologically comfortable today, absolutely inappropriate."

As the Cold War ended, new military and nuclear threats developed. Caldicott continued her advocacy about these new developments, particularly focusing on some of the corporations involved in nuclear arms development. As the administration of President George W. Bush pursued a new generation of nuclear weapons, Caldicott's book *The New Nuclear Danger* exposed the dangers of a new arms race with Russia and China if such a course should be pursued. One issue that especially concerned her was the use of depleted uranium bombs in U.S. military actions against Serbia and Iraq. She described the practice as "punishing the children. It's really wicked."

Nuclear power has also been a constant concern for Caldicott, seeing it as the second major medical threat to life on the planet after nuclear war. She criticizes all stages of the nuclear power industry, from mining to power plant production to the storage of spent nuclear fuel. So far there is no safe way to dispose of nuclear waste, even though some of these materials can remain an active threat to health and life for more than 500,000 years.

Throughout her career Caldicott has spoken as a physician, giving special attention to the health impact of nuclear weapons and nuclear power. However, she also sees the issues about human survival in the face of the nuclear threats as far larger than a medical problem. "This is the ultimate spiritual and religious issue ever to face the human race," she said. "For what is our responsibility to God to preserve the creation and evolution? We are the curators of possibly the only life in the universe and our responsibility is enormous. We must therefore dedicate every waking and sleeping moment to the preservation of creation."

CHAPTER 6

Tenzin Gyatso, The 14th Dalai Lama

(b. 1935)

In the practice of tolerance, one's enemy is the best teacher.

—Tenzin Gyatso

How do we sustain hope in the face of a seemingly hopeless situation? For me hope is rooted in faith, especially in my understanding of Christ. It's not a political or strategic calculation. Coming at the question of hope and the struggle for freedom from a Buddhist tradition, the Dalai Lama also challenges activists to go deeper. The heart of a peacemaker needs to be spiritually rooted for the hardest and longest struggles.

TENZIN GYATSO WAS BORN in a rural village in Tibet. Following the practices of Tibetan Buddhism he was recognized as the 14th reincarnation of the Dalai Lama, a term that means "Ocean of Wisdom." Dalai Lamas are believed to be the manifestation of the Bodhisattva or "enlightened being" of compassion and the patron saint of Tibet. As the Dalai Lama, Tenzin Gyatso began his monastic education at the age of 6. He received his doctorate in Buddhist philosophy at 23, but prior to completing his education, politics intervened to shape his life in a dramatic fashion.

In October, 1950, China invaded Tibet and seized control. During the next month the Dalai Lama assumed full political power in the Tibetan government where the Dalai Lama has traditionally been the absolute ruler. He initially sought to work within the Chinese Communist system, meeting with Mao Tse-Tung, Chou En-Lai and other Communist leaders. Then, in 1959, there was a failed uprising by Tibetans that prompted the Dalai Lama to flee to Dharamsala, India, and set up a government in exile. Tens of thousands of Tibetans followed him into exile, leaving Tibet for India and other parts of the world.

In articulating his three major commitments, the Dalai Lama sees himself first as a promoter of human values such as compassion, forgiveness, tolerance, contentment and self-discipline. He says, "Love and compassion are necessities, not luxuries. Without them humanity cannot survive." A central Buddhist ethical teaching is to do no harm. The Dalai Lama teaches, "It is necessary to help others, not only in our prayers, but in our daily lives. If we find we cannot help others, the least we can do is to desist from harming them."

Through his teaching the Dalai Lama addresses both the internal aspects of personal peace and the social and political dimensions of peace. Both are necessary. He said, "We can never obtain peace in the outer world until we make peace with ourselves." On the other hand he said, "It is not possible to find peace in the soul without security and harmony between the people." As a religious peacemaker he teaches and works for the inner and outer forms of peace.

The Dalai Lama's second commitment is to harmony and understanding among the world's religious traditions—a specific area of global peacemaking to which he has given much effort. He sees the exchange of ideas and feelings between leaders of different religions as a way to "open the door to a progressive pacification between people." He has met with almost every major religious figure in the world in his quest for understanding and harmony. He is more than the formal head of a major religious group appearing in global religious congresses. He has participated directly in the organizing and planning of such events.

Working with other contemplatives of different religions in the Monastic Interreligious Dialogue, the Dalai Lama helped produce the Universal Declaration of Nonviolence. In introducing the declaration he wrote: "This document is an attempt to set forth a vision of nonviolence within the context of an emerging global civilization in which all forms of violence, especially war, are totally unacceptable as means to settle disputes between and among nations, groups and persons. This new vision of civilization is global in scope, universal in culture and based on love and compassion, the highest moral and spiritual principles of the various historical religions. Its universal nature acknowledges the essential fact of modern life: the interdependence of nations, economies, cultures and religious traditions."

His third commitment is to the people of Tibet as their Dalai Lama. While in exile the Dalai Lama began a thorough overhaul of the Tibetan political system. He abandoned Tibet's traditional heavy-handed feudalistic system and established democratic reforms in both the government-in-exile and in the plans for a constitution for a free Tibet. He designed a process upon return to Tibet to have the Dalai Lama step down from his traditional position of political power and become an ordinary citizen, sharing in life under a fully democratic government. He has also set up many educational, cultural and religious institutions to preserve Tibetan identity and culture during the period of exile and Tibetan Diaspora.

The Dalai Lama has persistently sought nonviolent means for liberating Tibet. He has repeatedly taken the case of Tibet to the United Nations, resulting in the passage of a number of General Assembly resolutions in support of Tibet. In 1987 he proposed a Five-Point Peace Plan to deal with Tibet. He proposed making Tibet a zone of peace, halting the massive influx of ethnic Chinese into Tibet, halting nuclear weapon production and nuclear waste dumping in Tibet, and negotiating constructive relationships between China and Tibet. The Dalai Lama's peacemaking efforts were recognized with a Nobel Peace Prize in 1989, but they were not received positively by China. The Dalai Lama tried to accommodate China's interests, but he held that "whatever the outcome of the negotiations with the Chinese may be, the Tibetan people themselves must be the ultimate deciding authority."

In 2008, during the lead-up to the Beijing Olympics, another uprising and violent repression in Tibet focused world attention on the situation in that mountainous region. During this crisis, new contacts were made between the Dalai Lama and the Chinese government to open negotiations on the status of Tibet. Once again Tibetan hopes and dreams were shattered when the talks failed to achieve any political change.

The Dalai Lama's life and work are closely tied to the Tibetan political struggle, but he also has become a voice in the global quest for the peaceful survival of humanity. He said: "Today the world is smaller and more interdependent. One nation's problems can no longer be solved by itself completely. Thus, without a sense of universal responsibility, our very survival becomes threatened. Basically, universal responsibility is feeling for other people's suffering just as we feel our own. It is the realization that even our enemy is entirely motivated by the quest for happiness. We must recognize that all beings want the same thing that we want. This is the way to achieve a true understanding, unfettered by artificial consideration."

The light of his vision has attracted not just Tibetans or Buddhists, but people of many faiths and many nationalities.

CHAPTER 7

Desmond Mpilo Tutu

(b. 1931)

Peace involves inevitable righteousness, justice, wholesomeness, fullness of life, participation in decision making, goodness, laughter, joy, compassion, sharing and reconciliation.

—Desmond Tutu

Of course, I have followed Desmond Tutu in the news, but I had one brief moment alone with him. We were at The Carter Center in Georgia for the inaugural conference of the International Negotiation Network. I forgot some of my materials in one of the conference rooms and went to retrieve them. There was Tutu with his shoes off, feet up on a chair and an open Bible in his lap. He was working on a sermon but graciously took time to chat. He was as genuine in that moment with a younger, over-awed pastor-peacemaker as he was when standing before crowds of thousands.

DURING YET ANOTHER FUNERAL of yet another young black person slain by the police in South Africa, a policeman was discovered alone in the crowd. Angry youths turned on him and beat him to the ground. His car was torched. Then gasoline was poured on the screaming officer. Suddenly a small robed priest pushed through the mob to the bleeding policeman. In tears, the priest pleaded for the man's life. The young people turned their anger on the priest who did not give ground. He told them he understood their anger, knew they had been beaten, imprisoned and some of their friends killed. But he challenged them about the noble cause in which they were engaged—and argued that there was no need to kill in that cause. The policeman was saved by the priest's intercessions. It was another day in the courageous peacemaking journey of Desmond Tutu amid the crushing violence of apartheid in South Africa.

Desmond Mpilo Tutu was born to parents of mixed black ethnicity. He suffered many afflictions in his childhood and youth: polio, severe burns and tuberculosis. He also discovered the prejudices and injustices suffered by blacks in South Africa. He became a teacher, but following the passage of the 1953 Bantu Education Act, which aimed at degrading education so that blacks would only be eligible for manual labor, he and his wife, also a teacher, resigned.

Tutu turned to Christian ministry, describing his call as, "God grabbing me by the scruff of my neck." He joined the Anglican Church and studied in England. He then began working through a series of posts as pastor, university chaplain and teacher in South Africa and in neighboring Lesotho and Botswana.

Through his studies, teaching and experience, Tutu developed a theology centered on the African cultural philosophy of Ubuntu, sometimes summed up as: "A person is a person through other people." Our humanity is woven into the community we have with other humans, so the destruction of that community by violence and injustice is actually a destruction of our own humanity—both for the oppressed and the oppressor. The perpetrators of the apartheid system were, in Tutu's eyes, bound to their victims, and they were dehumanized by their own dehumanizing behavior. As Tutu said, "It was equally clear that recovering from this situation would require a magnanimousness on the part of the victims if there was to be a future. The only way we can be free is together."

That magnanimity along with tremendous courage and clarity of words made Tutu a prophet of hope amid a situation that seemed hopeless. Tutu was not a political priest, rather he was driven to politics by his pastoral heart for his people. His eyes could twinkle with joy or flood with tears, mirroring the profound heights and depths of life in his nation. In 1968, as the Black Consciousness Movement (BCM) was growing on the campus where Tutu was chaplain, police tried to break up a demonstration. Tutu joined the students and said, "If you are arresting the students you can count me as their chaplain with them." From that point on Tutu was a leader in the movement against apartheid. He held prayer vigils for those detained. He presided over funerals for victims of police violence, including the funeral of BCM leader Steve Biko. He preached, "Our cause, the cause of justice and liberation, must triumph because it is moral and just and right." He exhorted whites to condemn the repression.

Tutu was chosen as General Secretary of the South African Council of Churches, which gave him a national platform for his actions. He called for economic sanctions and boycotts against South Africa, acknowledging that there would be some increase in suffering for blacks as a result, but that if the end of apartheid was brought closer the cost would be worth it. He was arrested at demonstrations and responded by leading detainees in prayer and song. He also consistently called for nonviolent action, questioning activists during protests in Port Elizabeth, "Why must we discredit our cause by using methods that, if they were used against us, we would oppose?" He called people to press on with courage, "Being courageous does not mean never being scared; it means acting as you know you must even though you are undeniably afraid."

In 1984 Tutu was selected for the Nobel Peace Prize. That same year he was elevated to be Bishop of Johannesburg, the first black elected to such a post. Two years later he was named Archbishop of Cape Town, thus becoming head of the Anglican Church in South Africa, again a position no black person had ever held. As the situation in South Africa deteriorated with increasing government repression, Tutu refused to accept bans on his activities. He defied a ban against marches by organizing 30,000 South Africans, black and white, to march for peace. Tutu preached to the crowd, "Come and see what this country is going to become. This country is a rainbow country!" That march was a turning point, moving the government from confrontation to negotiation. The continuing protests within South Africa and global pressure from outside finally led to the release of Nelson Mandela from prison.

As apartheid was crumbling, violence erupted between Mandela's African National Congress and the Zulu-based Inkatha Freedom Party, violence that was later revealed to have been stimulated by pro-apartheid police. Tutu was frequently on the streets in black communities trying to defuse the rage that was boiling over into violence. He would repeatedly whip up the crowd with his words, using rhetoric many would consider provocative and inflammatory. He would bring the crowd together around his speech, and then carefully channel their anger into constructive peaceful action. He would tell them, "Because we know that we are going to be free, we can afford to be disciplined, we can afford to be dignified and we need to underline the fact of this struggle being a nonviolent struggle." He was a master at such "street mediation," even when the crowds were directing their hostility toward him.

In 1994, national elections were held with blacks voting for the first time. Mandela was elected President of the first majority government in South Africa. This breaking apart of the old apartheid regime opened a new chapter of Tutu's work. Now, instead of the prophet for liberation, he became the lead facilitator for reconciliation.

The Truth and Reconciliation Commission was set up to try to move the country beyond the traumas of the apartheid years, and Tutu, as the nation's clear moral authority, was selected as its chair. The new commission had two basic challenges. First, victims were provided a forum for telling their stories. The suffering of well-known figures like Stephen Biko and the hidden tragedies of the unknown victims of the apartheid repression were publicly aired, many accounts for the first time. During the testimony of one elderly victim of torture, Tutu broke down and wept with his head down on the table.

The second aspect of the Commission's work was controversial. The perpetrators of the atrocities under apartheid were also given the opportunity to confess with the offer of amnesty under certain circumstances. This generated very different emotions—anger for some people, but also great sorrow. For Tutu, people who could callously talk about their actions and the suffering they caused without any expression of remorse were denying their own humanity. Still, Tutu knew that these stories must come out, and ultimately forgiveness must be expressed.

Tutu's modeling of forgiveness through the Truth and Reconciliation Commission played a major role in moving South Africa from the horrific violence of apartheid to the possibility of building a peaceful interracial future for his country. He said, "This forgiveness is not about altruism. It is about regaining dignity and humanity and granting these, too, to the former oppressors." He feared that the violence of the past would resurface in the future, trapping the people in a terrifying and hopeless cycle. "If we are going to move on and build a new kind of world community," he said, "there must be a way in which we can deal with the sordid past. The most effective way would be for the perpetrators or their descendants to acknowledge the awfulness of what happened and the descendants of the victims to respond by granting forgiveness, providing something can be done, even symbolically, to compensate for the anguish experienced, whose consequences are still being lived through today." Forgiveness required steps toward restitution where possible, so Tutu spoke about the economic justice needed as part of the rebuilding of South Africa, especially in the black communities.

The post-apartheid process has been messy and full of conflict. The work of the Truth and Reconciliation Commission left much to be desired, Tutu acknowledged. But for all the shortcomings, the world saw South Africa emerge in far better shape than anyone had imagined. Instead of the feared bloodbath, Tutu and

Mandela led South Africa to become a global symbol of hope. For Tutu, this was a divine mission for reconciliation to be forged out of seemingly intractable conflict.

"Perhaps God chose such an unlikely place deliberately to show the world that it can be done anywhere." Certainly through Desmond Tutu's leadership, an example has been set to inspire the world and bring hope to situations that seem irreparable.

CHAPTER 8

Jim Wallis

(b. 1948)

Hope unbelieved is always considered nonsense. But hope believed is history in the process of being changed.

—Jim Wallis

*As a student, I attended a teach-in on campus led by Jim Wallis and the group from Trinity Evangelical Divinity School who founded **The Post-American** magazine. I scooped up copies of the first issues and kept them as treasured possessions. Much of the way I thought about the world was shaped by that magazine. **The Post-American** was first published in 1971 but renamed **Sojourners** in 1975. Many years later, following the Los Angeles uprising and the gang peace summits, I worked with Jim in support of Carl Upchurch (the former gang member who became a prophetic teacher of urban justice) in a nationwide movement to bring peace to our urban streets. I include this profile of Jim Wallis as the last chapter of Prophets and Visionaries, because I have seen the impact of Jim's work in the world—and in my own life.*

JIM WALLIS HAS BECOME one of the leading U.S. religious voices in the media. Deeply rooted in what he calls an evangelical faith, he has consistently campaigned for issues of peace along with economic and racial justice. Through Wallis, *Sojourners* magazine has lifted the voices of dozens of other activists, as well, and has spread their collective voices into receptive homes and communities around the world.

He was born in Michigan and raised in a conservative evangelical church. As a teenager Wallis encountered social divisions along racial lines. He visited black churches in Detroit, where he discovered a very different expression of the Christian faith than he had experienced in his home church. He found the same fervor about having a "personal relationship with Christ", but in the black churches, that intimately personal faith flowed directly to active involvement in social struggles over the injustices of racism and poverty. His persistent questions about the lack of connection between issues of race and faith asked in his home church sparked that congregation to oust him, though only in his teens. .

He went to Trinity Evangelical Divinity School near Chicago where he joined with other students in anti-war activities during the Vietnam War. They founded a magazine, *The Post-American*, which engaged in the anti-war and anti-racism discussions common at the time—but they did so from an evangelical perspective. This perspective understood their personal relationships with Christ as driving them to engage in direct, nonviolent social action. *The Post-American* quickly built a national readership, expanding beyond evangelical social activists to other Christian groups who were concerned about issues of justice and peace: African-American churches, progressive Catholics, liberal Protestants, historic peace churches and social activists from Pentecostal and charismatic traditions.

In order to more effectively serve this growing and diverse constituency, to improve their capacity for advocacy about peace and justice issues to the U.S. government, and to put substance to their radical vision, Wallis and those involved with the magazine moved to Washington, D.C., in 1975 and changed the name of the magazine to *Sojourners*. They were located in the inner city neighborhood of Columbia Heights, an area marred by blight and poverty. Since 1975 *Sojourners* has engaged in national discussions about major political issues all the way down to the local urban issues of poverty, racism and violence. They developed the Sojourners Neighborhood Center and the Freedom School to address these local concerns. Wallis' writing and preaching is a direct result of these neighborhood struggles.

Wallis also was active against apartheid in South Africa and the nuclear arms race. In the 1980s, the wars in Central America became the focal point for the peace movement. Wallis attended a retreat of religious peace activists in 1984 that developed the Pledge of Resistance that was then introduced to the nation in the pages of *Sojourners*. It called for individuals to be prepared to commit acts of civil disobedience to block a feared invasion of Nicaragua by the U.S. military under the policies of President Ronald Reagan. More than 30,000 people signed the Pledge of Resistance. As U.S. policy shifted from a threatened invasion to what was termed "low intensity conflict" the leaders of the Pledge broadened their focus to include any escalation of the wars in Central America. In 1985, Pledge activists, the majority based in religious groups, engaged in civil disobedience to stop the funding of the Contras in Nicaragua. As a result, thousands were arrested in cities across the U.S. *Sojourners,* with Wallis at the helm, continued to be the coordinating voice by telling stories that the U.S. mainstream media chose to minimize.

As the Cold War ended and the wars in Central America wound down, Wallis and the *Sojourners* community began to look at the systemic issues of poverty in the United States in a new light. They stimulated the gathering of a network of many religious groups to publish *The Call to Renewal* in 1995. *The Call to Renewal* sought to unite congregations and faith-based organizations from many different traditions and different political positions to address the concerns of the poor out of the biblical prophetic tradition. *The Call to Renewal,* in Wallis' words, was about "a new agenda, beyond both the Left and the Right, which combines personal responsibility and moral values with a frontal assault on racism and poverty." *Sojourners* magazine was the nerve center for the movement. Wallis went around the U.S. with singer Ken Medema in the tradition of old-time revivalists, but this time with a call to biblical justice in the contemporary context. In 2006, *The Call to Renewal* was merged with Sojourners.

Jim Wallis has published eight books, but his 2005 work, *God's Politics*, took on both Republicans and Democrats and called for a new moral agenda to address systemic problems of injustice, violence and discrimination in the U.S. He became a regular on news shows and panels of religious commentators. His voice moved from the columns of *Sojourners* to major newspapers and media networks nationwide. In this new role, it would be easy to dismiss Wallis as just another pundit—but that casual judgment ignores Wallis' life and witness. From the beginning, his peacemaking has been rooted in a faith community. *Sojourners* has gone through many changes over the decades. The form of the community has changed and ministries have been developed, phased out and new ones started. Despite its changes, *Sojourners* has always consisted of a band of Christians that has shared their lives together with a common vision for the peace and justice of their local neighborhood and the wider world. Most of the individuals connected with *Sojourners* have not been in the public spotlight, but work in various neighborhood ministries or with the organization and magazine. The reality of that community life, both in *Sojourners* and the D.C. neighborhood, is what has given Wallis his moral grounding.

Wallis doesn't just preach the vision of biblical prophets—he works within the daily relationships of a religious community and an urban neighborhood to make that vision real.

PART 2

Litany of Martyrs

"Presente!"

ON SEPTEMBER 15, 1963, a bomb exploded in the 16th Street Baptist Church in Birmingham, Alabama. Four girls were killed in the blast: Addie Mae Collins, Carole Robertson, Cynthia Wesley and Denise McNair. Twenty other people were seriously injured. Just a few weeks earlier Martin Luther King, Jr. had proclaimed, "I Have a Dream" in Washington, D.C, yet the nightmare of American racism was still tragically evident in this slaughter.

Alabama is tucked in the "Bible Belt," where the violence was especially shocking against these innocents who had just finished Sunday school and were putting on their choir robes. This horror stripped away the mask of piety covering a long history of Southern Christian racism. When King preached at their funeral service, he described them as "martyred heroines of a holy crusade for freedom and human dignity." To this day, the killing of these four girls remains a lasting symbol of the struggle for civil rights.

Martyrs are people who die, but live on as powerful symbols. The two most notable martyrs for peace are Mahatma Gandhi and

Martin Luther King, Jr., but they are among countless peacemakers who have perished.

Millions have died as intentional targets. The Holocaust during World War II saw six million Jews slaughtered along with Slavs, Gypsies, homosexuals and the disabled. "Never again," the world said, only to stand by as Cambodia, Rwanda and Darfur spun into genocidal horror. So many die in such struggles that sometimes no one is left to recall their lives, their personalities or even their names.

The martyrs in the next six chapters were drawn from a tragically long list. These six are meant to evoke the preciousness of what we have lost—and the powerful testimony offered through sacrifice. Archbishop Oscar Romero was, and still is, a towering figure in struggles for justice across Latin America. Others in the following chapters, such as Anne Frank, were unknown when their lives were taken. Her diary gave voice to many whose voices were silenced.

Though not mentioned in this book, the litany of martyrs continues and must also include names such as these:

Benigno Aquino was assassinated as he stepped off an airplane in Manila. He refused to stay in the safety of sanctuary in the United States, but returned to confront the injustice and despotism of Ferdinand Marcos in the Philippines.

Rachel Corrie died at 23 when she put her body between an Israeli bulldozer and the home of a Palestinian family in Gaza. The driver of the bulldozer ran over her, not once, but twice. She was one of many internationals in various organizations who have tried to stand in nonviolent solidarity with Palestinians.

Medgar Evers was gunned down in the driveway of his own home in Mississippi. He had been a leader for civil rights, especially working on the campaigns to register blacks to exercise their right to vote, a right guaranteed by the U.S. Constitution but not by the U.S. government nor the government of Mississippi at that time.

Imam Moussa Al-Sadr from Lebanon went to Libya as part of a peacemaking mission across the Middle East to try to halt the flow of arms feeding the civil war in Lebanon. Shortly after making his appeal to Colonel Gaddafi he disappeared, cutting short one of the few strong voices for interreligious reconciliation within Lebanon.

Mary Dyer was hanged in colonial Massachusetts for her refusal to recant beliefs she held as truth. She was the first martyr of religious freedom in a place where many people had fled for their own religious liberty.

Alexander Muge was killed in a car crash that was highly suspicious. He was a church leader who was a critical voice in Kenya against the attempts of President Daniel Arap Moi to hold onto power in dictatorial fashion. All the evidence points to assassination as a means of silencing the voice of a prophet.

Wu Fung was a mediator in Taiwan who offered himself before warring head-hunting aboriginal tribes to halt cycles of violence. Though greatly loved by all sides, he placed himself in a position to absorb violence and reveal its horrors at the cost of his own life.

Franz Jägerstätter was an Austrian killed by the German Nazis because he was a conscientious objector to the war. He viewed the Nazi movement as a train bound for hell, and he felt he would imperil his own mortal soul by participating in any way with the Nazi cause. He was beheaded in 1943 as an "enemy of the state."

And the litany continues…

A tradition of remembering martyrs arose during the wars in Nicaragua, El Salvador and Guatemala. At gatherings, especially around the Eucharistic table, the names of the dead were voiced. After each name was spoken, the people gathered would cry out: "*Presente!*" The martyrs were still among them, not forgotten, but held in their hearts and in their passion to see the struggle through until justice and peace came to fruition. Writing these stories is a way for me—and for you as you read them—to join those courageous circles of faith. When you remember these stories and share them with someone else, you are widening the circle of peacemakers. You are crying out:

"*Presente!*"

CHAPTER 9

Anne Frank
(1929-1945)

In spite of everything I still believe that people are really good at heart.

—Anne Frank

Names are essential in remembering the Shoah (better known as the Holocaust). Most Holocaust memorials include names, when names are known, because names help to replace inhumanity with the identities of real men, women and children. Anne Frank gave us not only a name, but a mind, a heart, a dream and a life of one among the millions. I read her diary first as a child. After visiting Auschwitz, Yad Vashem and other memorials later in my life, her words and spirit have only grown in power.

HOW COULD A TEENAGE girl be the voice that expressed a horror beyond words and at the same time brought a brilliantly simple articulation of hope to so many in despair? Anne Frank died in the bloodiest conflict in the history of our planet. Yet she also wrote words that brought to light a humanizing ideal that shines brightly out of that dark time.

Anne was born into a Jewish family living in Germany. As anti-Semitism rose with the growth of Hitler's Nazi party, Otto and Edith Frank moved their family to the Netherlands in 1933. Life there was safe until war broke out. In May of 1940, Germany quickly invaded and conquered the Netherlands, and almost immediately, the anti-Semitic laws of the Nazis were put into place.

June 12, 1942, was Anne's 13th birthday. One gift was a diary, and she immediately began to write in it. "I hope I will be able to confide everything to you," she wrote, "and I hope you will be a great source of comfort and support."

Less than a month later, the Nazis issued a call for Jews to report and be sent to work camps. The Frank family had prepared a hiding place in the back of a building owned by Otto Frank's company. They prepared a room for two families and quickly moved in to avoid the Nazi call-up. Anne confided in her diary, "My happy-go-lucky, carefree school days are gone forever." Employees of Otto Frank kept the hidden families supplied with food, clothing and books. Living in the cramped quarters, which they called the Secret Annex, put a great strain on everyone. They had to stay quiet during the day because work continued in the factory below. For Anne, her diary was her only safe outlet as she wrote about the tensions, the quarrels and the cursing which particularly bothered her.

Those in the Secret Annex knew about the extermination of Jews taking place through their daily interaction with those helping them. Anne wrote about the "dismal and depressing news" of friends being deported to the east in cattle cars. In 1944 they suspected the tides of war were turning. Anne wrote, "Where there's hope, there's life. It fills us with fresh courage and makes us strong again."

The news of the Allied landings at Normandy sparked excitement, but on August 4, 1944, a Nazi SS officer and Dutch police raided the Secret Annex. The eight people in hiding and some of their helpers were all arrested. Two helpers avoided arrest. Luckily, they found Anne's diary on the floor and rescued it.

The Jews were taken to Westerbrok transit camp, while the helpers were sent to prison. After a few weeks in Westerbrok, Anne and her family and friends were packed into cattle cars (70 to a car), and taken on a three-day trip that ended at Auschwitz-Birkenau. The men and women were separated. Anne and her sister Margot were eventually shipped to Bergen-Belsen where they succumbed to typhus in March, 1945, just weeks before the camp was liberated by the British Army. Of the eight Jews in the hiding place only Otto Frank survived; all four of those who helped them survived the war.

Miep Gies, the helper who had picked up Anne's diary, returned it to Otto after he made his way back to Amsterdam. It took Otto a while before he could read the diary of his dead daughter. He was surprised by the wonderful depth of feeling she showed—something she had never shared with her family. Because Anne talked in the diary about publishing a book about her experiences in the Secret Annex, Otto decided he would honor his daughter's dream.

The Diary of Anne Frank was first published in 1947 and later translated into many languages, becoming one of the definitive works on the Shoah. A stage play was adapted from the diary. Some citizens of Amsterdam restored the dilapidated building where the Franks had hidden, turning it into the Anne Frank House. Late in his life Otto Frank said, "The task I received from Anne continues to restore my energy: to struggle for reconciliation and human rights throughout the world." As young people wrote to him about Anne's diary before his own death in 1980, Otto Frank urged them to work for unity and peace.

Anne's own voice challenges people to this day to work toward peace and justice. She believed in the goodness of people, in spite of the most stunning evidence to the contrary.

Anne wrote, "How wonderful it is that nobody need wait a single moment before starting to improve the world." Our response is part of her enduring legacy.

Victor Jara

(1932-1973)

**I think I am passionate
because I am full of hope.**

—Victor Jara

*I first heard about Victor Jara
from Arlo Guthrie's song about
him. I loved the song and added
it to my own repertoire. I had
known about U.S. complicity in
the 1973 coup that brought down
Salvador Allende's democratically elected government in
Chile and replaced it with a brutal military dictatorship.
My proudest memory of a congressperson was when my
own U.S. Rep., Michael Harrington from Massachusetts,
revealed information to the American public about the
CIA's involvement in that coup, information he learned
in secret briefings of the House Intelligence Committee.
Harrington was censured by Congress and his political
career ruined, but I wrote a letter telling him how proud
I was that he had represented me in that way. Learning
about Victor Jara gave me another hero in the tragic story
of Chile—a hero who would not be silenced even by death.
I'll keep singing his song even with tears in my eyes.*

THE OLD ARENA IS now called Victor Jara Stadium—named
after a man who died there along with hundreds of other Chileans.
He had performed in that stadium many times as one of Chile's

leading folk musicians. His last burst of creativity was there, too, writing his poetry with a battered face, broken ribs and broken hands that would never again hold a guitar. He slipped his final poem to a friend just before the sadistic officer who had taunted him led him away to be shot.

Victor Jara was born to a peasant family. His mother taught him to sing, but by age 15 he was orphaned and on his own. After a brief sojourn in seminary and a stint in the army, he turned to a career in music and theater. He became a director, putting on plays ranging in style from the classical to the experimental. Eventually, his love for music drew him away from the theater, and he became one of the leading figures in the Nueva Canción Chilena (New Chilean Song) movement. Singers and songwriters of this movement incorporated Chilean folk traditions into music that spoke to contemporary contexts and struggles.

In 1970, the socialist Salvador Allende ran for President. Jara had been active in many justice movements, singing with miners and peasants. He had joined the Communist Party in Chile, one of the parties in Allende's Popular Unity coalition that was seeking nonviolent, democratic change in Chilean politics. Allende won the election, and soon elements in the Chilean military—with the support of the U.S. Central Intelligence Agency—began an intentional program to destabilize the country. Paramilitary brigades were formed that would beat people aligned with Allende, often with the support of the police. "Bosses' strikes" shut down many industries, crippling the economy. Students and other volunteers rushed to help out, trying to keep the country functioning.

Jara inspired people with his songs during Allende's campaign. Then, as the industries were being destabilized, he joined the volunteers and sang to them. The American activist folk-singer Phil Ochs traveled to Chile and joined him singing to the miners such songs as Pete Seeger's "If I Had a Hammer." Paramilitary gangs chased Jara a number of times and threatened him repeatedly as he had become a nationally recognized figure through his music.

On September 11, 1973, the Chilean military launched a violent coup. Fighter planes rocketed the Presidential Palace and

Allende was killed in the ensuing battle. Jara had left his wife Joan earlier that day to go to the university where he was on the faculty. The military surrounded the university with tanks, keeping all students and faculty inside. Jara sang to those trapped to keep up their spirits. The next day the army moved in and arrested everyone.

Joan Jara heard about the arrests and tried to find Victor, afraid to identify him because she knew he was a marked man. After a few days, she traced him to the Chile Stadium where about 5,000 people had been taken, but the soldiers surrounding the stadium made it clear that nobody would be able to get inside. A week after the coup, a stranger saying he was a friend took her to the city morgue. She saw hundreds of bodies piled up like cordwood. Most of the bodies would never be identified and would be buried in a common grave. But Victor's face had been recognized by one of the workers in the morgue, and so Joan had been found and taken to him. His body bore the marks of severe beatings. He had a head wound, and his wrists were clearly broken. His torso had been riddled with machine gun bullets. Joan and the friend loaded his body on a trolley cart and pushed it across the street for quick burial before the military disposed of it.

Over the years, Joan Jara pieced together the story of what happened to her husband. She interviewed survivors of the siege at the university and those detained at the stadium. She found that Victor had been recognized quickly when taken to the stadium and pulled out for special attention by the torturers. He was mocked and beaten severely, as were most of the other detainees. After three days with no food, no heat, loss of blood and broken bones, Jara wrote his last poem as he huddled with his university friends amid the stadium seats. He wrote with borrowed pencil and paper:

> ...*Oh God, is this the world that you created,*
> *For this your seven days of wonder and work?*
> *Within these four walls only a number exists*
> *Which does not progress,*
> *Which slowly will wish more and more for*

death....
How hard it is to sing
When I must sing of horror.
Horror which I am living,
Horror which I am dying.
To see myself among so much
And so many moments of infinity
In which silence and screams
Are the end of my song
What I see, I have never seen
What I have felt and what I feel
Will give birth to the moment...

The poem was unfinished, for the guards came to take him away as he was still writing. The paper was surreptitiously shoved into the sock of a professor from the university. Jara was taken away, tortured and then shot. His body was dumped outside with five others in a cemetery where they were found and taken to the morgue. A brief notice of his death appeared in one of the papers, then the military ordered that no mention be made of him in the media. Someone risked their life to play a few bars of one of his songs on a TV station in his honor.

Victor Jara's death crystallized the brutality of the military regime in Chile under General Augusto Pinochet. Through his bold music and through his death, he became a symbol for all those in Latin America suffering under the dictatorships of the 1970s and 1980s. Folk musicians from around the world sang about him. Rock bands such as The Clash and U2 told his story.

The vision of the Popular Unity government under Allende was violently overthrown, but it did not die. That vision was renewed through a nonviolent campaign that eventually brought down the Pinochet dictatorship in 1990. Then in 2006, Michelle Bachelet, a socialist like Allende, was elected president through a democratic process. Her father had been tortured to death during the 1973 coup. Her mother and she were both detained and tortured in the notorious "Villa Grimaldi" center.

Those supervising the torture and executions in the stadium have never been brought to justice. General Pinochet was the first person in history arrested under the doctrine of "universal jurisdiction," which holds that those who commit certain human rights crimes can be arrested any time in any country. Pinochet was arrested in the United Kingdom under orders from a Spanish judge. He was returned to Chile. However, he died from failing health while under house arrest before standing trial for the massive crimes committed under his authority.

Though Victor Jara died a brutal death under a brutal regime, his songs are not all about the horror he witnessed. They are also about the hope and courage of people who stand up to those who use violence to sustain injustice. He said, "Song is like the water that washes the stones, the wind which cleans us, like the fire that joins us together and lives within us to make us better people."

Among the last songs Jara wrote was "*Vientos del Pueblo,*" (Winds of the People) with a refrain that echoes long after his death:

Winds of the people are calling me,
winds of the people are bearing me,
they scatter my heart
and blow through my throat.
So the poet will be heard
while my heart goes on beating
along the road of the people,
now and forever.

CHAPTER 11

Stephen Biko

(1946-1977)

**The most potent weapon in
the hands of the oppressor is
the mind of the oppressed.**

—Stephen Biko

*An African-American friend
painted Biko's face on a T-shirt
along with the words, "Cry
Freedom," then gave it to me. I
wore it at various vigils including
one at a bank with money invested in South Africa. We
read the names of people killed under the apartheid
regime, including the name of Stephen Biko.*

A DEATH AND A funeral said so much about who this man was
and the evil system against which he struggled. He died alone,
naked, shackled, battered and bloodied in the back of a police van
that took a long, slow trip so he would die on the way to the hospital. He was a black man in the hands of white police officers.
Twenty thousand mourners attended his funeral even though
police had blocked roads and driven thousands of people away.
The story of his death would spread his teachings around the
globe, bringing one more huge indictment against the murderous
regime that tried to silence him.

His name was Stephen Bantu Biko. He died at 30 years of age
in 1977, but already he had become a champion for his people. He
founded The Black Consciousness Movement to resist the apartheid regime in South Africa.

His family supported Biko in the effort to improve his lot through education. But when he was a child, the South African government passed the Bantu Education Act that sought to limit education of blacks so that they would not be able to aspire to anything that did not include back-breaking labor. The author of the Act said, "There is no place for him (the Bantu or black) in the European community above the level of certain forms of labor." Faced with legislated limits on his education, Biko began to grow in his political awareness. His brother was arrested and jailed for nine months on suspicion of being connected with the military wing of the Pan Africanist Congress. Biko was interrogated and expelled from school, leaving him with a "strong resentment toward white authority."

Despite the government's legal suppression of education resources, Biko struggled to continue his education in both law and medicine, first at a Catholic school and later at the University of Natal. Despite all the structural discrimination he encountered, his political activism took shape. He began seeing that the consciousness of blacks under the oppressive system of apartheid was one of the key problems to be addressed. He said, "The most potent weapon in the hands of the oppressor is the mind of the oppressed." So he sought to change that mindset.

He encountered racism and paternalism in the National Union of South African Students (NUSAS). The NUSAS was open to students of all races, but he saw that blacks were not being allowed by the white students to assume leadership positions so he founded an all black, pro-black student group called the South African Students' Organization (SASO). Under Biko's leadership SASO adopted the doctrine that became known as Black Consciousness and began promoting it throughout the country. SASO provided legal aid and medical clinics for poor blacks as well as promoting small-scale industry to build up the economic base in black communities.

As The Black Consciousness Movement spread beyond the campuses, Biko helped launch the Black People's Convention (BPC) to give structure to the movement in non-student contexts.

The BPC grew to be a coalition of over 70 groups that embraced Black Consciousness. Biko was elected the president of the BPC, which led to his expulsion from medical school.

"The basic tenet of Black Consciousness," according to Biko, "is that the black man must reject all value systems that seek to make him a foreigner in the country of his birth and reduce his basic human dignity." Biko was not anti-white, but he did stand against forms of racial oppression, even from liberal whites who, despite their open-minded views, wanted to limit black leadership. He sought to break the chains of inner inferiority that blacks had given into under the weight of years of oppression. He taught that everyone—black and white—must realize and act upon basic humanity. As Biko put it: "As a prelude whites must be made to realize that they are only human, not superior. Same with Blacks. They must be made to realize that they are also human, not inferior." He would say, "Man, you are okay as you are; begin to look upon yourself as a human being."

Such teaching was too explosive for the controlling white apartheid regime to tolerate. Biko was banned, which meant that he was restricted to his home district in King William's Town; he was not allowed to teach, to speak to more than one person at a time, to be published, or to attend any educational institution. He also had to report weekly to the local police. In spite of the ban, Biko was able to continue organizing the movement and to set up a rural health clinic outside King William's Town for poor blacks who were not given access to city hospitals. He helped establish the Zimele Trust Fund to assist political prisoners and their families. He also continued to write for the SASO newsletter under the pen name Frank Talk.

In June 1976, Soweto erupted in protests as students rejected the government's demand that they be educated in Afrikaans, which they viewed as the language of the oppressor. The students went on strike, stirred by the teachings of Black Consciousness and the work of the BPC. In a confrontation with protesting students, police opened fire. The rioting and police violence lasted for two days. The world was shocked at the brutality of the repression.

Nobody knows how many people were killed, but international news agencies put the death toll at more than 500.

As the leader of the movement to raise consciousness, Biko was targeted for more serious treatment. On August 21, 1977, he was arrested under the Terrorism Act, which had been used to jail many black activists. Biko was brutally treated while in police custody. He was beaten on the head, and according to police reports began exhibiting signs of neurological injury as early as September 7. His condition was ignored for days, as he was kept naked and chained to a metal grille. Finally a police physician recommended that he be transferred to a hospital. Though he was in detention in the sizeable city of Port Elizabeth, he was taken, still chained and without even rudimentary medical treatment, in the back of a police Land Rover for a 1,200-kilometer journey to Pretoria. They drove slowly for hours as he bled to death from his internal injuries.

Police brutality continued at Biko's funeral as police hauled people off buses and beat them with truncheons. Biko's funeral went on for a long time, becoming an angry protest rally. The international criticism over Biko's death eventually prompted an inquest, but the police investigators said Biko died of self-inflicted causes. Nobody was held responsible. White journalist Donald Woods had known Biko and was able to take photos of his injuries at the morgue, images that Woods then smuggled out of the country. In exile, Woods wrote a book titled *Biko*, later followed by the movie *Cry Freedom*, which gave international prominence to Biko's work and martyrdom.

After the fall of the apartheid government and establishment of majority rule in South Africa, the Truth and Reconciliation Commission found that Biko's death was "a gross human rights violation." Law enforcement officials were found responsible for his death, but they had agreed to testify under the provision of amnesty that the commission gave as part of their regular procedures.

Stephen Biko was one of the great visionaries in the South African struggle. His pride in who he was became a model for the inner liberation that needed to precede the legal liberation of blacks and the other repressed people of South Africa. He spoke of his vision: "We have set on a quest for true humanity, and somewhere on the distant horizon we can see the glittering prize. Let us march forth with courage and determination, drawing strength from our common plight and brotherhood. In time we shall be in a position to bestow upon South Africa the greatest gift possible—a more human face."

Whatever human face is possible today in South Africa is a result in great part from Stephen Biko's vision and sacrifice.

CHAPTER 12

Rutilio Grande and Oscar Arnulfo Romero

(1928-1977) (1917-1980)

Nowadays it is dangerous, and practically illegal to be an authentic Christian in Latin America.

—Rutilio Grande

We can present, along with the blood of teachers, of laborers, of peasants, the blood of our priests. This is communion in love. It would be sad, if in a country where murder is being committed so horribly, we were not to find priests also among the victims. They are the testimony of a church incarnate in the problems of its people.

—Oscar Romero

In my own peacemaking work around the world, I've occasionally set out for places that frighten me. Sometimes on the night before heading out, I've watched the movie **Romero**

*with Raúl Juliá in the title role. I never met Romero,
but I spent a lot of my time in the 1980s resisting U.S.
policies in Central America. Romero was a courageous
beacon of truth for us. For me as a pastor/activist it
was the profound love of Romero's pastoral heart that
drove him out of safety into the risky path of faithful
witness. When I need courage, I think of Romero.*

TENS OF THOUSANDS OF people died in the war in El Salvador
in the late 1970s and 1980s. Many religious leaders also lost their
lives, mostly to death squads affiliated with the Salvadoran military. In that carnage, two people stand out for the clarity of their
witness for justice and peace and for the courage with which they
faced their deaths. They continue to inspire courage and commitment in peacemakers far from El Salvador.

The Rev. Rutilio Grande, a Jesuit priest, was not particularly
noteworthy early in his career, but following Vatican II, he experienced a transformation in his sense of ministry. He once viewed
his vocation to the priesthood as a call to perfection—a goal he
never could attain; he later came to see the priesthood as embody-
ing loving service and self-sacrifice. This liberated him to minister
with newfound joy and to help people apply the Christian gospel
to the social disparities that plagued El Salvador. For nine years he
taught in the seminary as director of social action projects, helping young priests refine their calling to join with the poor in a
quest for dignity and justice. Grande's teaching was viewed by
political authorities and by some of the Salvadoran bishops as too
radical, so he was forced out of the seminary. He became a parish priest in the small town of Aguilares. In his sermons there,
Grande began addressing some of the specific conditions of economic oppression that plagued the local peasants. He became a
popular preacher, but he also began to be watched by the town's
elite and the military.

In February 1977, following the expulsion of a Colombian-
born priest from El Salvador, Grande preached that Jesus himself

would have been denied entry into the country and would have been accused of being a rabble-rouser. Grande said that he had no doubts that the wealthy in El Salvador would crucify Jesus anew. A few weeks later on March 12, 1977, Father Grande's vehicle was attacked by machine gun fire as he drove through the countryside. He was killed along with an old *campesino* (farmer) and a teenage boy who were riding with him. Rutilio Grande was the first of a long line of priests, nuns and lay leaders who would perish as intentional targets in the war in El Salvador because they chose to speak out about issues of injustice and the suffering of the poor.

The murder of Rutilio Grande was the first crisis for the newly chosen Salvadoran Archbishop Oscar Romero. Romero had been selected as archbishop in part for his conservative views. He believed, as did the Catholic Church, that it was their duty to protect the status quo and minister only to people's "spiritual" needs. But two things changed Romero in a profound manner as he ascended to the position of archbishop. First, the Catholic Church had been going through major transitions since the Second Vatican Council, the global gathering of Catholic leaders in the 1960s that opened fresh relationships to the world's non-Christian faiths and changed the Mass from Latin to local languages universally. For many Catholic clergy around the world, the Second Vatican Council was an earthquake with aftershocks that continued for decades. In Latin America, these rumblings touched off a new commitment to justice for millions of ordinary families. A council of Latin American bishops met at Medellin and issued a call for Catholic leaders to take a "preferential option for the poor" in their work throughout the church. This idea was not welcomed by the majority of the Salvadoran bishops who still aligned themselves with the wealthy families and military leaders who ruled El Salvador. But Romero, formerly a conservative himself, took the Catholic's new vision of justice very seriously. He knew that this was a life-and-death struggle and that he was challenging his colleagues in El Salvador—but he raised a strong and prophetic voice on behalf of the massive poverty he saw all around him.

The second factor in Romero's radical change of heart was Grande's martyrdom. The men had become friends years earlier even though they had many disagreements about applying the Gospel to the realities of their country. Grande's murder directly confronted Romero, as the shepherd of the church, with the suffering of people close to him. Immediately following Grande's death, Romero went to Aguilares and led a long, highly emotional Mass. Then he cancelled Mass in churches throughout El Salvador on the day of Grande's funeral so that people would focus on a single nationwide Mass. More than 100,000 Salvadorans filled the cathedral, the square and surrounding streets for the service. On that day, Romero's voice seemed changed into the confident, powerful voice of a prophet.

Though Romero made it clear that he was aligning himself with those seeking social change, he called on all sides to turn from violence. He called on popular organizations—and the rebel groups that sprang from them—to turn away from violence and employ nonviolence in their quest for justice. But he held the ruling oligarchy and the military even more responsible for the state into which El Salvador had descended. He saw their violence against union organizers, peasant leaders, teachers and students as direct attacks against the entire Salvadoran people. Furthermore, he saw the church as needing to suffer with the people. He spoke out in defense of murdered priests even when other bishops said they had been "radicals" and thus had become legitimate targets of paramilitary violence. Romero also refused to attend state functions that previously had been a regular part of an archbishop's schedule.

Romero's weekly homilies were broadcast on the radio to an eager population throughout the country. He would tell stories of the people killed or "disappeared" each week, read their names, and weave the contemporary plight of those who suffered into the themes of Bible readings for the week. At one point the military blew up the radio station, so people came to hear Romero in person from parishes around the country armed with tape recorders to disperse his message to the waiting populace.

Outside El Salvador, Romero's reputation quickly grew as the violence in the country gained international attention. His courage and convictions resonated with many concerned with the issues of global poverty and the abuse of human rights. He joined many other Latin American bishops at the conference in Puebla, Mexico, that followed up the Medellin conference in trying to redefine how the Catholic Church should address the pressing concerns of the region. But Romero's international acclaim was not shared by the powerful in his homeland. Though the majority of priests and grassroots congregants loved him with a passion, only one of the other five bishops in El Salvador supported him.

In early 1980 the violence from both the insurgents and the military increased dramatically, spinning into civil war. Romero kept calling for an end to the violence. He received death threats and knew he had been targeted. Still he continued to speak out prophetically against the violence. His final message went on for almost 2 hours, but people were riveted to his words as he dealt in great detail with the interaction of God's Word, true liberation, and each sector of Salvadoran society. At one point he spoke directly to the enlisted personnel in the Army: "Brothers, you are part of our own people. You kill your own *campesino* brothers and sisters. And before an order to kill that a man may give, God's law must prevail that says: Thou shalt not kill! No soldier is obliged to obey an order against the law of God. No one has to fulfill an immoral law. It is time to take back your consciences and to obey your consciences rather than the orders of sin…In the name of God and in the name of this suffering people, whose laments rise to heaven each day more tumultuous, I beg you, I beseech you, I order you in the name of God: Stop the repression!"

The next day the military answered his prophetic appeal. He was celebrating Mass at a hospital chapel. He lifted the host and said, "May this body immolated and this blood sacrificed for humans nourish us also, so that we may give our body and blood to suffering and to pain—like Christ, not for self, but to teach justice and peace to our people." A few moments later a shot fired by a sniper from the rear of the chapel struck him in the chest.

Archbishop Romero was dead, but his words and witness had just begun to grow.

The suffering of El Salvador continued as the national cathedral and surrounding streets were filled with thousands of mourners. In the middle of his funeral, a bomb went off and soldiers started shooting into the crowd. Panicked people fled in all directions including into the cathedral. Romero's coffin, which had been on the front steps, was hastily pulled inside. Forty people died in the violence. Like his own final Mass, Romero's funeral Mass was never finished.

Because of the threats from death squads and the rising tide of violence in El Salvador, Romero had the opportunity to speak about the possibility of his martyrdom. Two weeks before he was killed he told a Mexican journalist: "If the threats are carried out, from this moment I offer my blood to God for the redemption and for the resurrection of El Salvador. Martyrdom is a grace of God that I do not believe I deserve. But if God accepts the sacrifice of my life, let my blood be a seed of freedom and the sign that hope will soon be reality. Let my death, if it is accepted by God, be for my people's liberation and as a witness of hope in the future. You may say, if they succeed in killing me, that I pardon and bless those who do it. A bishop will die, but God's church, which is the people, will never perish."

Romero was wrong in one respect: His humility allowed him not only to offer a sacrifice for the nation of El Salvador, but also become a prophetic gift to the whole world.

CHAPTER 13

Jerzy Popiełuszko

(1947-1984)

If we must die suddenly, it is surely better to meet death defending a worthwhile cause than sitting back and letting injustice win.

—Jerzy Popiełuszko

I've been a pastor for many years, but Jerzy Popiełuszko continues to challenge me. He was a pastor who found himself caught up in a historic, nonviolent, freedom movement. The Polish struggle for freedom was remarkable because so few people died—yet Popiełuszko was among the very few martyrs in that revolution. He died because he stood in the front, ferociously defending his sheep against the wolves of oppression. To this day, he makes me wonder how far my love as a pastor would go.

MORE THAN 250,000 PEOPLE attended the funeral of Polish Catholic priest Father Jerzy Popiełuszko in November 1984. His body had been found in a reservoir on the Vistula River, bound with ropes and badly beaten. For his relentless role as a firebrand in the banned Solidarity movement, police had kidnapped him eleven days earlier. He and his driver were stopped by three men while returning from a preaching engagement. The driver later escaped and reported the incident, igniting the search that found the priest's body 45 miles from where the kidnapping took place.

When news of Popiełuszko's death spread, Solidarity leader Lech Wałęsa said, "The worst has happened. Someone wanted to kill, and he killed not only a man, not only a Pole, not only a priest. Someone wanted to kill the hope that it is possible to avoid violence in Polish political life." At the funeral, the first time in three years that Wałęsa was allowed to speak to a large crowd, the union leader said, "Solidarity lives because Popiełuszko shed his blood for it." There were still years of struggle before Solidarity and democracy were to triumph in Poland, but Popiełuszko's death was a major focal point for clarifying the nature of the struggle and the commitment to freedom for the Polish people. He was only 37 years old.

Jerzy Popiełuszko attended seminary at a time when the conflict between the Communist regime and the Catholic Church was at one of its most intense moments. He and fellow seminarians witnessed the brutality of the government first-hand as they tended students who were beaten by police in anti-government riots in 1968. Popiełuszko eventually became the priest of the St. Stanislaw Kostka Church in Warsaw.

Polish history was changed in August 1980 when strikes erupted at the shipyards in Gdańsk under the leadership of Lech Wałęsa. The Solidarity Union was formed, and labor unrest spread rapidly throughout Poland. The workers at the massive Huta Warszawa steel plant joined the strikes and asked for Mass to be celebrated inside the occupied plant. Popiełuszko was selected by the archbishop and the strikers, and led 10,000 strikers in worship. He was chosen as the chaplain for the steel workers, and St. Stanislaw's became their official parish in Warsaw.

In December 1981 martial law was proclaimed in Poland. Solidarity was banned, and thousands of union leaders were arrested. The Catholic Church became the main place where people could still gather and voice their resistance. Popiełuszko attended some of the political trials and decided to hold a special worship service for the people in prison and their families. These rites became a new form of national Mass and incorporated Polish poetry and national songs. Popiełuszko's sermons attacked abuses of human rights and encouraged freedom of conscience. He compared the sufferings of Poland to Jesus on the cross. "The trial of Jesus goes on forever," he preached. "It continues through his brothers. Only their names, their faces, their dates and their birth places change." In his mind the church could not be neutral in the face of injustice, but must join as a defender of the oppressed.

On one hand, Popiełuszko said that the authorities should serve the people they govern. He proclaimed that God gives freedom to humans and that therefore any enslavement of freedom is a work against God. On the other hand, he spoke out against any form of violent revenge. He said Christians must pray not only for the oppressed but also for the oppressor. Poles were called to a "patriotic struggle to reinstate human dignity." Violence would undermine the very nature of their cause.

The machinery of repression quickly turned against this outspoken priest. His parish house was vandalized. He was repeatedly detained and interrogated for "abusing religion for political purposes." At one point he was given amnesty provided that he stayed away from his political activism for two and a half years. But days later he preached at a Mass for prisoners and called for the ban on Solidarity to be lifted, for allowing freedom of expression, for releasing detained leaders and for allowing crucifixes to be displayed in public places. Popiełuszko faced new threats, but felt that witnessing to the truth was how people overcame fear. He said, "If truth becomes for us a value, worthy of suffering and risk, then we shall overcome fear—the direct reason for our enslavement."

Less than two months later Popiełuszko was murdered. Knowing he was a target, he said, "If we must die suddenly, it is surely better to meet death defending a worthwhile cause than sitting back and letting injustice win." Though the government feared an outbreak of violence following his death—or perhaps even hoped for such an outbreak to justify another crackdown—the Solidarity activists maintained their nonviolent discipline. The struggle continued with Popiełuszko's murder as a rallying cry. When the Communist system finally fell and the once-imprisoned union leader Lech Wałęsa was elected president, the fallen priest's hopes were fulfilled. His monuments in stone, and tributes through music, film and poetry show that he lives on in the grateful hearts of the Polish people.

PART 3

Peace Theorists
Gaining Ground on Military Science

MILITARY SCIENCE BEGAN WITH the Chinese strategist Sun Tzu's "Art of War" in the 6th Century B.C.E. and grew through thousands of years of warfare. Entire libraries now march with military strategists across blood-soaked battlefields, trying to perfect tactics for the next skirmish, the next campaign, the next war. Military academies around the world research and prepare for future conflict.

Peace science is in its infancy. Research into nonviolent methods of bringing about social and political change is just beginning. Most peace-studies programs in universities are of recent vintage.

The U.S. government has supported research into peacemaking, but Congress has played politics with the U.S. Institute of Peace (USIP) since first establishing this "peace academy" in 1984. Unlike U.S. military academies, the USIP was decentralized and run in conjunction with a number of educational institutions. Its founding goals were to "prevent and resolve violent international conflict, promote post-conflict stability and development, and to increase conflict management capacity, tools and intellectual capacity worldwide." In 2011, a Washington D.C. headquarters building for USIP was scheduled for completion. Then, in early 2011, as this book was being printed, Republicans in the U.S. House pushed through a measure slashing all funding for the USIP. This "peace academy" may survive in some form, but its seesaw history represents far less support than Washington gives to military academies.

In the mid-19th century Henry David Thoreau's essay, *On the Duty of Civil Disobedience*, sketched some of the theory behind nonviolent resistance to governments engaged in violent behavior. Thoreau practiced tax resistance—in his case refusing to pay the poll tax that was used to finance the U.S. war with Mexico in 1848. Thoreau said, "If a thousand men were not to pay their tax bill this year, that would not be as violent and bloody a measure as it would be to pay them and enable the State to commit violence and shed innocent blood." His resistance only resulted in a single night in jail. Thoreau's real contribution was thinking through the philosophy of civil disobedience. He spoke about the authority of a person's conscience over their actions. "If injustice is legally sanctioned, such as in slavery or an imperialist war, then a citizen is duty-bound to resist", Thoreau insisted. "Under a government which imprisons any unjustly, the true place for a just man is also a prison," he wrote. Thoreau's writings about civil disobedience had an impact on Leo Tolstoy, Mahatma Gandhi and Martin Luther King, Jr., who quoted Thoreau in his historic *Letter from Birmingham Jail*.

Gandhi and King were activists who carefully explained their ideas in speeches and writings. The success of their work caused thinker-activists and scholars to examine what they did more thoroughly.

World religions have a great deal to say about conflict, but the message often is muted or even deliberately garbled. Buddhism represents one of the oldest peace traditions that still resonate around the world. Christianity has both a strong body of teachings on peace—and a history of conflict. Many contemporary conflicts involve predominantly Muslim nations and groups. Islam as a religion has been drafted into the service of political campaigns from the nationalism of Palestinians in Hamas to the international terrorism of al-Qaida. Debate swirls around the meaning of perhaps the most famous word in the Quran: *jihad*, or spiritual struggle. The word has withstood various interpretations in various times and places—but today, *jihad* often is misinterpreted as a call to "holy war." Some Muslim scholars and theorists now are digging into their scriptures and traditions to resurface and restore an Islamic tradition of peace.

The Syrian philosopher Jawdat Said went to the Quran itself in 1966 to provide a basis for nonviolence in Islam. From his study, he published an important book, *Path of Adam's Son*, exploring the ancient story of Cain and Abel as it is recorded in the Quran (even though the two figures are not specifically named in the Muslim text of the story). In studying that ancient passage, Said was trying to discern the first action of nonviolent prophetic self-sacrifice. In translation, the text in the Quran reads: "One said, 'I will surely kill you.' The other answered, 'If you stretch out your hand to slay me, it is not for me to stretch my hand against you to slay you. For I fear Allah, the Lord of worlds.'" For Said, Abel's statement means, "I will not make my death validate killing." Living in a part of the world where the killing of one's relatives or neighbors can justify lethal cycles of retribution, Said understands the significance of Abel's sacrificial action in that story. In Said's view, Abel's choice represents a major rejection of such violence, even at the cost of his own life. Said is among a handful of courageous Muslim scholars trying to restore a Muslim tradition of teaching peace—and, in Said's analysis, that tradition dates to the very first killing on the planet.

In Christian thought, most of the discussion has focused on the debate between pacifism and Just War Theory: Should Christians participate in war and, if so, under what conditions? St Augustine (fourth century) and St. Thomas Aquinas (13th century) challenged the pacifist view of the early church by suggesting that participation in war could be ethically acceptable under certain conditions. Various theologians and philosophers have debated those conditions for a "just war", but generally they have included: A just cause; a legitimate authority waging the war; a just intent (defense rather than aggression); proportionate use of force; that war be the last resort and that there be a probability of success.

Glen Stassen, an activist ethics professor at Fuller Theological Seminary in California, turns the discussion to "How can we participate in forging peace?" He argues for a positive option: "just peacemaking." He edited a book by that title in which a number of Christian thinkers and peacemakers examine the ten specific practices that Stassen says are already preventing, halting or limiting wars. The ten "just peacemaking" practices range from nonviolent direct action to just and sustainable economic development; from building international institutions to building democracy and respecting human rights and religious liberty. Stassen is working to expand the ethical discussion of "just peacemaking" beyond the Christian community in presentations to Muslim and Jewish ethicists. He is preparing a new edition of *Just Peacemaking* that has reflections in support of each of the ten practices by Muslim and Jewish thinkers as well as by Christians.

One of these practices is the use of cooperative conflict resolution, which has become a major stream of academic exploration. With the growth of the labor movement, the art of negotiating contracts between workers and management was recognized as a valuable skill. Conflict resolution soon became a well-established field of study. Negotiation moved out of the refined sphere of diplomacy into the realm of ordinary workers. Methods of teaching conflict resolution became a major topic all the way from business schools to elementary school playgrounds. As recently as 1986, Dean Pruitt, who could write with a bit of intentional exaggeration, said: "Negotiation and mediation today can be likened, in some respects, to medicine and surgery in the early 18th century. Both sets of fields consist almost entirely of practitioners; training is heavily in the direction of the apprenticeship; practitioners operate more or less intuitively, each with a distinct individual style; and the literature in both fields, to the extent it exists, derives mainly from the experience of practitioners and consist largely of aphorisms about appropriate action." Since Pruitt's assessment, academic programs have multiplied. Where once there might have been a course or two at an academic institution, now there are masters degrees and doctorate-level programs. The rapid expansion of peace building, conflict resolution, mediation and nonviolent activities has provided a wealth of material for analysis, reflection and systematization.

Most of the theory of nonviolent struggle continues to be developed by men and women personally committed to justice and freedom, but in this new millennium they are strengthened by university-sponsored research and training. Finally, peace science is gaining ground on military science—making up for lost time.

CHAPTER 14

Paulo Freire

(1921-1997)

To surmount the situation of oppression, people must first critically recognize its causes, so that through transforming action they can create a new situation, one which makes possible the pursuit of a fuller humanity.

—Paulo Freire

*I tried reading the famous Brazilian theorist's **Pedagogy of the Oppressed** years ago, but the book was so dense—I gave up. Yet Freire's teaching method was passed down to me through experiences over the years that I found engaging and effective. My own teaching style was revolutionized through what I picked up from Freire's insights. So after understanding his methodology through practical participation, I went back to Freire's book. Reading it still was a tough slog, but finally the book made sense. It's best to learn Freire in practice rather than as a mere intellectual exercise.*

PAULO FREIRE SPENT 70 days in prison when the military *junta* seized power in Brazil during a 1964 coup. He had been working on a literacy campaign, teaching the rural poor how to read. His work was done under the auspices of the University of Recife and the Brazilian government. So why was this educator branded a "traitor" by the military?

Freire became one of the most influential educational theorists, developing what has been called "critical pedagogy." He educated people marginalized in society so that they could participate in the analysis and transformation of their own situation. That idea about the power of grassroots education now has circled the globe. Education is not a top-down project, but rather a dialogical partnership, or as Freire puts it, "a pedagogy which must be forged with, not for, the oppressed."

The Great Depression of 1929 threw Freire's middle class Brazilian family into poverty. His experience with hunger forged a concern for the poor that he maintained throughout his life. Poverty and hunger severely restricted his access to education and his ability to take advantage of it. "I didn't understand anything because of my hunger," Freire said. "I wasn't dumb. It wasn't lack of interest. My social condition didn't allow me to have an education. Experience showed me once again the relationship between social class and knowledge"

As his family recovered financially he was able to go to law school, but soon shifted over to the study of language and phenomenology, at the time a new approach to analyzing the way humans think and communicate. He began teaching secondary school. He met Elza Maia Costa de Oliveira, also a teacher. They married and then worked together throughout their careers as educators.

Freire was appointed by the government of the state of Pernambuco, where his home city of Recife is the capital, to work among the illiterate poor. Brazilian law required voters to be literate, thus disenfranchising vast numbers of the poor. Freire's thinking was shaped by his Christian faith and by liberation theology, which taught that freedom and justice are central biblical themes, as he began developing the teaching methodologies that would make him famous. In 1961 he was appointed director of the Department of Cultural Extension at Recife University, and he began to put his ideas into practice more extensively. He worked with 300 sugar cane workers, enabling them to read and write in 45 days. One of the educational programs had the slogan, "Bare feet can also learn to read." His work was so successful the Brazilian government supported the establishment of thousands of literacy projects based on his model. Students said, "I now realize I am a person, an educated person," and, "We were blind, now our eyes have been opened."

The key for Freire was to connect the educational task, such as learning to read, with the issues of oppression people experience in their daily lives. He helped students analyze their own conditions and begin to speak out publicly. In a "problem-posing" approach to education, the particulars of an oppressive situation are turned into problems to be solved by the students in a critical co-investigation with the teacher. In the process the students' consciousness is awakened, moving from passive fatalism to becoming active in bringing about change to relieve their oppression. The "culture of silence" among the dispossessed is overcome, and they are able to discover their own voices and transformative capacity.

As part of the change in consciousness, both the teacher and the student must transcend the dichotomy of what Freire called the "banking" concept of education: where the all-knowing teacher makes "deposits" of the selected knowledge into the empty vessels of the students. Instead, students need to recognize their own capacity to be teachers themselves. They are, in fact, the ones with the clearest vantage point of their situations in life. The teacher must be humble enough to also be a student, learning from the participants in the educational setting. Freire wrote, "The humanist, revolutionary educator...must be imbued with a profound trust in people and their creative power. To achieve this, they must be partners of the students in their relations with them." Together then the teacher/student and student/teacher enter into dialog to bring about change. Praxis is the term for "reflection and action upon the world in order to transform it."

Freire knew such thinking would not be acceptable to those who benefitted by the oppressive situations throughout Brazil. The military coup of 1964 seemed to confirm his fears for he was imprisoned and then exiled. Freire ended up in Chile where he worked for five years with the Christian Democratic Agrarian Reform Movement and UNESCO. His work there played a major role in helping Chile achieve one of the best records in the world for overcoming illiteracy.

By 1969 Freire's work was so widespread and acclaimed that Harvard University invited him to become a visiting professor. His book *Pedagogy of the Oppressed* had been released in Portuguese and later in English. However, the book was banned in Brazil. Freire later left the U.S. to become the special education advisor to the World Council of Churches in Geneva, Switzerland. In that capacity he became a consultant for education reform around the world, especially in the former Portuguese colonies of Guinea Bissau and Mozambique.

The world-renowned educator was finally allowed to return to his homeland in 1979. He worked on adult literacy with the Workers' Party, and when they won municipal elections he was appointed Secretary of Education for São Paulo. In 1986 he was awarded the UNESCO Prize for Education for Peace.

Freire was heavily influenced by Marxist thinking as well as by radical Catholic writers. He wrote, "I never understood how to reconcile fellowship with Christ with the exploitation of other human beings, or to reconcile a love for Christ with racial, gender and class discrimination. By the same token, I could never reconcile the Left's liberating discourse with the Left's discriminatory practice along the lines of race, gender and class. What a shocking contradiction: to be, at the same time, a leftist and a racist." His work is full of revolutionary terminology, but he also provides a devastating critique of revolutionary leaders who return to the same paternalism and manipulation of their oppressors in order to seize and maintain their own power. Revolutionary leaders who speak for the people ultimately do not transform the culture, he argued. Rather, a true revolutionary lovingly enters into a genuine dialogue with the people and is humble enough to be changed by that dialogue. The leader then speaks with the people.

Around the world, popular education has been strongly influenced by Freire's work. Teachers who follow his theories are less lecturers presenting information in packaged formats and more facilitators who raise questions to awaken the participants to search for their own answers. Freire did not live to see the new millennium, but his life continues to reshape our world.

CHAPTER 15

Gustavo Gutiérrez

(b. 1928)

The faces of the poor must now be confronted... There was a time when poverty was considered to be an unavoidable fate, but such a view is no longer possible or responsible. Now we know that poverty is not simply a misfortune; it is an injustice.

—Gustavo Gutiérrez

I received my theological training at a conservative evangelical seminary. But one professor challenged his students with the social teaching of Jesus and included a healthy dose of liberation theology, beginning with Gutiérrez. At the time, I received this "foreign" wisdom— from a Peruvian Dominican priest—with the arrogant criticism of a young American academic. Later, I read Gutiérreez's study on the book of Job, **We Drink from Our Own Wells,** *and was humbled and moved by his deep love of God and passionate faith lived out amid human suffering. By the time I discovered that book, I had learned more of the world and was ready to receive this wisdom that was far richer than Gutiérrez's critics recognized.*

THROUGHOUT THE HISTORY OF Latin America, the Catholic Church has been a dominant institution supporting the status quo and ruling powers. But in the 1970s and 1980s, in many countries, priests and nuns were arrested and many were killed. Bible study leaders were murdered by the thousands. What turned the Church from a pillar of power to such a threat to the established order that its leaders were targets for systematic violence? This transformation bears witness to the power of ideas to change people and to change the history those people create.

Gustavo Gutiérrez has been called "the father of liberation theology." He does not like that appellation because he believes the theology of liberation is a project of "the people," ordinary Christians who apply their faith and the teachings of the Bible to the historical context in which they live. In Latin America that has been a context of extensive, grinding poverty and repressive regimes, often military dictatorships. Gutiérrez has been one of the leading lights in a movement of church authorities preaching a new theology that takes the plight of the poor seriously.

Gutiérrez was born in Lima, Peru, as a *mestizo*, mixed race, with both Hispanic and Quechuan Indian blood. His early childhood was marked by illness; he was bed-ridden for years with osteomyelitis (inflammation of the bone). His illness prompted him to plan for a medical career, but he later felt a calling to the priesthood. He studied theology in Europe, but on his return to Latin America, he found his studies upended.

What Gutiérrez had learned in his classical education and what he encountered in the poor *barrios* of Lima seemed completely at odds. He had been taught that poverty was a virtue to be accepted, but he saw it as a destructive reality that needed to be changed. He had learned that poverty was the result of laziness or bad luck; instead he saw structures of oppression and political decisions that were made to keep the poor in horrible living conditions so others could benefit. He had learned that poverty was inevitable, but he saw that there was a power in the poor if they could organize themselves.

Gutiérrez had found deep images in the Bible that spoke to the realities he encountered with the poor, images that called for liberation. These images were not at the fringes of biblical teaching, but at the very center. One image was that of the exodus of the

Hebrew slaves out of the bondage of Egypt. In their captivity, the Hebrews' labor contributed "to increasing injustice and to widening the gap between exploiters and exploited." So God acted to bring these slaves to freedom and, "The God of Exodus is the God of history and political liberation."

As a Christian theologian, he saw God taking flesh in Jesus as an act of divine solidarity. In Jesus "God became poor," he taught. This was a powerful affirmation that Christ wasn't isolated in churches—rather, Christ was located mainly among the poor in Latin America. Since Christ was living among the poor, then efforts toward social justice were a natural part of the Kingdom of God, the work of salvation. "Messianic practice is the proclamation of the kingdom of God and the transformation of the historical conditions of the poor. It is the word of life, backed up by the deed of deliverance."

In 1971, Gutiérrez published his landmark book that later would be published in English as *A Theology of Liberation*. Many other theologians, church leaders and activist clergy wrote in this same vein, a movement called "Liberation Theology." Soon, this river of teaching and preaching branched into other cultures, giving rise to Black Theology, Feminist Theology, Asian Liberation Theology and African Liberation Theology.

For Gutiérrez, the voices of the marginalized ones needed to emerge by both honestly retelling old stories and writing new chapters of history: "I believe that our job today is to rewrite history in terms of the poor, the humiliated, and the rejected of society, to rewrite the struggles and the fights that have taken place in the last century." Re-envisioning history in a powerful new way transformed current challenges. "Development" was a term he rejected as more passive than the word "liberation." The poor could make their own history, and the Church should join with them as a stimulus toward liberation.

What made the work of Gutiérrez and the other Latin American liberation theologians so powerful was that they did not design this new approach from some ivory tower. They worked through hundreds of thousands of "base communities," small groups that met in urban barrios and in rural villages to discuss the Bible. The Exodus imagery, the concept of God taking flesh among us, the suffering of the cross of Christ and the hope of his resurrection were all interpreted within the setting of peasants being driven off their land, of the poor going hungry, of those who protested being imprisoned, tortured or killed. The theology burned with incendiary fervor in the hearts of people for whom religion was their life's blood.

Government response was harsh. Gutiérrez and other liberation theologians were called Marxists. Sometimes Gutiérrez and others used Marxist terms in their writing and teaching, but most of them rejected Marxist politics as incompatible with Christianity. For Gutiérrez, the liberation theology that he expressed throughout his writing and teaching sprang from a deep Christian spirituality and echoed the biblical tradition of prophets courageously speaking out against injustice. His own prophetic engagement sprang directly from his understanding of how faith, hope and love must be rooted both in love of God and in love of the poor with whom God became identified in Christ. Some priests joined revolutionaries in the jungles, but Gutiérrez believed one did not need to kill in order to love the poor.

Gutiérrez participated in discussions at the highest levels of the Latin American Catholic Church that shaped what eventually was expressed in formal statements throughout the Americas as "the preferential option for the poor." Conservative bishops tried to bar Gutiérrez from attending the crucial 1979 Puebla, Mexico, conference, but Gutiérrez and other liberation prelates including Oscar Romero participated at Puebla anyway. If they could not be formal delegates, they would serve as personal advisors to others at Puebla. Gutiérrez was advisor to eight bishops, so his thoughts were introduced into discussions by high-powered advocates. Gutiérrez understood that this was high-octane fuel, so potent that, he wrote, "The denunciation of injustice implies the rejection of the use of Christianity to legitimize the established order."

The revolutions, both violent and nonviolent, that shook Latin America and that eventually replaced most military dictatorships with democracies would not have happened without liberation theology. The ideas of Gustavo Gutiérrez and other liberation theologians transformed the lives of ordinary Latin Americans, turning religious communities into social and political forces. Religious-based passivity was replaced by religious-inspired activism. Of course, this work and Gutiérrez's hopes have not been fully realized. Poverty remains a massive problem. But the call, the theoretical and spiritual fuel, is still there—"a demand that we go and build a different social order."

CHAPTER 16

William Ury
(b. 1953)

Getting along is not the absence of conflict, but the strenuous processing of conflicting needs and interests.

—William Ury

*Steps to win-win solutions have become a centerpiece in my own workshops to train peace activists. Ury and Roger Fisher's 1981 book, **Getting to YES: Negotiating Agreement Without Giving In**, put this process together in such a clear way that I've been able to teach it to my children. I remember overhearing my daughter Janelle use a rough form of it as she mediated between two elementary-age playmates. In various corners of the world, I've taught insurgents negotiating with governments how to work toward win-win solutions—and afterward I've heard Ury's terminology in press statements. Sometimes transformation comes when simple ideas are set down in plain language.*

"WIN-WIN" IS COMMON PARLANCE in almost any discussion of conflict from politics to labor-management issues. This is the gift of William Ury and Roger Fisher, who wrote *Getting to YES: Negotiating Agreement Without Giving In*. First published in 1981, the book is already a classic in the field of conflict study and the practice of conflict resolution. Translated into more than 30 languages, their ideas have been the subject of doctoral dissertations and grassroots training in conflict zones.

Fisher and Ury challenge readers to move away from negotiating over positions, which inevitably is adversarial and becomes a conflict in which one party wins and the other loses, or perhaps both lose. Instead, they focus on the needs and interests of the parties, separating the people from the problem. "A basic fact about negotiation, easy to forget in corporate and international transactions, is that you are dealing not with abstract representatives of the 'other side,' but with human beings." They urge, "Be hard on the problem, soft on the people." Their approach challenges people to begin by focusing on collective needs and interests, which usually moves people past initial defensiveness and fear. Soon, participants are collaborating as they brainstorm ways to meet their needs.

Ury and Fisher also provide guidance in the communication needed to reach win-win solutions: "Speak about yourself, not about them…If you make a statement about them that they believe is untrue, they will ignore you or get angry; they will not focus on your concern. But a statement about how you feel is difficult to challenge. You convey the same information without provoking a defensive reaction that will prevent them from taking it in." What Ury and Fisher lay out in their book now is foundational in conflict resolution, mediation and negotiation.

Shortly after their collaboration on the book, Fisher and Ury co-founded the Program on Negotiation (PON) at Harvard Law School. Established in 1983, the PON is "a university consortium dedicated to developing the theory and practice of negotiation and dispute resolution." The PON has drawn together scholars, students and practitioners to work on creating a new generation of negotiators in many spheres of social, political and economic life.

Ury is not just a scholar. He has been a mediator in many conflicts and an advisor to mediators in others—from high-level corporate mergers to wildcat strikes in Kentucky coalmines. During the Cold War, Ury helped create nuclear crisis centers to prevent the outbreak of accidental nuclear war between the U.S. and the Soviet Union. That idea met the needs and interests of both adversaries. Following the Cold War, he helped to negotiate an end to the civil war in the Aceh region of Indonesia, and he helped to keep civil war from erupting in Venezuela. Ury joined with former President Jimmy Carter and founded the International Negotiation Network to assist in ending civil wars around the world.

Before his books and success in conflict resolution, Ury originally studied social anthropology. He was trained at Yale and Harvard, and studied negotiation practices in diverse settings from Western boardrooms to gatherings of indigenous people in southern Africa and New Guinea. In *The Third Side: Why We Fight and How We Can Stop*, Ury draws on wisdom from many traditional societies where a third party—the community surrounding a conflict—plays a role in resolving the crisis. He outlines 10 roles for people on this third side: for example, they can provide security, respect and recognition. They can teach skills for handling conflict. They can act as mediators or arbiters. They may need to contain conflict by acting as witnesses or may need to interpose themselves between factions.

More recently, Ury has turned his attention to the Middle East and helped to establish the Abraham Path Initiative, which encourages cultural tourism to foster understanding. Participants walk together along the traditional routes of the patriarch Abraham's journeys—and experience culture and hospitality along the path. Despite entrenched conflict in that region, Ury sees his methods bearing fruit around the world. He says, "Violence is not the only contagious phenomenon. So is cooperation."

CHAPTER 17

Gene Sharp
(b. 1928)

You get rid of violence only if people see that you have a different way of acting, a different way of struggle.

—Gene Sharp

I first read **The Politics of Nonviolent Action** *in 1989 as the uprisings in China's Tiananmen Square were unfolding. Sharp's analysis highlighted both the power of the students' actions and the false steps along the way that made the movement toward democracy vulnerable to the government's crackdown. Sharp's analysis helped me to turn unfolding history into a learning laboratory. Since then, I've used Sharp's works in much of my teaching and have carried his resources, often in translated versions, into many countries.*

GENE SHARP HAS BEEN called the "Machiavelli of nonviolence" and the "Clausewitz of nonviolent warfare." He has been the leading academic theoretician about nonviolent struggle with an activist's heart. Unlike Gandhi or King who developed their theories in the middle of specific struggles, Sharp has steeped himself in the history of conflict and examined peaceful methods of engagement in great detail. From that analysis, he teaches others how to use these nonviolent strategies effectively.

Raised in Ohio, Sharp participated in early sit-ins to desegregate a lunch-counter in Columbus, Ohio. He engaged in civil disobedience protesting military conscription during the Korean War and spent nine months in prison as a result. Then he left the U.S. for10 years of work, study and teaching in England and Norway. Upon returning, Sharp became a researcher at Harvard University's Center for International Affairs and was later professor emeritus of political science at the University of Massachusetts Dartmouth.

In 1983 Sharp founded the Albert Einstein Institution to advance "the study and use of strategic nonviolent action in conflicts throughout the world." The institution is "committed to the defense of freedom, democracy, and the reduction of political violence through the use of nonviolent action." Sharp chose to name the center after Einstein because late in his life, the world-renowned scientist and intellect saw the potential for nonviolent struggle to profoundly address his deep concerns about war, violence and nuclear weapons. Einstein said, "On the whole, I believe that Gandhi held the most enlightened views of all the political men in our time." This nonprofit center has given Sharp a vehicle to move beyond classrooms and books to consult with leaders in various struggles around the world. Sharp's works on nonviolent action have been translated into more than 45 languages—and many are available through free downloads from the center's website. Books that used to be smuggled into various countries for freedom movements can now be accessed directly via the Internet.

Perhaps Sharp's deepest impact in regional struggles has been in Eastern Europe and the former Soviet Republics. When the Soviet Union was breaking up, the Baltic nations knew they could never resist a Russian invasion through violence. So Sharp and his assistant at the Albert Einstein Institution worked with the defense ministers of the governments of Estonia, Latvia and Lithuania to explore and put in place plans for "civilian-based defense." The basic idea was to plan for widespread non-cooperation so that an occupied country would become ungovernable by a larger power. This kind of resistance was used successfully by Danes and

Norwegians against Nazi occupiers in World War II. As the Soviet Union crumbled, the three Baltic republics gained independence with relatively little loss of life.

His principles proved so effective that his book, *From Dictatorship to Democracy*, became "the bible" for nonviolent *PORA!* activists in the Ukraine who led the Orange Revolution in 2004. The young Otpor activists in Serbia who brought down Slobodan Milosovic had also studied Sharp's writings. The Albert Einstein Institution provided thousands of copies of his works for free to stimulate these freedom movements. Sharp had actually met with activists in many countries as well.

The centerpiece of Sharp's understanding of nonviolence is that all power is derived from the consent of the governed gained through both legitimate and illegitimate ways, but it is given nonetheless. This is an empowering insight, because an oppressed people can decide to withdraw that consent. They don't have to obey. As Sharp says: "Nonviolent action is possible, and is capable of wielding great power even against ruthless rulers and military regimes, because it attacks the most vulnerable characteristic of all hierarchical institutions and governments: Dependence on the governed."

To give shape to that withdrawal of consent and resistance to oppression, Sharp outlined 198 different nonviolent methods with specific historical illustrations. Power is not monolithic, so a key to nonviolent struggle is breaking down that power into its constituent parts: What are the pillars that hold up the power structure? If the supports for oppressive power are properly analyzed, then strategies can be developed to undermine those pillars and forces that once upheld the oppressive power. They can be transformed into allies in a movement for change.

When Sharp first published his three-volume *The Politics of Nonviolent Action* in 1973, the luminaries for nonviolent struggle were Gandhi and King. There had been various peace movements related to the nuclear arms race and the war in Vietnam. There were also historic struggles forgotten by most people: the nonviolent defense against a military coup in Germany in 1920, the nonviolent overthrow of the brutal Maximiliano Martinez dictatorship in El Salvador and the Jorge Ubico dictatorship in Guatemala, both in 1944. In his landmark book, Sharp pulled all these lessons together in a coherent way, spelling out the dynamics of power and struggle as well as the tactics and methodologies that could be employed. With the explosion of the People Power movement in the Philippines, movements in Latin America, South Africa, Burma, China and Eastern Europe, Sharp's theories became a key for activists to interpret what was happening and plan further engagements.

For Sharp, commitment to nonviolent alternatives is not necessarily a moral or religious matter—it can be pragmatic. It may be the most effective strategy for forcing change and it may avoid the horrendous damage that results from violence.

As this book was in the final editing stages, nonviolent revolutions toppled governments in Tunisia and Egypt. As the leaders of these revolutions began to emerge, they spoke of the roots of their ideas for resistance—specifically about reading the works of Gene Sharp. They had studied the Serbian nonviolent resistance movement, Otpor, which took them to Sharp's booklet *From Dictatorship to Democracy* (available in Arabic—which is one of the many languages offered for free downloads). The Arab activists followed up their reading with nonviolence training. This became the core of decentralized leadership, which is changing the Arab political landscape today. As the media spotlight turned to Sharp, he was quick to say, "The people of Egypt did that—not me." This is true, because it takes committed, courageous people to make a nonviolent revolution. However, for these people, Sharp's ideas have proved their value in some of the harshest testing grounds imaginable.

"I don't think you get rid of violence by protesting against it," Sharp says. "I think you get rid of violence only if people see that you have a different way of acting, a different way of struggle.... Part of my analysis is that if you don't like violence, you have to develop a substitute. Then people have a choice."

CHAPTER 18

John Paul Lederach

(b. 1955)

The primary practical task of those working for reconciliation is to help create the space where Truth, Mercy, Justice and Peace can truly meet and thresh things out.

—John Paul Lederach

We had just listened to a church leader from Burma deliver a riveting appeal for help to bring peace to his country. This was a high point for me while attending the first international Baptist peace conference held in Sweden in 1988. A Mennonite guest, John Howard Yoder, challenged us Baptists to get involved and not just listen to a good presentation. He told us of the Nicaraguan peace process and the work of John Paul Lederach. So the church leader from Burma and I met with John Paul. With his counsel we launched an initiative that was my first step in direct mediation.

THE MOB CHASED AFTER the truck, pointing at John Paul Lederach: "There's the gringo! Get him! Get him!" The windows were smashed by rocks. A two-by-four slammed into Lederach's shoulder. A rock bloodied the head of his Nicaraguan companion and driver—but he managed to maintain consciousness and drive to the hospital.

Lederach was part of a team trying to set up a speaking engagement as part of the Nicaraguan peace process. The revolutionary Sandinista movement had deposed the Samosa dictatorship in 1979 and had become the ruling party in Nicaragua. Then, for almost a decade, the Sandinista government had been under siege by a coalition of insurgent forces known collectively as "the Contras," who were supported by the United States with money and military advisors. Along the eastern coast of Nicaragua, the Contra groups were mostly indigenous Indians from three tribes. At the meeting where Lederach and his driver were injured, Miskito Indian insurgent leaders were coming home from the border areas where they had carried out their insurgency. This step to open up direct communication between the two sides had been agreed to in the negotiation process, but Sandinista sympathizers turned the event at a local stadium into a riot.

During the Nicaraguan peace process Lederach also faced threats of assassination, a threat to kidnap his 3-year old child, and accusations of being a CIA informer on the one hand and a Sandinista spy on the other. Staying committed to peacemaking for Lederach is a spiritual journey often grappling with his own anger and fear. He writes, "To pursue reconciliation, we must accept the long sleepless nights of fighting in ourselves with God before we can journey toward and look for the face of God in our enemy."

Lederach is the Professor of International Peacebuilding at the University of Notre Dame. He also helped found the Conflict Transformation Program and Institute for Peacebuilding at Eastern Mennonite University in Harrisonburg, Virginia. He has written many books from the popular level to the highly technical level. That sounds like life in an ivory tower, but that is hardly the case. Not many academics find themselves at the center of a riot.

Lederach's father was a Mennonite pastor. He retains a deep commitment to the Christian faith as expressed in the pacifist Mennonite tradition. His spirituality has been a great source of direction and sustenance. For twenty years he was on the staff of the Mennonite Central Committee (MCC). He wrote reference material, many articles and training guides. Some of his works were written and published in Spanish under the name Juan Pablo Lederach.

The effort to bring peace to Nicaragua was Lederach's greatest mediation achievement. Representing the MCC, he worked with a team of Moravian and Baptist Nicaraguans to open communication between the Contra insurgent groups from eastern Nicaragua and the Sandinista government. Most of the Moravians were from the same English-speaking Miskito Indian groups as the insurgent leaders, and they linked up with Gustavo Parajón, a Baptist leader on the National Reconciliation Commission who was trusted by the Sandinistas. Together they built the bridge of trust that could reach to the two sides.

Many rounds of talks took place between the mediation team and the two sides. Sometimes when Lederach was back in the U.S. he spent most of his time making calls to various government officials, insurgent leaders or members of the mediation team, racking up the phone bills as he relayed messages and proposals between the sides. Everyone persevered through all the threats and disruptions, including the riot where Lederach was injured. In 1988 an agreement was reached that ended the war between the Nicaraguan government and the Indian insurgents. This was a major step, along with the Esquipulas II agreement of the Central American presidents mediated by Oscar Arias, in bringing an end to the decade-long war that had plagued Nicaragua. Besides his work in Nicaragua, Lederach has participated in various peace-building and mediation efforts in Somalia, Northern Ireland, Colombia, the Philippines and Nepal.

However, Lederach's biggest impact has come through his ideas and teaching methods. He has combined theory and practice—each supporting the other. He likes to think of himself as a "reflective practitioner." In this way, Lederach has influenced a generation of peace-builders working around the world and touched many places of conflict far beyond his own direct involvement.

In one of his books Lederach writes, "I have a rather modest thesis: I believe that the nature and characteristics of contemporary conflict suggest the need for a set of concepts and approaches that go beyond traditional statist diplomacy." He sketches a pyramid of actors who play roles in peace building, with the top leadership at the narrow end of the pyramid, middle-range leaders in the center, and grassroots leaders at the bottom. News reports usually focus on the actions of top leaders; that is the level where government diplomacy works. But the keys to peace often lie in the middle and grassroots levels, which is where Lederach focuses most of his efforts. His educational methods help people find their own solutions. Trainers using his theories are catalysts to help participants discover their own creativity and draw upon their own cultural strengths and practices.

In Nicaragua, one catalyst was a Bible verse translated from Spanish into English, which proclaims: "Truth and Mercy have met together. Justice and Peace have kissed" *Psalm 85:10.* Through Lederach's training tools, Nicaraguan pastors began using this verse before every mediation session during that peace process. Lederach writes that, indeed, Truth, Mercy, Justice and Peace came to life. "I could hear their voices in the war in Nicaragua. In fact I could hear their voices in any conflict....They became people, and they could talk." In training sessions, he would form groups around each concept, and then ask people to treat that concept as a person. He would ask, "What is Truth (or Mercy or Justice or Peace) most concerned about in the midst of the conflict?" Lederach would interview the spokesperson for each group, addressing them as "Sister Truth" or "Brother Peace." Through that dialog, many of the elements of the conflict could be examined from fresh perspectives.

"Conflict Transformation" is the overarching concept for much of Lederach's work. He sees this concept as going beyond and uniting the "revolutionary" camp of those engaged in nonviolent social change and the "resolutionary" camp of those engaged in mediation. Conflict transformation seeks to build constructive patterns of relationship to replace the destructive dynamics between people and groups. Those involved in conflict transformation seek "to maximize the achievement of constructive, mutually beneficial processes and outcomes." This involves personal as well as systemic change. He even incorporates trauma recovery into the process. Lederach has provided a thorough and integrated understanding of what is necessary to build peace in conflicted societies and how they can achieve reconciliation.

John Paul Lederach has been creatively driven by questions such as How do we move from merely talking about peace to actually building peace? and How can we promote a concern for human life and justice in settings of devastating violence and oppression? His answers have placed creative tools in the hands of people often overlooked in major conflicts—the mid-level and grassroots men and women who can truly transform their communities and bring enemies together to reconcile.

PART 4

Advocates
Pulling the Levers of Change

ADVOCATES MAY SPEAK WITH prophetic fervor, and most great advocates understand underlying theories of making peace—but the hallmark of true advocates is this: They know how to steer organizations and institutions through complex processes in search of peace and justice. They may labor for reform and even radical change in the basic structures and laws of their nations, but they try to work within existing systems as they reach toward ideals.

Advocates may be political figures who raise their voices within the government. They may be part of non-governmental organizations standing outside a country's formal structures, speaking on behalf of marginalized people or specific issues. Sometimes advocates use a newspaper or a magazine as their platform. Advocates may work within their home country or as part of networks that transcend national boundaries.

Within the halls of political power, bold advocates include U.S. Rep. Abraham Lincoln, who cast the sole dissenting vote against going to war with Mexico in 1848. U.S. Rep. Michael Harrington from Massachusetts made public the congressional hearings about U.S. involvement in the overthrow of President Salvador Allende in Chile in 1973. Harrington knew that this step would ruin his career—and it did lead to censure by Congress—but in his heart he felt that Americans had a right to know that their government was behind the overthrow of another democratically elected government.

One of the greatest political advocates was British Member of Parliament, William Wilberforce, who led the fight in the late 18th century and into the early 19th century to abolish the slave trade within the British Empire. He knew that lasting change depended on advocates who could enshrine ideals in law that would stand for years to come. Building a successful movement took 20 years before Wilberforce and his allies could topple entrenched interests that controlled the government. Finally, in 1806, a bill was passed outlawing the slave trade. As an advocate, Wilberforce refused to give up on a cause that at first looked politically hopeless in spite of its morality. He said: "Never, never will we desist till we have wiped away this scandal (of the slave trade) from the load of guilt which we at present labor, and until we have extinguished every trace of this bloody traffic which our posterity will scarcely believe have been suffered to exist so long, a disgrace and dishonor to our country."

In the U.S., a leading advocate against the institution of slavery was William Lloyd Garrison. Garrison was not elected to any office, but was a spokesperson for a broad citizens' movement seeking the legislative, social and economic changes to eliminate slavery. His newspaper, *The Liberator*, became the organ for the abolitionist movement. He continued publishing *The Liberator* until the 13th Amendment of the U.S. Constitution was adopted, abolishing slavery.

Advocates are crucial in campaigns around the world today. Jody Williams led the International Campaign to Ban Landmines. The campaign eventually coordinated the advocacy work of more than 1,300 non-governmental organizations in 85 countries demanding an end to the production and deployment of anti-personnel landmines. In 1997 an international treaty banning landmines was affirmed by 156 countries, not including the United States, Russia or China. As the treaty was signed, Williams said, "It wasn't until the voice of civil society was raised to such a high degree that governments began to listen, that change began to move the world with lightning and unexpected speed."

Human rights lawyers, yet another group of advocates, are leading voices for a basic standard of treatment for other human beings. One example is Jennifer Harbury, who began her work in a small legal aid clinic on the Texas-Mexico border. Talking with people, Harbury discovered that many Guatemalans living there, mostly indigenous Mayans, had fled the repression and death squads of the Guatemalan military government. She traveled to Guatemala to see the situation herself and eventually married a Mayan activist. Her husband was seized, tortured and murdered without trial. Harbury investigated the case and eventually exposed not only the Guatemalan injustices but also U.S. complicity as some members of the C.I.A. had participated in the torture and murder of her husband. Harbury has most recently exposed torture used by U.S. interrogators at the infamous Abu Ghraib prison in Iraq and the Guantanamo Bay facility in Cuba where al-Qaida and Taliban terror suspects are held. Harbury wrote: "We are reacting out of fear instead of thinking our way through the difficult process of conflict resolution. In the end, our use of violence and repression can only sow seeds of hatred and trauma, which in the end will produce only greater violence against us."

Advocates may coordinate large networks and coalitions when raising an issue, but sometimes one person can make a striking appeal. Cindy Sheehan had such an impact after her son Casey Sheehan was killed during the war in Iraq. She was stirred to action by her son's death, wanting to end the war so that other mothers would not know her grief. She organized the support and advocacy group called Gold Star Families for Peace, linking families whose relatives had been killed in military service and who wanted to put an end the war in Iraq. In August 2005, Sheehan set up camp outside the gate to President George W. Bush's

Texas ranch. She demanded to speak to the president about what she viewed as an unjust war, not the "noble cause" that Bush proclaimed. This grieving mother's personal advocacy helped re-energize a moribund peace movement in the United States.

Many journalists have also become advocates, exposing truth that leads to change. Sometimes journalists around the world risk their own livelihood—and even their own lives. The latter is especially true if journalists find their own employers are colluding with the very forces they are exposing. Sometimes their reports are presented in major news outlets, but often these feisty advocates have to create their own means of publishing the news. Dahr Jamail was not a journalist, but rather a mountain guide in Alaska when the U.S. invaded Iraq. He was deeply disturbed that the American news media cooperated with the U.S. military. So from 2003–2005 he traveled to Iraq in search of the true "collateral damage" that was not being reported. He revealed the burns that civilians suffered from white phosphorus, the shootings of men and women carrying white flags, and the corporate profiteering of American-based contractors. Jamail was rigorous in getting corroboration from many sources. No news agency hired him, so he published his stories via e-mail and his own website. Eventually the quality of his reporting caused his stories to be picked up by the Inter Press Service, *The Asia Times*, BBC and Democracy Now. Jamail says, "Since an informed citizenry is the basis for a healthy democracy, independent, non-corporate media are more critical today than ever before."

Jamail survived his reporting in Iraq, but advocates—especially independent journalists—understand that they face risks each day. This is not a recent development. The pioneering African-American journalist Ida B. Wells took on the issue of lynching in the late 19th and early 20th centuries. She was co-owner of the *Free Speech and Headlight* newspaper in Memphis, Tennessee, and waged her campaign from her editorial page. White businesses boycotted the paper, her office was attacked and destroyed, and her life was threatened. But Wells continued her advocacy campaign and, in 1909, became a co-founder of the National Association for the Advancement of Colored People (NAACP). Wells wrote, "I'd rather go down in history as one lone Negro who dared to tell the government that it had done a dastardly thing than to save my skin by taking back what I said."

During the Vietnam War Daniel Ellsberg had worked for the RAND Corporation and was a consultant with the U.S. State Department, Defense Department and the U.S. embassy in Saigon. As a first-hand witness of the "patterns of official deception" by the U.S. government concerning the war, he copied 7,000 pages of documents that were published as *The Pentagon Papers*. Ellsberg's revelations added to the pressure to get the U.S. out of the war, but for his efforts he was arrested and tried for revealing secret documents. His case was dismissed when burglars working for the Nixon White House broke into the office of Ellsberg's psychiatrist looking for evidence against him.

For every new law that creates a more just society, there was an advocate who started the political momentum. For every new institution that oversees justice or maintains peace, there was an advocate who pushed to institutionalize those values. For every hidden crime exposed in high places, there was an advocate who revealed the truth. Advocates bring substance to dreams of peace and justice by steering government toward those lofty ideals.

CHAPTER 19

Frederick Douglass
(1818-1895)

I would unite with anybody to do right and with nobody to do wrong.

—Frederick Douglass

I have chosen only two figures who lived prior to the 20th century to profile in full chapters of this book. Thomas Clarkson, who Douglass met in 1846, is profiled in the Organizers section. In this section on advocates, Douglass' passion for justice and his struggle to achieve it led him to a series of daring innovations in peacemaking. I include him here not out of a sense of nostalgia or obligation (there were many noteworthy peacemakers in earlier eras) but because Clarkson and Douglass were pioneers whose legacies still shape our work today. If Douglass were to somehow resurrect himself today, his restless mind and heart would continue to raise hard questions about injustice. His powerful image continues to march before us all.

FREDERICK DOUGLASS WAS A man who claimed his own freedom by a dramatic escape from slavery—then became a liberator of others by helping fellow slaves escape. He was a powerful voice for abolition. He also advocated for the rights of women. He liberated the U.S. Constitution from its own inner contradictions so that it truly could become an instrument of freedom.

He was born into slavery and named Frederick Augustus Washington Bailey. As a boy he was sold to a family in Baltimore, Maryland. His master's wife began teaching him to read, though her husband disapproved. Slave owners at that time realized that if slaves learned to read they would be better equipped to pursue freedom. Douglass was an avid reader, teaching himself through any newspaper or book he could find. Later he was sold to a farmer known for his cruelty to slaves. Douglass was whipped frequently until he finally fought back against his master and was never beaten again. When he was 20 years old, he obtained a uniform and identification papers from a free black seaman and began a train journey that took him to New York and freedom. He abandoned his slave name and took the last name of Douglass from the hero of a Sir Walter Scott novel.

Douglass settled in Massachusetts where he met the famed abolitionist William Lloyd Garrison. At 23 years of age he gave his first speech, detailing the horrors of slavery. Though he was nervous, his passion riveted those who heard him. He became a popular speaker, traveling across the country with the abolitionist message. He said: "Where justice is denied, where poverty is enforced, where ignorance prevails, and where any one class is made to feel that society is an organized conspiracy to oppress, rob and degrade them, neither persons nor property will be safe."

Douglass wrote his autobiography—later to be updated in two subsequent versions. *The Narrative of the Life of Frederick Douglass, an American Slave* became a best seller and was published in Europe as well. But this notoriety also was dangerous for he was still an escaped slave who could legally be returned to his owner. At the urging of his friends he went to Ireland and Great Britain for two years. English friends officially purchased his freedom.

While in Ireland, Douglass' advocacy regarding struggles for justice broadened. He met with Irish nationalists and spoke out for Irish Home Rule. Seeing the deplorable working conditions of the early industrial revolution, he advocated for fair treatment of workers. He also supported feminism, and after returning to the United States, participated in the historic 1848 Seneca Falls

Convention for women's rights. Douglass was a whirlwind in that era, launching an abolitionist newspaper called *The North Star*, which proclaimed a broad view of freedom on its masthead: "Right is of no Sex – Truth is of no Color – God is the Father of us all, and we are all brethren." While most Americans still thought of slavery as the only racial issue the country was facing, Douglass already was identifying other related injustices on the horizon. In New York, a free state, the schools were segregated. Black schools received far less money per student than white schools. Since he believed that education was the key to freedom, he advocated for court action to desegregate schools.

Abolition of slavery remained his major concern. He served as a "stationmaster" on the Underground Railroad personally helping hundreds of people escape from slavery in the South and make their way to freedom. As the struggle intensified, Douglass wrote: "Those who profess to favor freedom and yet depreciate agitation, are people who want crops without ploughing the ground; they want rain without thunder and lightning; they want the ocean without the roar of its many waters. The struggle may be a moral one, or it may be a physical one, or it may be both. But it must be a struggle. Power concedes nothing without a demand; it never has and it never will." He met with John Brown, the radical abolitionist who planned a violent raid at the federal armory at Harper's Ferry. Douglass believed Brown's plans for a slave revolt would not work and strongly disagreed with him. After Brown's raid failed, Douglass fled briefly to Canada fearing that he would be targeted through guilt by even a brief association with Brown.

Douglass split with William Lloyd Garrison over this issue of the U.S. Constitution: Garrison saw the Constitution as an inherently pro-slavery document and even called for the dissolution of the United States but Douglass did not want to abandon the slaves in the South and argued that the Constitution could be turned into an instrument for freedom. (Douglass lived to see amendments to the Constitution that eliminated slavery and gave blacks citizenship, equal protection under the law and the right to vote without discrimination because of race.)

But first was the great struggle! For Douglass, the Civil War was always about slavery. He advised President Lincoln to free the slaves. When Lincoln's *Emancipation Proclamation* was announced Douglass spoke about it: "We were waiting and listening as for a bolt from the sky...we were watching...by the dim light of the stars for the dawn of a new day...we were longing for the answer to the agonizing prayers of centuries." Douglass also urged Lincoln to allow blacks to join the Union Army so they could participate directly in the fight for their freedom. Two of his sons fought in the first black regiment to engage in battle.

After the war, Douglass continued as an advocate for justice for newly liberated African-Americans. He served as President of the Freedman's Savings Bank to help former slaves in the Reconstruction period. He supported President Ulysses Grant in passing a law against the rising violence of the racist terror group, the Ku Klux Klan. Following passage of the Klan Act, Grant sent federal troops to arrest more than 5,000 Klansman, a move that Douglass applauded but that was unpopular among whites. Among many of Douglass' appointments to government service, he was a diplomat to Haiti and the Dominican Republic. He consistently pressed for voting rights, not only for blacks but also for women. Douglass' last public appearance was at a meeting of the National Council for Women in 1895; he died of a heart attack that night.

Though many people, blacks and whites alike, played important roles in the struggle to abolish slavery in the United States, nobody had as broad, as long, and as strategically important an impact as Frederick Douglass. He mobilized public support, counseled presidents and provided a positive interpretation of the Constitution that allowed fundamental reform to take place within the structure of American law. His goals were so high that many were not realized in his lifetime, but his constant focus enabled political systems to eventually achieve these ideals.

CHAPTER 20

Jeannette Rankin

(1880-1973)

There can be no compromise with war. It cannot be reformed or controlled; cannot be disciplined into decency or codified into common sense, for war is the slaughter of human beings, temporarily regarded as enemies, on as large a scale as possible.

—Jeannette Rankin

*John F. Kennedy's **Profiles in Courage** praises U.S. senators throughout American history who stood against overwhelming popular sentiment to vote their conscience. That book and similar stories inspire me. Abraham Lincoln cast the sole vote of opposition against going to war with Mexico back in 1848 when Lincoln was in the U.S. House. Then I learned about another representative who had stood in that courageous line with Lincoln and the senators whom Kennedy profiled: Jeannette Rankin. Her votes against entering World War I and World War II were castigated by many as disloyal, but she was always clear about her convictions to her constituents and her colleagues in Congress. She was a mother for the peace movement and a founding member of the Women's International League for Peace and Freedom, which continues today. I've been honored to march for peace alongside many of Rankin's "daughters."*

ONLY ONE PERSON IN Congress voted against participation in both World War I and World War II. That person was Jeannette Rankin, daughter of a rancher from Montana. She was the first woman elected to the U.S. House of Representatives—in fact, the first woman elected to a national legislature in any Western democracy. She was a tireless advocate for peace.

Rankin worked briefly as a teacher and a social worker before jumping into politics and the women's suffrage movement. She was the first woman to speak before the Montana legislature, urging them to give women the right to vote. In 1912 she became the field secretary for the National American Woman Suffrage Association. Thousands of suffragettes marched in Washington, D.C. demanding the vote. She returned home to help organize the campaign to win the right to vote for women in the state of Montana, which happened in 1914.

Rankin was then elected to Congress in Montana in 1916 before women could vote nationally. A mere four days into her term she had to take a stand on the monumental question: Should the United States enter the Great War in Europe? She voted with a minority against going into World War I, declaring, "I want to stand with my country, but I cannot vote for war." She was vilified in the press, and women's suffragist groups cancelled her speaking engagements claiming she had hurt their movement by being "sentimental." Rankin defended herself, "The first time the first woman had a chance to say no against war—she should say it!" She maintained her anti-war convictions against the harsh criticism, though once the country was at war she voted for some of the measures that maintained U.S. involvement.

Rankin also took historic action when she opened the debate on what was known as the Susan B. Anthony Amendment. The legislation passed both houses of Congress, was ratified by the states, and became the 19th Amendment, giving women the right to vote. Her earlier anti-war vote would cost her re-election. Her district was cut out in a gerrymandering scheme. She ran for the Senate and lost overwhelmingly.

After her term in Congress ended Rankin became a lobbyist, especially for issues of child and maternal health. She also was the first Vice-President of the American Civil Liberties Union and a founder of the Women's International League for Peace and Freedom (WILPF). She became the field secretary for the WILPF working on various anti-war efforts.

In 1940 war had broken out in Europe once again. She decided to run for Congress, specifically on an isolationist platform, and the voters of Montana returned her to the U.S. House. This time she was one of six women in the House, but soon she would be standing alone again. After Japanese forces attacked Pearl Harbor, the vote for war came to Congress. Rankin was the only person to vote against the declaration of war. As she stood alone to cast her vote she said, "As a woman, I can't go to war and I refuse to send anyone else. It is not necessary. I vote NO." Later as Germany and Italy declared war against the United States, she merely voted "Present" on those declarations of war. Though she had been open about her anti-war stand when she ran and had acted consistently, she knew that war fever would prevent her re-election. She chose not to run for another term.

Though Rankin consistently voted against going to war, she was a supporter of the ordinary men and women who ended up in the military. She blamed politicians for wars, not the soldiers and sailors who fought them. She was a spokesperson for veteran's rights and introduced the GI Bill to Congress, which provided education and other benefits to veterans returning from World War II.

Rankin's peacemaking was far from over. She traveled to India seven times to study Gandhi's strategy of nonviolent conflict resolution—and later participated in anti-war activities especially during the Vietnam era. For the 1968 March on Washington, she organized more than 5,000 women as the "Jeannette Rankin Brigade" to demonstrate there against the war. In 1970, she was still marching in the streets for peace at the age of 90.

CHAPTER 21

Peter Benenson

(1921-2005)

The candle burns not for us, but for all those whom we failed to rescue from prison, who were shot on the way to prison, who were tortured, who were kidnapped, who 'disappeared.' That is what the candle is for.

—Peter Benenson

When Amnesty International was awarded the Nobel Peace Prize in 1977, I felt as though I had played a small part. I was one of the thousands around the world who wrote letters on behalf of prisoners of conscience, prompted by Amnesty International. At that time, I never knew about Peter Benenson, the founder of the group. He lit candles of hope for thousands of prisoners and victims of torture—but didn't spend time shining light on himself in the process. Now, it's time to write Benenson back into the pages of our history books.

HOW MANY TIMES HAVE you read a small news item about an injustice, felt a momentary pang, but then swiftly moved on with your life? One man, Peter Benenson, changed the world by not moving on from the small story he had just read. Instead, he turned his anger from the reported injustice into a creative new strategy that mobilized millions to save tens of thousands of lives.

Benenson was born Peter James Henry Solomon but later took his mother's maiden name to honor his grandfather. He attended privileged schools in Britain and trained as a barrister. In 1957, he joined with a group of British lawyers to form JUSTICE, a human rights and reform organization. He also tried his hand at politics, but failed to win an election to Parliament.

In 1961 as he rode the London Underground on his daily commute, he purchased a copy of *The Observer* newspaper. He saw a report about the arrest of two students in Portugal during the dictatorial regime of António de Oliveira Salazar. The students' crime was that they had raised their glasses to toast "freedom!" They were sentenced to seven years in prison. Benenson was shocked at the injustice and knew he must do something.

Benenson immediately headed to the Portuguese embassy to lodge a protest, but on the way he detoured to a church. He sat inside for a long time in thought. One voice wouldn't matter much to authorities. As he later put it, "I went in to see what could really be done effectively, to mobilize world opinion. It was necessary to think of a larger group which would harness the enthusiasm of people all over the world who were anxious to see a wider respect for human rights." As he sat in the church, Benenson conceived the idea that would become the central practice of an organization he would found, Amnesty International.

Benenson said, "The newspaper reader feels a sickening sense of impotence. Yet if these feelings of disgust could be united into common action, something effective could be done." To spur the common action he took out a full-page ad called "The Forgotten Prisoners" supported by a front-page article in *The Observer*. He called for others to join by sending letters to the Portuguese government about the students' case. Newspapers from other countries picked up the appeal. More than a thousand letters were written.

In order to build a network of letter writers and coordinate these campaigns, he founded Amnesty International (AI) with a group of other concerned human rights advocates. Benenson was appointed general secretary. Within a year, a dozen countries had

Amnesty International groups, committed to research and action on human rights abuses, especially to end torture, end extra-judicial executions, and to bring freedom for prisoners of conscience. Cases were researched and publicized by AI along with specific steps people could take to support prisoners of conscience.

The candle burning inside a coil of barbed wire became AI's symbol. "The candle burns not for us, but for all those whom we failed to rescue from prison, who were shot on the way to prison, who were tortured, who were kidnapped, who 'disappeared.' That is what the candle is for," Benenson said.

Benenson only led the group for a few years. In the mid 1960s, he stepped down from leadership, due to ill health, and by 1967 he resigned over conflict within the group's leadership. Later, the leaders reconciled and Benenson occasionally was involved in special AI projects, but he was a humble man who never sought personal credit. Over the years, many world leaders wrote to him—and he always wrote back turning the subject to human rights issues they should address. He was especially outspoken in telling British officials that if they wanted to honor his work, they should address abuses in the UK.

From that day when Benenson was seized by the story of two prisoners of conscience—and thought of a way to respond—the organization he founded has grown to one of the largest civil society movements in history. There are nearly 3 million members of Amnesty International with chapters formed in more than 60 countries. Some 45,000 cases that Amnesty has pursued have been successfully resolved, drawing a flood of thankful letters from former prisoners of conscience and victims of torture. This work has helped create an international climate in which torture has now been officially banned, though it is still practiced by many countries in one form or another. The International Criminal Court has been established to bring some of the worst systematic offenders to justice. At AI's 40th anniversary, Benenson said, "Only then, when the last prisoner of conscience has been freed, when the last torture chamber has been closed, when the United Nations'

Universal Declaration of Human Rights is a reality for the world's people, will our work be done."

CHAPTER 22

Alison Des Forges

(1942-2009)

Governments hesitate to call the horror by its name, for to do so would oblige them to act.

—Alison Des Forges

The Rwandan genocide was personal for me. I had a Rwandan friend who was involved in peacemaking efforts—and was caught up in the violence. He was missing for a month before we heard from him in a camp in another country. We had been praying daily for him and his family. Alison Des Forges made the numbing scale of those slaughtered personal. Voices like hers are needed if we are ever to fulfill that oft-empty promise: Never again!

A PLANE CRASH TRIGGERED her greatest work. Another plane crash stilled her voice that had advocated tirelessly for the victims of genocide. Alison Des Forges was one of the first raised and most persistent voices protesting Rwandan genocide, a voice that leaders around the world deliberately chose to ignore until it was too late. Then she became the voice describing in great detail what had happened so the world would never forget.

Born Alison Liebhafsy, she earned both her master's and doctoral degrees in history studying the Central African country of Rwanda and the impact of colonization. She volunteered with Human Rights Watch, but soon she was working with the organization full-time focusing on Rwanda. She became the senior advisor on Africa with a focus on the Great Lakes region, which encompassed Burundi, Rwanda and Zaire, later renamed the Democratic Republic of Congo. She developed a deep understanding of the history and politics of the conflicts in the region, an understanding that was different and more complex than the simplistic view popular in U.S. government circles— that these conflicts were all ancient tribal enmities.

When Tutsi soldiers in Burundi assassinated the Hutu president, massive killings erupted in that country. Tens of thousands of Tutsi were killed, and extremist Hutus in Rwanda were watching. As they later said during the genocide, "Look what happened with Burundi. Nobody gave a damn, so we can do the same thing here, and no one will give a damn." A 1993 peace accord between the Hutu-dominated government and Tutsi rebels was rejected by extremists on both sides, and Des Forges feared something terrible was going to happen.

She was back in the U.S. when the plane carrying the presidents of Rwanda and Burundi was shot down on April 6, 1994. Her Rwandan friend and human rights monitor Monique Mujawamariya immediately called. "This is it. We're finished, " she said. Mujawamariya described over the telephone what she could see and hear as militiamen went door-to-door pulling people out of their homes and hacking them to death. When they came to her door she told Des Forges, "Please take care of my children. I don't want you to hear this." The phone went dead. A few days later Des Forges heard back from her friend who managed to flee and find shelter at the Hôtel des Mille Collines depicted in the movie *Hotel Rwanda*.

As Des Forges kept gathering reports, she realized that the slaughter was systematic, targeting all Tutsis as well as Hutus who supported Tutsis in some way. The killing fit the legal definition of genocide in the United Nations' Genocide Convention that defines it as an attempt to eliminate, in whole or in part, the people of a given group. Ten days into the killings it was clear that it was more than just a spontaneous outburst of violence; the massacres were planned, coordinated and politically motivated. Radio broadcasts from the independent Radio RTLM, mapped out the killings down to local details of specific roadblocks and particular people to murder. Des Forges went to the United Nations and lobbied members of the Security Council, but nobody would talk about genocide. Calling what was happening "genocide" would mean the U.N. would be compelled to act at a time when foreigners were leaving the country and the U.N. peacekeepers were even being scaled back.

Des Forges took her appeals to the U.S. State Department, where African desk officials agreed with her, but those higher up refused to listen. She worked her way up to Tony Lake, President Clinton's National Security Advisor, where it was clear that policies were being shaped. Lake would not support calling the slaughter "genocide" and condemn it as such, which would have changed the entire complexion of how the crisis was being interpreted. Des Forges pleaded for safe zones to be created to which refugees could flee, for Radio RTLM to be jammed, and for governments like the U.S., France and Belgium to condemn the slaughter and say no aid would be given to the government carrying out such actions, but her appeal fell on deaf ears.

When the Tutsi rebel forces seized control of Kigali (the capital city of Rwanda) and the rest of the republic, the genocide stopped. But killing continued. The Tutsi forces had killed more than 20,000 civilians. The Hutu extremists fled to Zaire pursued by the now Tutsi-dominated Rwandan army, sparking the war in Zaire/Congo that became the worst conflagration since World War II. Amid all the horror, Des Forges held consistent standards for human rights. She differentiated between "war crimes," which all sides committed, and "genocide," which one side committed. But her unwillingness to gloss over Tutsi crimes eventually got her banned from Rwanda.

Following the genocide and the minimal response from the international community, Des Forges undertook a massive four-year study of what had happened. She and her team of researchers interviewed survivors and killers. In 1999, she published the 800-page report that was titled, from a killer's cry, *Leave None to Tell the Story*. Des Forges knew that telling the stories of the victims was important for truth and justice to have any hope in the region. Des Forges meticulously documented her report and was careful not to embellish the facts. She estimated that about half a million people died in the genocide, less than some reports of up to a million. For her, the credibility of human rights advocacy lay in the accuracy of what was reported.

As the story of the Rwandan genocide moved to trials, Des Forges became a frequent witness against the perpetrators. She testified at the International Criminal Tribunal for Rwanda in Tanzania. She also testified at trials held in Belgium, Switzerland, the Netherlands and Canada. She served on various panels investigating the alleged genocide for the United Nations, the African Union and various national legislatures.

Alison Des Forges' voice as the storyteller of the genocide in Rwanda will stand as a challenge to the international community for years to come. She died with 50 other passengers and crew when her plane crashed near Buffalo in February 2009.

CHAPTER 23

Shirin Ebadi

(b. 1947)

How can you defy fear? Fear is a human instinct, just like hunger. Whether you like it or not, you become hungry. Similarly with fear. But I have learned to train myself to live with this fear.

—Shirin Ebadi

As I complete this book in early 2011, my country's conflict with Iran is a global flash point. If more Americans knew our history in Iran we might be more humble and sympathetic about Iranian suspicions and hostility. We won't be able to threaten or browbeat Iran into positive change. The transformation will come from courageous Iranians with their own vision. Ebadi may be a forerunner of that change.

DURING THE 2003 CEREMONY at which she was to receive the Nobel Peace Prize in Oslo, Norway, Shirin Ebadi did a simple thing which evoked criticism from many sides. She chose not to wear the *hijab*, the traditional head covering for Muslim women. Since the 1979 revolution in Iran, women have been required to wear the *hijab*. As a tireless advocate for women's rights, Ebadi chose her form of dress to highlight freedom of choice: "I want Iranian women to make their own choice whether they want to use the *hijab*." The *mullahs* (who are usually Islamic *clerics)* in Iran were not the only ones upset. Non-religious Iranian women were also dismayed and planned to protest because Ebadi was seeking equality using the Quran as the moral and legal basis. Her action was not a rejection of her Islamic faith, rather an expression of trying to live out the demand for justice and respect for human rights she finds deep within it.

Shirin Ebadi was born into a family of legal professionals. Her father was a professor of commercial law and the chief notary public in Hamadan. She studied law at the University of Tehran, and in 1969 she became a judge. In 1975 she was the first woman in Iran to preside over a legislative court.

Then in 1979, the Iranian revolution changed everything. The ruling clerics insisted that Islam prohibited women from being judges, so Ebadi and the other women judges were demoted. Ebadi became a clerical worker in the judicial office over which she once presided. Unable to overturn the policy against women judges, she was even restricted from practicing law, and so she retired. From her home she began to write extensively on legal and political matters, which moved her into a brighter spotlight within Iranian society.

The election of reformist Mohammad Khatami as president led to a change in legal opportunities for women. In 1992 Ebadi's law license was reinstated and she returned to her legal practice, specializing in cases of minorities and dissidents. She represented the family of one such intellectual who had been murdered along with his wife. Eventually the murders were traced to a team from the Iranian Ministry of Intelligence. The controversy climaxed when the head of the Ministry of Intelligence allegedly committed suicide before the case came to trial. Ebadi also provided legal representation in the high-profile case of a young man who was killed in the 1999 student protests. In a startling development, a videotape circulated that appeared to link the killing to high-level conservative officials. Ebadi was accused of circulating the tape; she was arrested and sentenced to five years in prison. A higher court eventually overturned her conviction, and Ebadi was released.

Ebadi established the Defenders of Human Rights Center in 2001 with four other human rights lawyers. Through the center, Ebadi has continued her defense of those in need. She has defended the rights of refugees—particularly Afghans fleeing to Iran. She has also advocated for the right to circulate media journals banned by the government and of people who have been sentenced for merely expressing their views.

Ebadi has made a special cause of dealing with issues of child abuse and domestic violence. She challenged the child custody laws in divorce cases that separate children from their mothers, giving priority to the fathers. She established the Society for Protecting the Rights of the Child in Iran, and served as the group's president. Then, she helped draft a law against the physical abuse of children, which passed the Majilis, the Iranian national assembly in 2002. The next year, she was awarded the Nobel Prize for Peace, especially for defending the rights of women and children.

For Ebadi, her work on human rights is consistent with her Muslim faith. She wrote: "In the last 23 years, from the day I was stripped of my judgeship to the years of doing battle in the revolutionary courts of Tehran, I had repeated one refrain: an interpretation of Islam that is in harmony with equality and democracy is an authentic expression of faith. It is not religion that binds women, but the selective dictates of those who wish them cloistered. That belief, along with the conviction that change in Iran must come peacefully and from within, has underpinned my work." Ebadi earlier opposed the Shah and, in recent years, has supported critics of the Islamic revolutionary regime, but she does not support those who call for outside intervention against Iran. "The fight for human rights is conducted in Iran by the Iranian people," she says, "and we are against any foreign intervention in Iran."

In May 2008 the Iranian government continued the harassment of believers of the Bahá'í faith. This disrespect has been on going since the establishment of the revolutionary government. Ebadi claimed that Iran's respect of human rights was regressing, and she cited her own harassment, including death threats when she agreed to represent imprisoned Bahá'ís. The government attacked her in the state-controlled media, accused her of links to the Bahá'ís, connection to the West, support of homosexuals, not wearing the hijab, and protecting CIA agents. The office of the Center for the Defense of Human Rights was raided by police and shut down. Ebadi's computers and files were seized. Demonstrators connected with the government attacked her office and her home.

Ebadi understands that there is strength in personal connection, both globally and in local communities. In 2006, Ebadi joined with five other women who had received the Nobel Peace Prize to launch the Nobel Women's Initiative. Betty Williams, Mairead Corrigan Maguire, Wangari Maathai, Jody Williams, Rigoberta Menchu and Ebadi decided to pool their resources and experiences to encourage women's rights around the world. Ebadi also encourages all Iranian women to link together through an elaborate campaign to collect one million signatures to protest their lack of legal rights. In launching the drive, 400 women were trained as grassroots educators and organizers. They spread through the country, talking to women and raising awareness of this issue. The government has tried to repress the effort, shutting down the petition website and arresting three journalists who wrote in support of it. Ebadi says, "By getting one million signatures, the world will know we object to these conditions."

Whether encouraging one woman at a time to sign her name for change, or joining with Nobel laureates to speak for peace and justice around the world, Shirin Ebadi refuses to be trapped by anyone's definition of what she should be and say. She speaks for freedom for all, and practices that freedom in the face of relentless persecution.

CHAPTER 24

Leymah Gbowee

We will keep walking until peace, justice, and the rights of women is not a dream, but is a thing of the present.

—Leymah Gbowee

When I went to Liberia in 2004, I saw signs posted all over proclaiming slogans of peace and the name of the Women in Peacebuilding Network (WIPNET). These signs sprouted amid the rubble that marked the path of fighting during the civil war. I asked my host what this was all about, and he told me about vigils at a fish market. Later, when the documentary **Pray the Devil Back to Hell** *came out, I learned the depth of the women's actions. You've got to see that movie—two thumbs up, five stars!*

NO PEACE TALKS HAD ever been so disrupted. Two hundred women formed a blockade with their bodies, locking the negotiators inside the hotel conference room. Peace talks were being held in Accra, Ghana, to seek a settlement to the Liberian civil war. Talks had dragged on for weeks with the various warlords showing no seriousness about ending the conflict that had cost more than 200,000 lives. Then the women acted, women who had been demonstrating daily for peace in Liberia and finally had traveled to Accra. They surrounded the place where the negotiators were gathered and refused to let them out until they came up with a peace agreement. Soon the negotiators were negotiating with them, and the women set the terms for how the peace process would be handled. The women's action changed the nature of the talks and precipitated an end to a conflict that had gone on since 1989. At their head was Leymah Gbowee.

When Leymah Gbowee was a teenager, the civil war in Liberia erupted. Charles Taylor started the war in 1989, and soon other warlords entered the fray. President Samuel Doe was killed, but the fighting continued. Taylor had his "small boys unit," children ages 9 to 15 who were often drugged as they fought. They were notorious for their brutalities, including hacking off the limbs of civilians. As part of a peace plan, elections were held in 1997 and Charles Taylor was elected President, more out of fear that he would continue the war than out of respect or support. Fighting exploded again in 1999 with a rebel movement known as LURD, Liberians United for Reconciliation and Democracy. In spite of the noble-sounding name, LURD forces were as brutal as Taylor's. The rebels seized whatever they wanted. They stole, killed and raped at will. As the fighting spread, one out of three Liberians was displaced by the war.

Gbowee knew the horrors of war. She had to flee an attack on her village when she was five months pregnant, bringing her 3-year old son and 2-year old daughter with her. They had no food. She experienced the anguish of a mother with nothing to give her hungry children. Eventually, Gbowee became a social worker with an emphasis on trauma counseling. She worked with soldiers who as children had fought in Charles Taylor's army. She saw the damage done from violence to their young lives.

As the war continued to grind down the country, Gbowee shared a dream at her home church in Monrovia. She dreamed of the women from all churches gathering together to pray for peace. From that dream the Christian Women's Peace Initiative was born. A Muslim woman, Asatu Bah Kenneth, inspired by Gbowee's dream, pledged to organize the Muslim women. At first there was some difficulty bringing the Christian and Muslim women together, but the leaders said, "Can the bullet pick and choose?

Does the bullet know a Christian from a Muslim?" The coming together of these women from the two main Liberian religions formed WIPNET, the Women In Peace-building Network.

WIPNET leaders organized women across Liberia. They went into the sprawling displaced-persons camps on the outskirts of Monrovia. They had heard stories of horrific abuses, yet the WIPNET leaders were struck by the hopefulness of these women who had lost everything. Since Taylor attended church, and the leaders of LURD their mosques, the women began challenging their respective pastors and imams to pressure the two sides to stop the war.

By April 2003 the war was getting worse, so Gbowee decided to do something more dramatic. WIPNET broadcast a call on the radio for women to come out to protest. They drew their image from the Bible story of Esther protesting to protect her people. The women wore plain white clothes as a sign of peace, and set aside their usual hair adornments popular with Liberian women. They gathered at the Fish Market, a strategic place alongside the road where Taylor would have to pass every day to go to his presidential office. With T-shirts, signs and songs they made their message clear: "The women of Liberia want peace now!" Every day Taylor's convoy would pass, but he never stopped to talk with the women. Instead he harshly criticized them to the press: "Nobody can embarrass my administration!" Soon there were as many as 2,500 women holding vigil at the Fish Market, waiting in the sun with hand-made placards: "We want peace, no more war."

The women employed many methods to get their message across. They developed a white T-shirt uniform. They launched a sex strike, refusing to have sex with their husbands until the men mobilized for peace. They put up billboards: "The women of Liberia say peace is our goal. Peace is what matters. Peace is what we need." WIPNET groups were organized in 9 of Liberia's 15 counties, taking the message of peace far and wide.

LURD's forces seized control of most of the rural areas and began moving toward Monrovia. They attacked the displaced-persons' camp, and the civilians were trapped between the violence of both sides. Meanwhile Taylor and the rebels refused all appeals to negotiate. So the women wrote a formal statement demanding peace talks. They marched to Parliament in Monrovia. All along the route, women streamed out to swell the numbers. Finally Taylor agreed to receive the women. As hundreds of white-clad women sat in the sun, Gbowee presented their statement. Boldly she faced the President who had killed so many and said, "We are tired of war. We are tired of running. We are tired of begging for bulgur wheat. We are tired of our children being raped. We are now taking this stand to secure the future of our children." Taylor finally agreed to peace talks.

Next WIPNET leaders went to Freetown in Sierra Leone to present their appeal to the rebel leaders. The women challenged the rebels that their mothers were coming to tell them to go to the peace talks and that the rebels were as involved in human rights abuses as Taylor had been. LURD agreed to participate, mainly seeing the peace process as another way to oust Taylor.

The talks were held in Accra, Ghana, hosted by the Economic Community of West African States (ECOWAS), which had earlier sponsored peacekeeping operations in Liberia and Sierra Leone. Meanwhile WIPNET had been raising money to get as many women as possible to go to Ghana to support and monitor the peace talks. They mobilized Liberian refugee women in the camps in Ghana. On June 4, 2003 the talks began, and the women were in place along the travel route to the hotel. They kept vigil with their signs and songs just as they had in Monrovia.

Early in the talks, stunning news was announced: Charles Taylor had been indicted for crimes against humanity related to the war in Sierra Leone. Taylor quickly returned to Liberia to avoid arrest, leaving his delegation in Accra to continue talks. Almost immediately full-scale war hit Monrovia. Once again, civilians were caught in the fighting and endured incredible suffering. The women in Accra worried and wept as they followed the grim news reports.

Gbowee and the other WIPNET leaders kept going back and forth between the delegations to urge them toward peace, but they grew increasingly frustrated. The war was claiming countless victims back home, but the leaders of LURD were enjoying themselves living in luxury at the hotel rather than the bush. The rebels poured out insults on the women as they passed them. After six weeks, there had been no movement in the talks. Gen. Abdulsalami Abubakar, chief mediator and former President of Nigeria, acknowledged they were getting nowhere.

On July 21, the US embassy was hit by rockets, which fell among the displaced people camping inside the compound. This atrocity fueled fresh anger in Leymah Gbowee, who proclaimed: "Today is showdown." She had the women sit at the door of the conference hall with their arms looped together. They blocked anyone from coming in or going out. Gbowee said, "We're going to keep them in that room without water, without food, so they at least feel what the ordinary people in Liberia are feeling at this particular point in time." On the loudspeaker someone announced: "Oh, my God, the peace hall has been seized by General Leymah and her troops!" Security guards confronted Gbowee saying she was "obstructing justice" and tried to arrest her. That charge was the final insult to Gbowee. She stood and began to strip off her clothes. In West Africa it is a curse to see the naked body of one's mother. Her action prompted a quick and desperate response.

Gen. Abubakar came out to meet with Gbowee in front of the women and media. Gbowee spoke of their frustration with the warlords and the insults they endured. Abubakar listened and joined in challenging the warlords, saying they weren't real men for killing their own people. "Because you are not real men," he said, "That's why the women are treating you like boys." Abubakar negotiated with the women: An agreement would be reached within two weeks; otherwise thousands of women would converge. Also, the warlords would have to attend sessions regularly, pass the women each day and speak no insults. Gbowee said, "This peace talk has to be a real peace talk, not a circus."

The women's blockade dramatically changed the mood at the talks. Within two weeks an agreement was reached. Charles Taylor was exiled to Nigeria where he was later arrested to be tried in The Hague for his war crimes. U.N. peacekeeping forces were deployed, and a transitional government was established.

Gbowee and the WIPNET women kept close watch on the implementation of the peace agreement. They continued their vigils in the streets. They worked in the communities on reconciliation, disarmament and forgiveness. They knew firsthand about the terrible things perpetrators had done, but understood that many of the "child soldiers" were victims as well. WIPNET challenged the U.N. peacekeeping operation when the disarmament process turned into chaos. Gbowee and other women went to the streets and got directly involved in calming the situation. They talked directly to the soldiers on the streets, getting them to surrender their weapons.

The women of WIPNET mobilized to teach about democracy and participation in the upcoming election. They did not support any of the warlords. Instead, in January of 2006, Liberia elected Ellen Johnson Sirleaf as president, the first female president of an African nation. Johnson Sirleaf praised the women of WIPNET in her inauguration speech, acknowledging "the powerful voice of women…. It is the women who labored and advocated for peace in our region." Gbowee said about their achievement, "We stood out and did the unimaginable."

After almost three years of transforming action, WIPNET dissolved. Gbowee continued her peace work, first becoming the Liberia Coordinator for the West Africa Network for Peacebuilding. She served on the Liberia Truth and Reconciliation Commission. In 2006 she co-founded and then directed the Women Peace and Security Network Africa, based in Ghana. WIPSEN Africa, as it is known, promotes women's strategic participation and leadership in peace, security and governance throughout Africa, with a particular focus on Liberia, the Ivory Coast, Sierra Leone and Nigeria.

The actions of Gbowee and the Liberian women were publicized through the award-winning documentary *Pray the Devil Back to Hell*. Gbowee continues to pray that the forces of evil are halted and supports the flowering of peace in places long plagued by war.

PART 5

Trainers and Teachers

Opening New Toolboxes

MILITARY FORCES OFTEN ENGAGE in war games. Peacemakers need similar training. They need to learn how to quickly and accurately assess a conflict, choose the best tactics and work effectively with other people to wage a nonviolent struggle. Opening up peacemakers' toolboxes is the work of teachers and trainers.

A huge challenge these educators face around the world is the wide variety of educational models they encounter. Hierarchical societies have developed top-down educational practices to support that distribution of power. In these systems, teachers have all the knowledge—or at least the currently acceptable version of knowledge; students are empty vessels; questions are discouraged; correct answers are praised. This form of education is the norm in many countries around the world, especially in places where oppression is widespread.

Over the past century, however, new forms of education are blossoming. Some of the brightest peacemakers have developed new pedagogical philosophies and teaching methods. These new systems of education rest on the belief that justice requires that education spread throughout the grassroots level and that students develop their own fresh insights—questions are highly valued and the answers are not necessarily pre-determined; teachers become learners themselves; students become teachers. This kind of education stimulates creativity and the birth of new ideas. These teachers don't fill empty vessels—they encourage students to develop and adapt their own sets of tools for peaceful change.

Nikolaj Grundtvig in Denmark developed a philosophy of popular education that took shape in the folk school movement. He saw a gap in educational institutions in the mid-1800s, mainly the huge number of young men and women who were not learning about their own history, culture and values. Grundtvig believed that schools should impart dignity to people and instill a life-long love of learning. He believed people should take pride in their culture. So he developed "Schools for Life," based on his belief that people have the capacity to learn together and to create just and peaceful societies. He also believed music was important for transformational learning, so he stressed group singing. Folk schools spread across Scandinavia, and later their influence shaped the philosophy and practice of popular education in other parts of the world.

In the early 1900s, the civil rights educator Septima Clark shaped her educational methods on Johns Island off the South Carolina coast. She got rid of the rote reading books filled with irrelevant sentences and pictures of white children. Instead, she taught illiterate adults how to read by starting with their life experiences. Clark became an activist with the NAACP and eventually found her way to the Highlander School in Tennessee where she was hired as director of workshops. There, she developed a program that became known as "citizenship schools" to teach illiterate blacks throughout the South how to read and write and educate them about their civic rights so that they could register to vote.

Literacy was necessary as part of voter registration because the segregationist Southern counties often used difficult literacy tests as a bar to the ballot box. Clark taught the teachers and trainers who, in the late 1950s and into the 1960s, spread throughout the South educating and equipping new voters. One practical result was that many African-American men and women soon owned small copies of the U.S. Constitution that they kept in wallets, purses and on bedside tables in their homes. By the time Clark retired in 1972 more than 10,000 citizenship schoolteachers had been trained and a huge number of African-Americans had been taught to read, write and join the struggle for their full rights as U.S. citizens. The voter registration drives in Mississippi and Alabama that broke the oppressive yoke of segregation could never have succeeded without this extensive educational campaign.

At the core of the liberation movements in Latin America in the last half of the 20th Century was a decentralized philosophy of education. The Catholic Church was a dominant institution across that region. Liberation movements turned the Catholic hierarchy on its head for millions of poor people. Education was refocused into thousands of "base communities"—small groups that met in many different settings and raised practical questions about the struggles of daily life. This kind of religious education became potent political fuel as people examined structures of land ownership, control of political decisions, access to resources and the prevalence of poverty.

Education that forms effective new peacemakers cannot be controlled. A typical strategy begins with teachers and students talking about their lives and the challenges they face daily. Sometimes, common experiences are recreated through simulations and role-playing. New questions are raised, and as learners explore a particular situation, they are nurtured to develop fresh insights about a larger society. How does this lesson connect with larger challenges? Education becomes a way of living; life itself becomes the laboratory for learning.

Peacemaking trainers and teachers have carried their insights into workplaces, houses of worship, community halls and any place a small group can gather. Today, they are reshaping entire educational institutions. As new generations transform the world, peace activists are opening new toolboxes thanks to these pioneering educators.

Myles Horton

(1905-1990)

**If people have a position on
something and you try to argue
them into changing it, you're
going to strengthen that
position. If you want to change
people's ideas, you shouldn't try
to convince them intellectually.
What you need to do is get
them into a situation where
they'll have to act on ideas, not argue about them.**

—Myles Horton

*Millions know "We Shall Overcome" by heart, but dig back
into the history of this song—past Pete Seeger and the
civil rights movement on your way to the song's roots in
gospel music and spirituals. On that journey, you'll pass
through the Highlander Folk School, where Myles Horton's
wife, Zilphia Horton, was the music director and found
that song had a particular power to help union activists
keep their spirits high. Zilphia used the song regularly
and taught it to Pete, who added a couple of verses and
carried it far and wide. That's how the peacemaking
family tree grows—many branches spread across the
landscape. In my own peacemaking work over the years,
I came to respect Highlander because of the talented
people who were trained there. However, most of the
Highlander branches were invisible to me. I wasn't aware
of Myles Horton until I began to fully study our collective*

family tree. In part, I am repaying debts to these often-overlooked pioneers by naming them in these chapters.

JAMES BEVEL REFERRED TO this white educator as "the Father of the Civil Rights Movement." Myles Horton was the co-founder and director of the Highlander Folk School in Tennessee, the training center for most of the great names in American civil rights history. The school also was vilified as a "communist training center."

Horton was born in 1905 into a poor, white Appalachian family. As a young man he traveled to Denmark to study the folk school movement and its impact upon the people and culture of Scandinavia because he was impressed with their philosophy—that they upheld the dignity of people and empowered them to bring about social transformation. He embraced the view that when gathered, educated and mobilized, oppressed people can build strategies for their own liberation.

In 1932 Horton and Don West founded the Highlander Folk School on a farm in Grundy County, Tennessee, donated by Lillian Johnson, a friend and a suffragette. The initial focus was on both rural and industrial labor issues in Appalachia. Horton saw the center as a training ground and meeting place for coal miners, textile workers, farmers and others to build a progressive labor movement. He trained people for leadership in unions, teaching them how to organize and engage in strikes. Workshops would be held from two days to eight weeks in length, usually with 15-40 participants.

Within its first two years, the Highlander School had its first black speaker at a workshop. However, out of fear of reprisal from the local community, the workshops were not fully integrated until 1942, though field projects held outside of Highlander were. The commitment of Horton and his staff to integration brought them into conflict with some Southern unions, but Horton believed that the labor movement could not succeed until it also confronted the evils of segregation and racism.

In that era, Highlander was such a magnet for restless young activists that a feisty, classically trained musician from Arkansas, Zilphia Mae Johnson, showed up for a training course in the mid 1930s and soon wound up marrying Myles Horton. Their marriage brought together powerful new elements in Highlander's training. The Hortons combined Zilphia's musical talents with the insights of the Danish folk school movement about group singing. That change at Highlander wound up changing the world. Though she was the music director, Zilphia didn't compose "We Shall Overcome"—but she and her husband saw the power of moving existing songs to help champion the struggle for justice, where they took on explosive new meanings. Highlander also played a role in moving "This Little Light of Mine" and "We Shall Not Be Moved" into the repertoire of peacemaking.

By 1953 the Highlander leaders felt a shift in focus was necessary—from the labor movement to the emerging civil rights movement. The school's long history of working toward integration gave it credibility. Workshops were held on desegregating public schools in 1953, one year before the landmark Brown v. Board of Education decision by the U.S. Supreme Court that mandated school desegregation. Black activists, including Rosa Parks and Martin Luther King, Jr., streamed to the school and participated in workshops that helped shape their strategies for the Montgomery bus boycott shortly thereafter. Horton also launched Citizenship Schools in various southern states as part of a voter education campaign, especially addressing illiteracy, which was often used to block black voters from access to the polls.

Rosa Parks spoke about Horton's disarming and healing sense of humor, especially in the face of the hardcore racism of Southern segregationists. She told about reporters asking Horton about how he got blacks and whites to eat together at Highlander. Horton responded, "First the food is prepared. Second, it's put on the table. Third, we ring the bell." Parks said about that encounter: "I found myself laughing when I hadn't been able to laugh in a long time."

The success of the Highlander Folk School provoked a back-lash. A sustained campaign by opponents tried to smear it as a "communist training school." A famous photo of Martin Luther King, Jr. at a Highlander workshop was published as evidence of his "communist" connections. There was an investigation by the Tennessee legislature, a police raid and two trials. Then, in 1961, the State of Tennessee revoked the Highlander charter and confiscated its land and buildings despite protests from high-profile figures like Eleanor Roosevelt, theologian Reinhold Niebuhr and U.N. Under-Secretary Ralph Bunche. The school survived by re-incorporating as the Highlander Research and Education Center and moving to Knoxville, Tennessee, where it remained until 1971.

In 1971, the school moved back to a rural setting outside New Market, Tennessee, and returned to emphasizing Appalachian issues again, such as: strip mining, environmental degradation, control and abuses by large outside corporations, and poverty. Two years later, Horton retired as the Highlander director. The school continues to provide training for activists in grass-roots movements for justice and social change. Its impact has expanded beyond Appalachia, even to India and Nicaragua, training new generations of leaders to empower and transform their communities.

CHAPTER 26

James Lawson

(b. 1928)

When you are a child of God, you try thereby to imitate Jesus in the midst of evil. Which means, if someone slaps you on the cheek, you turn the other cheek, which is an act of resistance. It means that you not only love your neighbor, but you recognize that even the enemy has a spark of God in them, has been made in the image of God and therefore needs to be treated as you, yourself, want to be treated.

—James Lawson

*As I watched **A Force More Powerful**, a 2000 documentary series on nonviolent struggle, I experienced a revelation. One of the episodes showed Nashville lunch counter sit-ins during the civil rights movement. I watched scenes of James Lawson's workshops preparing activists, including his lessons from Jesus' Sermon on the Mount and his use of role-plays. I realized that my own training methods were not new but that I was standing in a large group of mentors, including James Lawson. He's a hero I revere as a role model in my own work.*

SITTING BRAVELY TOGETHER, BLACK and white students withstood vicious name-calling, milk being poured over their heads, cigarette ash being flicked into their hair. They were pushed and shoved. But this was not taking place at a segregated lunch counter. It unfolded in a church, part of a role-play to prepare them for what they would face as they tried to desegregate the lunch counters in Nashville, Tennessee. It was part of the training program designed by James Lawson.

Civil rights leader John Lewis called James Lawson "the architect" of the civil rights movement. Lawson stood out as a trainer of many of the nonviolent activists who sat, marched and rode into the teeth of the racist violence that ruled the South in the 1950s and 1960s. He taught them the philosophy of nonviolence, overcoming their skepticism about the relative strength of non-violent action compared to the use of violence. Lawson built up their courage until they stood strong in the face of beatings, dog attacks and fire hoses. He taught them how to think strategically about campaigns that eventually would bring unjust structures tumbling down.

Lawson grew up in the home of a Methodist minister in Ohio. He learned about practical nonviolence from the teachings of Jesus passed on by his mother. He was so grounded by his love of God and the love of his family that he was able to stand up— even as a child— to the threats and assaults of bullies and racists. In college Lawson discovered the work and teaching of Gandhi, which shaped his pacifist convictions. Just before the Korean War broke out, Lawson returned his draft registration card because of his conscientious objection to war. His refusal to participate in the draft system cost him a year in prison. Following his release, Lawson volunteered for three years of missionary service in India. While there, he furthered his studies of Gandhi's philosophy, and deepened his understanding of the power and moral character of nonviolence, which he'd learned from his mother and the teachings of Jesus.

When Lawson returned to the U.S., he joined the Fellowship of Reconciliation (FOR), a leading U.S. pacifist group that had long been engaged in resistance to racial segregation. The FOR assigned Lawson to serve as Southern Secretary, working as a troubleshooter in places such as Little Rock, Greensboro and Birmingham. His main focus during this time, though, was in Nashville. The Rev. Kelly Miller Smith was the leading voice of civil rights in Nashville and head of the Nashville Christian Leadership Council (NCLC). The NCLC had been inspired by the Montgomery bus boycott and the work of Dr. Martin Luther King, Jr. The NCLC decided to sponsor a series of weekly workshops about how to break down the system of segregation.

Smith and Lawson got to work recruiting students for the workshops held at the Clark Memorial United Methodist Church adjacent to the Fisk University campus. Their small group quickly grew. Many of these students went on to become the long-term leaders of the civil rights movement: Diane Nash, James Bevel, John Lewis and Bernard Lafayette. Lawson designed the workshops using the Gandhian approach of investigating a situation and then looking for the best place to begin undoing the injustice. He trained the students on the nonviolent teachings of Jesus in the Sermon on the Mount, on the example of Jesus' suffering, on the teachings of Gandhi, and on the principles of nonviolence. Instead of turning on the emotive passion of typical black preachers, Lawson would grow cool and calm in his intensity. He challenged the students not to act out of anger, but out of a deep commitment and conscience.

As they analyzed the situation in Nashville, Lawson and the young activists realized that the system of segregation was based on humiliation and dehumanization. One place they encountered this was in the downtown shopping district. Lawson asked African-American women from Nashville to talk to the students about their experiences of shopping in stores where they were not allowed to eat and where signs reminded of them of their lower status. The focal point for the undoing of segregation in Nashville became the downtown lunch counters.

Next, Lawson turned to the workshops needed to launch such an action. First, he disempowered the racist epithet "nigger," so that participants began to see it as a word that did not define them. Rather, it defined people who would use such a word. The students learned to immunize themselves to racist epithets that otherwise might cause them to lose their self-control. They role-played scenarios that they might encounter. Lawson taught them to curl into a fetal position to save themselves during a beating. These weren't just political struggles, but moral ones, Lawson taught. "It was a moment in history when God saw fit to call America back from the depths of moral depravity and onto His path of righteousness."

In February, 1960, the students Lawson trained launched sit-ins in Nashville with teams of black and white students sitting together at lunch counters, violating the system that kept blacks separate from whites. The students were orderly, polite, disciplined and well-dressed as they occupied their stools at the counters. First they were ignored, then the counters were closed. Students were arrested and hauled off to jail. Their places at the counters were taken by fresh waves of students. At first the police kept angry whites away, but after two weeks of sit-ins the police unleashed the thugs. Police stood back while the demonstrators were viciously assaulted, then they arrested the injured demonstrators for "disturbing the peace." Even in the face of such violent intimidation, the students refused to end the sit-ins.

Pushing the campaign further, African-American residents of Nashville brought their economic power to bear in a boycott of downtown businesses. When the home of a black lawyer supporting the movement was bombed, the students quickly organized a silent march to City Hall—a story completed in the Diane Nash chapter later in this book. When the movement prevailed in Nashville, Lawson's training regimen became a model for civil rights activists in other cities. Martin Luther King, Jr. worked with Lawson to spread this kind of training throughout the South.

But Lawson was more than a trainer. In the John Lewis chapter, later in this book, you'll read more about the role of Lawson who also trained students in the 1961 Freedom Ride that was so crucial to the civil rights movement. Lawson himself rode on part of that journey and wound up with Lewis and others at the infamous prison known as Parchman Farm. After Lawson's release, he continued as a leader in the struggle. In 1966, when activist James

Meredith was shot during the March Against Fear from Tennessee to Mississippi, Lawson played a role with other civil rights leaders in keeping Meredith's march moving to its triumphant conclusion.

During this time, Lawson had become a Methodist pastor, although his path to the pulpit was an agonizing struggle as well. Because of his activism in Nashville, the Divinity School at Vanderbilt University expelled him. He later enrolled in Boston University to finish his theological training and returned to Tennessee as pastor of Centenary Methodist Church in Memphis. (The expulsion from Vanderbilt later became an embarrassment to the university. They finally apologized in 2006. Lawson teaches at Vanderbilt today.)

Even as a pastor, Lawson continued his activism. In Memphis, he advised the city's sanitation workers who were paid so little that they defined the phrase "working poor." As that campaign for justice became more intense, Lawson invited Martin Luther King, Jr. to help. Both men felt that the civil rights movement needed to focus on poverty. That's why King was in Memphis on April 4, 1968, when his assassination shocked the nation and devastated civil rights leaders. Lawson regarded King as the most important world leader since Gandhi. Nevertheless, living out his core convictions as a pastor and peacemaker, Lawson began regular visits to King's killer, James Earl Ray, in prison.

In 1974, Lawson left the South to pastor a church in Los Angeles. There he hosted a national TV talk show on justice from a faith perspective. He continued his leadership in various movements against racism and U.S. military action. He trained poor workers on how to organize unions and struggle for justice through nonviolent methods. Even after official retirement he continued his activism, joining in protests with groups ranging from "Janitors for Justice" in Los Angeles to gay and lesbian United Methodists in Cleveland.

In all his training workshops, Lawson taught that fear and injustice ultimately are overcome by love: Love of God, love for one another, love for justice—and even love of our enemies.

CHAPTER 27

Hildegard Goss-Mayr and Jean Goss

(b.1930) (1912-1991)

Christ came to show that only self-giving love can overcome injustice and its roots in the heart and mind and conscience of people…. So it is the task of the Christian to show this way in the revolutionary process and this can be done only if the Christian is with the people, with those who suffer, and not above them, but one with them.

—Hildegard Goss-Mayr

I've never met Hildegard, but I've appreciated the counsel and friendship of Richard Deats, a former executive director of the Fellowship of Reconciliation in the U.S. Richard led training in the Philippines with Jean Goss and Hildegard Goss-Mayr, and he told me much about them. Richard taught me how events like the People Power movement of 1987 don't just happen, rather they are a harvest from seeds planted through much training and organizing. News media may note 10 percent of an iceberg above the water level of history, but the wise activist pays special attention to the 90 percent below the surface where transformation is born.

HILDEGARD GOSS-MAYR IS NOT a name you'll find in head-lines. She works with the 90 percent of the iceberg most of us don't see. Working along with her husband Jean Goss, the benefits are multiplied in the lives of the people she trained.

Born into an Austrian Catholic family, Hildegard learned the principles and practices of pacifism from her parents. Her father, Kaspar Mayr, was one of the first Catholics to join the International Fellowship of Reconciliation (IFOR) and taught his children to respect all people. When Hitler and the Nazis seized Austria, nine-year old Hildegard engaged in her first act of civil disobedi-ence—refusing to salute when the dictator passed.

Later while sitting in a bomb shelter waiting for Allied bombs to fall, Hildegard came to a life-changing decision: To "either sub-mit to the forces of death, of bitterness, hatred and the spirit of revenge—or to reject violence radically and to seek the forces of life that are able to overcome evil at its root in the minds and hearts of human beings as well as in the structures of society... I could not go on living unless I dedicated my life to peacemaking through the power of nonviolence."

After the war, Hildegard's calling became crystallized in the teachings and self-giving love of Jesus. In 1953 Hildegard was invited to join the Secretariat of the IFOR. She began working on East-West dialogue, especially through European churches. She also taught about issues of nonviolence and conscientious objec-tion to war, and began to develop the workshops that would define the core of her career.

Through her work with IFOR, she met French peace activist Jean Goss. Jean had been a French soldier and was imprisoned by the Nazis for much of the war. During his imprisonment, Goss became convinced that God's love as seen in Jesus Christ demanded nonviolent love from his followers. Beginning in prison and then in the larger community following the war, Goss sought to put this radical love into practice. When he met Hilde-gard, they each found a perfect life partner.

Hildegard and Jean became part of the "peace lobby" that formed to provide input into the consultations of the Roman

Catholic Church during the Second Vatican Council. They prepared documents about the indiscriminant destruction of modern warfare, the dangers of weapons of mass destruction, nonviolence and the protection of conscientious objectors. The peace lobby helped many leaders at this historic Vatican council recognize that the traditional Just War Theory was inadequate to address the current ethical challenges of modern war. For the first time since the founding of Francis of Assisi's order, the Catholic Church affirmed and encouraged the practice of the nonviolence of Jesus as well as affirming conscientious objection to war.

A majority of the Goss-Mayrs' work, however, lay in their training programs, particularly in three significant areas of struggle: Latin America, the Philippines and Africa. In the 1960s, Latin American countries were usually ruled by military dictatorships, and there were many movements of revolutionary fervor that even drew priests into the violent liberation struggles. The Goss-Mayrs teamed up with bishops like Dom Hélder Câmera of Brazil who supported nonviolence as the way to break cycles of oppression and violence. They conducted seminars across Latin America, teaching nonviolence both from religious-philosophical foundations and in its pragmatic strategies. In Brazil, the term *firmez permanente*, or relentless persistence, captured the Goss-Mayrs' active spirit of nonviolence.

During a trip to Uruguay, Hildegard was arrested on suspicion of supporting the Tupamaro guerilla movement. During her time under arrest and questioning she was able to stay calm and express compassion for her interrogators. She was eventually released, and as she was being driven to the airport to be deported, her accompanying policewoman broke into tears that her country had arrested such a person as Hildegard.

One of their deepest friendships was with Adolfo Pérez Esquivel, a leading organizer from Argentina whom you will read about in the section on Organizers. Hildegard often traveled with him and other activists to provide nonviolence training throughout Latin America. They were arrested once in Brazil where they were interrogated and tortured. Later, when Esquivel was imprisoned again, the Goss-Mayrs played a major role in the international campaign for his release.

Catholic leaders in the Philippines had heard of the Goss-Mayrs' work in Europe and Latin America, and in 1984 invited them to their country to train nonviolent activists. At the time, dictator Ferdinand Marcos ruled the Philippines. One of the leading voices of nonviolent resistance, Senator Benigno Aquino, had been assassinated in 1983 at the Manila International Airport as he returned from exile. The Goss-Mayrs met with Aquino's widow, Corazon, and son, "Butz." Together they began to develop a network of people interested in nonviolent action against the Marcos dictatorship. Jean and Hildegard facilitated workshops that included small groups working on strategies and tactics. They analyzed the pillars of power supporting the Marcos regime and developed specific strategies for toppling those pillars.

Throughout the preparation of this movement, spirituality was central. Workshops included worship. Hildegard saw personal transformation as a foundation for the process of liberation: "The seed of the violence is in the structures, of course, and in the dictator. But isn't it also in ourselves? ... Unless we each tear the dictator out of our own heart, nothing will change." Besides a deepening spirituality, the Goss-Mayrs challenged the Filipinos to access their own cultural traditions and historical experiences to shape their movement. The people trained by the Goss-Mayrs held hundreds of workshops on nonviolence—dramatically multiplying the number of people ready to engage in the struggle.

When Marcos called for a presidential election to endorse his rule, Corazon Aquino ran against him. The movement was ready to take action, mobilizing the public and monitoring the polls. Although Marcos declared victory, Aquino's supporters announced their own monitored results. Eventually, two generals and a few hundred soldiers declared support for Aquino. When Marcos ordered his army to arrest the generals, church leaders and the movement activists quickly organized tens of thousands of unarmed Filipinos to create a human shield to protect the generals. News media from around the world called it People Power.

After a three-day standoff, the military refused to follow Marcos' orders anymore, and the dictator fled.

In April, 1991, Jean died suddenly. Hildegard continued her work, shifting the focus to Africa where she conducted workshops throughout the continent. Tapes and books by Hildegard and Jean were carried far and wide. They were used especially in Madagascar to help church leaders confront the dictatorship of Didier Ratsiraka. Jean had visited Madagascar just before his death. Hildegard visited to help the movement leaders explore how to continue their nonviolent pressure. A nonviolent movement had developed that brought more than 100,000 people into the streets every week. These leaders helped the republic transition away from the dictatorship and into an elected government.

The mark of the long-term impact of Hildegard Goss-Mayr and her husband Jean is the number of people who use their tools of analyzing power, their process for developing strategies and their methods of teaching nonviolence. Hildegard said, "We should remember that no effort, no action that we carry out through the force of Love and Truth is ever lost."

CHAPTER 28

George Lakey

(b. 1937)

The essence of the work I do is to love.

—George Lakey

I know George through various activist projects in the Philadelphia area. I've even gone to "folk sings" at his home in West Philly—one of my unfulfilled goals is to join him in singing Handel's Messiah. But things changed when I attended my first Training for Social Action Trainers (TSAT). George went from a friend and colleague to a mentor. My wife is also a TSAT grad and as trainers and activists George taught us new ways to think and to create learning opportunities on the spot. We've both participated in more of his workshops and seldom leave an encounter with George without finding ourselves creatively stretched. We joke about wearing WWGD bracelets—What Would George Do?

IN A FAMILY TREE of activists for peace and justice, George Lakey is surely a common mentor for people in many different movements in countries around the world. He has facilitated over 1,500 workshops on five continents and his name appears in many profiles throughout this book as an influence on other leaders. He's best known for his Training for Change center in Philadelphia, a catalytic stop for many of the world's peacemakers.

As a bread baker, Lakey enjoys the image of yeast: Mass movements begin with the "fermenting" work of a small group. Like yeast, visionary minorities have the capacity to make a huge difference in the larger group. Enabling such small groups, and then the growing movements they engender, to make a difference—that has been Lakey's work as a trainer of trainers.

As a college student, Lakey discovered the Quakers and became a pacifist. Quaker spirituality is a major source of self-awareness, guidance and strength in his peacemaking. He attributes prayer as the most reliable means to achieving results in his life, especially this prayer, "Please, God, help me to see this from a different point of view." He points out, "That prayer is always answered!"

Lakey jumped into the anti-war and civil rights movements in the late 1950s and 1960s. He taught at the Martin Luther King School for Social Change, inspiring the training work that would be refined throughout the years. Soon, he was involved in international activism as well. In 1967, he served on the crew of the peace ship, Phoenix, which set sail several times during the war on a mission to carry medical aid to Buddhist peace activists in South Vietnam. In 1971, along with several other leading Quaker activists, he co-founded the Movement for a New Society. Later, he founded and directed the Philadelphia Jobs with Peace Campaign. Lakey wanted his work to represent more than an anti-war message; he pushed for a transformation from war-industry employment to an economy that was life affirming. He also was a founder of Men Against Patriarchy, a pioneering men's anti-sexism movement. His voice spread through his books as well. *A Manual for Direct Action* was often called the bible of direct action by civil rights activists.

In 1992, Lakey founded Training for Change, an organization to train leaders and groups to stand up for peace, justice and the environment through strategic nonviolent action. Lakey turned his spacious Victorian home into a training center, producing weekend TSAT workshops that revolutionized the way many activists taught and trained. He designed a three-week "Super-T" program that included the TSAT as well as classes in Creative

Workshop Design, Adventure-Based Learning, and an advanced workshop on emergent design and group process. Besides training the trainers, he created workshops for those interested in nonviolent struggle, undoing racism, sexism and classism, developing strategies and transformational training. He utilized the experiential education model that begins with an experience, reflects on the experience, then generalizes and applies what is learned to develop a new experience. Through it all, he modeled a willing vulnerability that encouraged self-awareness in the men and women whose lives he touched.

Wherever they were held around the world, George Lakey's workshops touched as diverse a group of people as you could imagine: coal miners, therapists, homeless people and prisoners, lesbians and gays in Russia, Buddhist monks in Sri Lanka, ethnic insurgent rebels in Burma, anti-apartheid activists in South Africa. He and one of the younger activists he mentored, Daniel Hunter, developed the "Super-T" to help launch the International Nonviolent Peace Force. Activist leaders from almost every type of global struggle have come to Training for Change to refine their skills in transformative education, nonviolent activism, leadership, strategizing and group work.

Through his spirituality and activism, Lakey has found ways to welcome both the world's grief and joy. His training programs involve tears and laughter, which Lakey uses to fuel transformation. Along the way, his playful nature saps the power of oppression inside a person and in the structures around us. He teaches not only the principles of peacemaking and how to implement them, but becomes a role model for peacemakers. If this all sounds too calculated, then these words still have not captured the full essence of George Lakey. As usual, he sums up it up eloquently: "The essence of the work I do is to love."

CHAPTER 29

Mubarak Awad

(b. 1943)

In the end it is a question of life or death. I think all human beings want to live. They want to enjoy life. It doesn't matter what their religion or politics are; they want to live and allow others to live. When I speak of civil disobedience and nonviolence, I'm saying that I want to live, but I want you all to live with me. I think that is a powerful message.

—Mubarak Awad

I've never met Mubarak but my path has crossed his repeatedly. I've been in the office of the Palestinian Center for the Study of Nonviolence in Jerusalem, but he had already been exiled by Israel. I spoke at Bethlehem Bible College where his brother, Bishara, is president. I've worked with Michael Beer of Nonviolence International, an organization founded and directed by Mubarak. Although we haven't met, I have seen his influence around the world.

AN OLD MAN CAME to Mubarak Awad asking for help. Israeli settlers near his home in Tekoa had put up a fence, seizing several acres of the land belonging to his village. The old man had heard Awad's teaching about nonviolence. He said, "You told us that if we are not afraid, anything is possible."

Awad thought, "Oh my God! Did I say that?" He considered himself an educator, but this old man was pushing him beyond teaching to organizing action. Awad agreed to lead the villagers if they agreed not to bring guns or throw stones or run away if they were shot at or arrested. They mobilized 300 unarmed people to confront the armed settlers at the fence. "We refused to run.... We were hugging each other," he recalled as the military governor came and allowed the Palestinians to remove the fence.

In 1943, Awad was born into a Palestinian Christian family in Jerusalem during the period when the region was still controlled by the British Mandate. When war broke out in 1948 between Arabs and Jews, his father was killed while trying to bring wounded civilians into their home so that Mubarak's mother, who was a nurse, could care for them. When the fighting ended and the state of Israel was established, the family house was in an Israeli-occupied area. So the surviving Awads moved into the old city as refugees in Jerusalem, under Jordanian rule.

Mubarak's mother warned him that "the one who killed your Dad left a widow and seven kids. So don't ever carry a gun and kill anyone." When he was in the St. George secondary school in Jerusalem, the Jordanian soldiers began to drill students with guns. Awad refused to participate. The instructors tied him up with a gun in his hands and had all the other students spit on him.

In 1967 Awad gave up the right to Israeli citizenship and kept the Jordanian citizenship he obtained as a Palestinian prior to the 1967 war. The citizenship issue later became a key issue in his life. He moved back and forth between Jerusalem and the United States. While studying in the United States he became a U.S. citizen. He also married Nancy Nye, an American Quaker. He returned to the West Bank of Palestine to direct an orphanage in the Christian town of Beit Jala. Awad allowed students to join in protests against the Israeli occupation. As a result, Awad was jailed by Israeli authorities. The Mennonites for whom he worked negotiated his release on the condition that he go back to the U.S. for further studies.

Awad returned to Jerusalem in the early 1980s to set up a center to teach counseling skills to Palestinian educators. Nobody was interested in therapy—political confrontation with the Israeli occupation was the main concern. So Awad decided to put on a three-day workshop on "how to get rid of the occupation." Expecting 50 participants, more than 400 people showed up including angry members of the Palestinian Liberation Organization (PLO) who thought he was trying to replace their organization. Awad challenged participants saying, "We are under occupation because we choose to be under occupation," and then he introduced the concepts of nonviolent resistance. He said, "Nonviolence would go a long way toward paralyzing Israel's destructive war machine."

In 1985, Awad established the Palestinian Centre for the Study of Nonviolence, based in two small rooms in East Jerusalem. He taught nonviolence as a method for resisting the Israeli occupation. He was so committed to bringing the insights of nonviolence to the Arab world that he translated many key works into Arabic, including Gene Sharp's *The Politics of Nonviolence* and works by Gandhi and Martin Luther King. Given that the vast majority of Palestinians were Muslims, he also translated the biography of Abdul Gaffar Khan into Arabic. He established a mobile library to carry these books throughout Palestine.

Following the successful action of removing a fence at Tekoa, Awad helped villages organize actions over disputed lands. He brought Palestinians together with Israeli peace activists to plant olive trees on the land, an action that reflected Zionist rituals of planting olive trees in support of Israel. Sometimes settlers ripped out these saplings, but Awad had made his point. He was giving Palestinians nonviolent opportunities to confront the Israeli occupation.

Awad developed a "12-page blueprint for passive resistance in the territories," which included a list of 120 specific nonviolent steps such as: Instead of riots, Palestinians could engage in prayer protests, silent processions, wearing yellow badges or prison garb; they could block the paths of bulldozers with their bodies; they could boycott meetings at which Israeli officials or

Palestinian collaborators were present; they could ignore documents in Hebrew including official summonses; they could refuse to pay taxes and violate curfews. He even supported physical sabotage such as cutting phone lines and electric lines; he encouraged people to refuse to produce their identity cards, filling the jails if necessary. He encouraged the formation of alternative institutions under Palestinian control, a "completely autonomous infrastructure" that would be a prelude to the administration of an independent state. Instead of using Israeli courts, they would engage in their own traditional tribal system for adjudicating cases. Schools that the Israelis oversaw would be boycotted, and education would take place through classes held in homes instead. He organized a campaign to eat and drink Palestinian-produced products. The Israelis began to oppose the ideas Awad and his center were promoting, which created a positive response from some Palestinians: "If the Israelis say this is something bad, for the Palestinians it is good."

When the First Intifada (Palestinian uprising against Israeli rule) erupted in late 1987, Awad began organizing nonviolent actions. He organized "popular resistance," which referred to action involving the whole population in civil disobedience as contrasted to "armed struggle," which was carried out by the PLO and other groups. Awad did not reject armed struggle outright, which earned him much criticism outside the Palestinian community, but he encouraged Palestinians to see nonviolence as a way they could all participate. He also encouraged youths to throw flowers at the Israeli soldiers instead of rocks. At first the United Command for Fatah, which coordinated the Intifada resistance, rejected Awad's ideas of nonviolence, but eventually many of the leaders realized that Awad offered a clearer vision of both the goals and methodologies of resistance that would draw in the broad Palestinian populace. Whereas weeks earlier he had been hooted down while speaking to Fatah loyalists, now major portions of his proposals were adopted for action. Demonstrations were organized along with strikes. Palestinians stopped paying rent to Israelis, and shopkeepers refused to collect sales taxes. Tax revenues from the occupied territories dropped by 40 percent.

The Israeli government ordered Awad's deportation. They viewed any action against Israeli rule as seditious whether it was violent or nonviolent. Awad's citizenship became an issue. He appealed the expulsion, but the Israeli Supreme Court rejected his appeal. So he engaged in a hunger strike from jail and was even joined in a solidarity fast by Jewish supporters outside the police station. In May, 1988, Awad was forced to return to the U.S. Though he was deported, the bulk of the resistance by Palestinians during the First Intifada continued to practice the "popular resistance" they had learned from Awad. His proposal to set up their own governing infrastructure and announce the establishment of a Palestinian republic grew after his deportation. Many local "popular committees" sprang up to administer affairs in the "liberated areas."

Though many Palestinians practiced nonviolent resistance in a broad and systematic way during the Intifada, Hamas began to initiate a commitment to reinvigorate the violent struggle against Israel. In the years that followed, especially with the Second Intifada beginning in late 2000, many Palestinian activists opted for the violence of Hamas instead of the nonviolent approach advocated by Awad. Looking back, Awad thinks the Intifada came too soon. Nonviolent resistance requires a mobilization of the head and the heart, and not enough had been done to get people to shift their beliefs from violent struggle to the dedication and commitment needed for nonviolent engagement in the face of Israeli force.

As he settled in Washington D.C. in 1989, Awad formed Nonviolence International, an organization to promote nonviolent resistance and human rights around the world. The vision and practices Awad had developed for use in the Palestinian struggle were shared with people in other struggles. He also began teaching in the Department of International Peace and Conflict Resolution at American University.

In the years since he left Jerusalem, Awad's vision for the Palestinian struggle has been eclipsed by many other events and forces, including the barrier wall between Israel and Palestine begun in 2003 and the deep split between the PLO and Hamas that has led to further violence. As this book is published in 2011, Awad's work on nonviolence is spreading throughout the world, where people in many other lands are learning from his insights. We wonder what lies ahead for such an influential peacemaker. Will his own people someday embrace Awad again as a pragmatic prophet?

CHAPTER 30

Ouyporn Khuankaew

(b. 1963)

The method that touches only at the head level will not transform people. At most it can make people believe what they have heard or discussed, but their personal behavior will not change. Transformation happens at the heart level.

—Ouyporn Khuankaew

Ouyporn and I met years ago in a small group during one of George Lakey's workshops to prepare trainers. I was heading to Asia and needed help in determining what training tools would work well; Ouyporn helped me refine my thinking. Over the years, I kept hearing about her through various activists. Then, one day while I was in Thailand, I opened the Bangkok Post and saw a huge, section-front profile of her life and work. I was delighted to see the impact and the public recognition of her work. I can acknowledge that she helped me along the way, too.

SIXTEEN YEARS AFTER HER father died she still burned with anger at him. Ouyporn Khuankaew had been born into a peasant family in the rice-farming regions near Chiang Mai, Thailand. Her father was a devout Buddhist, giving over half of the family's money to the local temple and spending much of his time with the abbot. Meanwhile, his family struggled with poverty. He beat the children and threatened their mother. One daughter fled the violence at home when she was 13. When Ouyporn was 14, she challenged her brother-in-law who had violently insulted her sister. When her father was ailing, she urged her mother not to care for him so he would die and they could all have peace—but her father's death did not bring her peace.

"People don't see domestic violence as a kind of war," Ouyporn said. "That's why violence against women is the worst kind of violence, because it can happen every day, at any moment, in your own home, and most of the time by the one you love." She lived as an emotional refugee of that kind of war even as she got her education and began a career. She set out working on the crushing issues women faced when male-oriented programs for rural development left women in a worse situation than before. Under oppressive policies, many girls wound up involved in prostitution. Such tragedies were met with religious acceptance—Karma simply worked this way. Women were at a lower level than men. Out of frustration at this injustice, Ouyporn turned to feminism, but found that "head-oriented" Western forms of feminism drew negative reactions from "heart-oriented" Thai women.

Then in 1994 Ouyporn came to a new understanding of Buddhist "right practice" and committed herself to it. "It helped turn my feelings of anger, frustration, resentment and despair into compassion, loving, forgiving and hopefulness," she said. She reconnected with her rural roots and discovered the meditative dimensions of simple actions connecting one to the soil. Through meditation, she understood what Buddha really taught about suffering and how to end it—and she finally reached a spiritual reconciliation concerning her late father, finding inner joy to replace the anger. As she put it, "If I cannot heal and transform myself from my own ignorance, it is very difficult trying to transform other people."

This inner transformation also empowered her to work constructively on the gender justice issues that were of such deep concern to her. Ouyporn founded and directs the International Women's Partnership for Peace and Justice (IWP). She has also been the director of the Women & Gender Program for the International Network of Engaged Buddhists. She has conducted workshops on a wide range of topics throughout Asia, including nonviolence, anti-oppression work, conflict resolution, peacemaking, democracy and politics, community and team building, women's rights and trauma. She brings two major themes to her training: Buddhist spirituality and gender. Using "emergent design," where much of the shape of the workshop develops through the interactions with the participants, gender issues always arise. These are vital matters, since gender discrimination throughout Thailand leaves women more vulnerable to forced labor, especially in the sex trade. She designs her workshops so that women and men encounter each other in a non-threatening way, allowing women to express themselves.

Gender oppression is a crucial challenge, Ouyporn believes, because this is the setting in which humans first learn to oppress and to accept it as a way of life. To undo such a deeply engrained principle, Ouyporn offers extended training for several groups of women leaders in Asia. These women share their stories and also find male allies, so the process becomes more than a "woman's problem." As they explore the structural issues of gender discrimination, women realize that their suffering is not a product of their individual karma, but rather the "structural karma." Men and women begin to work together on solutions.

Ouyporn pushes the challenge of patriarchy back into Buddhism itself, while at the same time drawing her inner strength from the compassion, peace and mindfulness of Buddhist spirituality. Starting in the mid 1990s, Ouyporn became heavily involved in training programs with monks and nuns, challenging the patriarchy within Buddhism that often leaves nuns in tragically vulnerable positions. At first, even progressive monks were timid to tackle the sexist views of women's karma so prevalent in Buddhism. Through a Tibetan Buddhist abbess in Dharmasala, India, who had been raped by Chinese soldiers, Ouyporn discovered the healing power of "compassion meditation." Ouyporn sees this as a tool at the center of Buddhist spirituality that helps victims of violence transcend the destructive forces of trauma. Wherever she works now, she encourages activists to develop a spiritual practice as they build social movements so they will not burn out, fall prey to addictions or get caught up in struggles for power and fame. She helps people grow in personal awareness and inner peace as they work together.

Her eyes are always focused on individuals as well as larger issues. Across Thailand, she facilitates workshops for women and men who live with HIV to help them deal with the violence they encounter. Since 2008, she has worked with gay, lesbian and transgender activists in Thailand to build a movement to end homophobia and injustice.

As a trainer, she acknowledges many influences: George Lakey, a model for men who learned to support women in the quest for gender justice; Thich Nhat Hanh, the Vietnamese Zen Buddhist teacher and peace activist; and Kathryn Norsworthy of Rollins College, who taught feminist practice and methodology. Ouyporn has woven these streams of influence through her own experience and into training methods that help to transform some of the most marginalized people of Asia into peacemakers—both within themselves and in the world around them.

PART 6
Organizers
Making the Muscles Move

CHANGE OFTEN BEGINS WITH prophetic voices joined by theorists, advocates and educators. But how are people mobilized to join this movement toward change? That's where organizers play a major role. They connect people together to form a force for change—and get these new muscles moving in the same direction.

Fred Ross, Jr., who worked with Cesar Chavez and the United Farm Workers, wrote about this form of peacemaking: "...the organizer works quietly behind the scenes, patiently asking questions, listening respectfully, agitating, teaching new leaders, pushing them to take action, and creating hope *con animo*, with great enthusiasm. The organizer finds people one at a time, teaches them to develop their own powerful voices, turns their anger about injustice into hope by encouraging them to take action, raises hell, stirs up trouble, and has fun doing it."

Don't look for most organizers at the front of their movements. Their preferred place is working alongside or behind other people. Organizers help people find and unleash their own passions. Organizers are believers, not only in the cause of justice and peace, but especially in people—sometimes having more faith in people than they do in themselves. Oppression can grind people down into pessimism and despair. Organizers jump-start action by believing in the capacity of marginalized people to rise up and change their own reality. Organizers don't create the energy—they summon it from within the people forming a movement.

One of the frequent chants heard in street demonstrations is "The people united can never be defeated." That is the mantra of the organizer, who weaves people together into a united fabric. Smart organizers know that the thread of each individual life adds a slightly different hue to the beauty of the final pattern.

Organizers also present a huge challenge to people, because getting involved in struggles for justice or freedom can be very dangerous. Bernice Johnson Reagon, founder of the Grammy award-winning music group, Sweet Honey in the Rock, was a leader in the civil rights movement, not only with her powerful singing, but also in mobilizing people to join the cause. She said, "Organizing is not gentle. When you organize somebody, you create great anxiety in that person because you are telling them to risk everything." Even getting a local store owner to simply put up a civil rights worker in their home could risk having racist thugs firebomb the store or shoot at the house, possibilities that can understandably cause great fear and trepidation. Reagon went on to the express the courageous determination that is called forth by the organizer: "You decide to take that risk because this is important enough."

Good organizers are not control freaks, for such domination can snuff out a rising spirit of hope and unity. Instead, good organizers are servants to the people. A movement's direction arises from the dreams of the people. If organizers try too hard to shape that dream, the group can implode in a tragic power struggle. As groups grow, new leaders arise. Talented organizers help to discern and position those new leaders—then step back in satisfaction at a job well done. Organizers try to multiply themselves, developing a tree of organizers reaching from the top of a movement to the grassroots.

Sometimes, the leading figure in a movement is also a talented organizer. In 1931, Jane Addams was the first American woman to be awarded the Nobel Peace Prize. Known for her work as a social reformer through Hull House in a poor area of Chicago, she also organized women for peace. She organized the Women's Peace Party and the International Congress of Women to try to halt the move toward World War I. After the war she became president of the Women's International League for Peace and Freedom. Addams also was a co-founder of the American Civil Liberties Union and the National Association for the Advancement of Colored People. She clearly saw the value of strong organizing: "Peace is not merely something to hold congresses about… It has come to be a rising tide of moral feeling, which is slowly engulfing all pride and conquest and making war impossible."

Identifying the organizers from outside a movement isn't always easy. Many are not public figures, but spend their time toiling behind the scenes, working out the details of making contacts, talking with individuals and small groups, checking and double-checking commitments and giving solid data to spokespersons. Organizers generally are a humble lot. At their best, they are the connective tissue that allows a great movement to arise, flex its muscles, move and change the world.

CHAPTER 31

Thomas Clarkson

(1760-1846)

....and if I had sixty years more they should all be given to the same cause.

—Thomas Clarkson

*William Wilberforce and John Newton are well known in the campaign against the slave trade in Britain. Once, I even preached a first-person sermon about Newton, taking on his role as he wrote "Amazing Grace." But I didn't know about Thomas Clarkson until I read **Bury the Chains** by Adam Hochschild. As Americans, we often arrogantly assume that we've invented everything, so it first was humbling to me—and then inspiring—to learn that many years ago Clarkson was using peacemaking tools and even inventing tools we use today.*

IN JUST FIVE YEARS, an issue that was not even a topic of public discussion became a national cause that began to unravel the slave trade in the British Empire. It took more years to actually abolish slavery, but the movement in Great Britain started with twelve men who met in 1787 to bring down what they viewed as an iniquitous and unjust system. One of those twelve, Thomas Clarkson, was to be the only full-time organizer for the movement. He developed strategies and ideas that not only laid the basis for success against the slave trade but also became models for countless social and political movements that have followed.

Clarkson was a young divinity student who won a prestigious scholarly prize for a Latin essay about the slave trade. As he rode his horse home from a reading of the essay, he stopped, overwhelmed by what he had written: "…if the contents of the essay were true, it was time some person should see these calamities to their end." It didn't take him long to realize that he was that person.

In the next two years he was introduced to a circle of abolitionist Quakers. Since Clarkson was an Anglican churchman, the group quickly realized that he would be more accepted by the British mainstream as a voice for the movement. His own inner passion and organizing genius launched him into the new role. He began by developing an information resource to notify the public about the issue. He translated his winning essay into English, and had it published, not by a scholarly publishing house with only a small circle of academic readers, but by a Quaker publisher with a broad audience. Titles in those days were verbose! It was called: *An Essay on the Slavery and Commerce of the Human Species, particularly the African, translated from a Latin Dissertation, which was honoured with the First Prize in the University of Cambridge for the year 1785, with Additions.*

Clarkson's second step was to do more research. He read firsthand accounts of slavery and the slave trade. Then he went down to the docks in London to see the ships for himself. He wrote "I found soon afterwards a fire of indignation kindling within me" for the horrors were taking on tangible forms to him. Then he went to the ports of Bristol and Liverpool, which were the key centers for the slave trade. There he risked beatings to find people who would testify about the destruction of life that was commonplace. Besides the hideous and often deadly conditions for the African slaves, Clarkson discovered that 20 percent of sailing crews did not survive voyages due to disease and physical brutality, a point that would be of value in trying to persuade the British Parliament to outlaw the trade.

Then Clarkson began to develop a network of supporters for the cause. The original group of abolitionists formed the Society for Effecting the Abolition of the Slave Trade—an innovative idea in itself to establish an organization for social change. Then they recruited people to join them: nobles and members of Parliament; women and laborers who couldn't vote but who could express their opinions; Quakers and other religious dissidents as well as Anglicans. Clarkson traveled tens of thousands of miles organizing countless local committees to facilitate organizing and spreading the message in each community.

They had a huge challenge—the majority of the people in England viewed the slave trade as normal. Britain profited from it economically through countless jobs and the prosperity it brought to ports and London. Even the developing industrial sector benefited from the cotton grown by slave labor. So why should people bother with human rights for people they'd never seen, who were of a different race and an ocean away? Clarkson believed that if he could arouse basic human empathy in people they would see the gross injustice that needed to be halted.

Besides organizing the small groups, Clarkson and his abolitionist partners developed methods now used in all kinds of social causes around the world. One was the petition, a form of expressing opinion that was recognized hundreds of years earlier in the *Magna Carta*. But Clarkson used it as an organizing tool, having each community group gather signatures that were added together and taken to Parliament. A mere year after starting the campaign they presented 103 petitions with up to 100,000 signatures, more than all the other petitions on all other issues received by Parliament combined.

They also developed a movement logo, thanks to Josiah Wedgewood. He drew a symbol of a kneeling African in chains with uplifted arms, encircled by the words, "Am I not a Man and a Brother?" The logo was used as a seal for letters, put on books, cufflinks for men and ornamental pins and broaches for women. Clarkson would carry hundreds with him to disperse in his travels.

Women began to talk of a sugar boycott. Since all sugar was produced by slave labor, and they were the ones who prepared the food and tea, this gave ordinary people something substantive they could do. Clarkson pounced on the idea and added it to the actions taken by the campaign. In a few months, about 300,000 people stopped consuming sugar. Sugar sales dropped by more than a third. Clarkson and his colleagues even developed a version of "free-trade" labels for sugar produced in non-slave regions, including eventually liberated and independent Haiti. They read, "Produced by the labour of FREEMEN."

An image can be worth a thousand words, and Clarkson came up with the image that is iconic regarding the slave trade to this day: The sketch of how many people can be stacked into the hold of a slave ship. Clarkson took the first recorded measurements of a slave ship, where each person was chained into a bunk only 2 feet 8 inches high. He was careful not to exaggerate, showing how 482 slaves were crammed into the hold. Clarkson used this drawing in books, in his testimony to Parliament and in training small groups throughout the abolitionist movement.

The goal was to get Parliament to vote to abolish the slave trade. Besides the public pressure, they needed a member of Parliament to lead the cause. Clarkson helped to recruit William Wilberforce to be that leader. Wilberforce introduced bills against slavery every year. The petitions were presented. Clarkson hunted up witnesses for hearings, including doctors who had been on voyages to try to maximize profits by keeping the slaves alive. Pressure grew each year until victory seemed near in 1792. A bill was passed against the slave trade, but opponents inserted the word "gradually," which destroyed its effect.

War with France sidelined the movement. Then as the radicalism unleashed by the French Revolution took hold, the social radicals in Great Britain came under increased suspicion of being unpatriotic. Clarkson had to lie low for a few years, in large part due to fatigue from overworking. He took up farming. In 1803 Clarkson rejoined the abolitionist committee and helped re-ignite the cause. With the success of the revolt in Haiti and the return of

British soldiers from the bloody wars in the Caribbean, the economics and politics had changed. The abolitionists re-introduced the issue to Parliament, and in 1807 the bill passed to abolish the slave trade throughout the British Empire. What Clarkson referred to as "one mass of iniquity from the beginning to the end" had been undone through a multi-faceted public movement that he had organized.

But the work was not finished. Although the trade in slaves was halted, several decades passed before the Slavery Abolition Act of 1833 finally made slavery illegal throughout most of the British empire. Even then, some colonies related to the East India Company weren't required to comply until 1838. A new abolitionist society was formed with a new generation of leaders. Clarkson was now the grand old man of the movement, the only one of the original 12 abolitionists to see full emancipation.

Five weeks before Clarkson died, he was visited by two young American abolitionists: Frederick Douglass and William Lloyd Garrison. They talked about the slavery that still existed in the United States. Douglass recorded what Clarkson told about struggling for sixty years for the cause and quoted Clarkson as saying, "and if I had sixty years more they should all be given to the same cause." The torch was now passed to a new generation of activists, and the ideas and methods of organizing social movements that were originated or refined by Thomas Clarkson are staples in movements for change to this day.

CHAPTER 32

Ella Baker

(1903-1986)

In order for us as poor and oppressed people to become a part of a society that is meaningful, the system under which we now exist has to be radically changed. It means facing a system that does not lend itself to your needs and devising means by which you can change that system. That is easier said than done.

—Ella Baker

Ella Baker is mother to many in the peacemakers' family tree. I claim her as grandmother, because she shaped the life of George Lakey, who was one of my mentors. Yet, far too many women like Ella Baker are invisible in histories of the struggle for civil rights in the U.S. I confess that I wouldn't have discovered this grandmother except that George Lakey insisted on retelling her story. Now I am sharing that story with you, and this may be the first moment you have ever seen her name. Remember Ella Baker and tell someone else.

AT ELLA BAKER'S FUNERAL in the famed Abyssinian Baptist Church in New York City, long-time civil rights activist Bob Moses asked all those who considered themselves to be Ella's children to come to the front of the church. Hundreds of people gathered at the front in testimony to the impact this woman had directly made on their lives. She wasn't the most well-known name in the civil rights movement, but Baker probably did more than any single person to shape the substance of the movement and the lives of the activists who would change the course of U.S. history.

Ella Baker's credo was that "strong people don't need strong leaders." She said, "You didn't see me on television, you didn't see news stories about me. The kind of role that I tried to play was to pick up pieces or put together pieces out of which I hoped organization might come." As an organizer she frequently critiqued the male-dominated, top-down leadership of the various civil rights organizations with which she worked. She believed leadership should help people connect to the power within themselves, then they could rise up with strength, courage and creativity to challenge the unjust systems around them. Through her behind-the-scenes work she turned dreams into realities, visions into substantive programs, and did the hard work to make the movement a transformative force.

Baker began her life of activism in Harlem during the Depression. She helped organize consumer cooperatives to develop economic power in the black community through the Young Negroes Cooperative League. In 1938 she joined the staff of the National Association for the Advancement of Colored People (NAACP) and began traveling through the South to build up local NAACP branches. She resigned eight years later, frustrated at not getting organizational support for efforts toward mass protest that she felt were needed to attack segregation in the South.

When the Montgomery Bus Boycott was launched in 1954, Baker quickly stepped forward to help. She organized support for the Montgomery movement, coordinated publicity and raised financial aid from around the country. In the bus boycott she saw the beginning of the "mass force" of which she had dreamed.

Following the successful desegregation of Montgomery's buses, the momentum of protest stalled. Baker was frustrated that male clergy were not expanding the movement across the South—thereby squandering the outstanding work done mostly by women—to mobilize the men and women who had actually carried out the Montgomery campaign. Baker, along with Bayard Rustin and Stanley Levison, drew up plans for a broad-based movement with black ministers in the lead. They invited about one hundred of the best-known black ministers to Atlanta's Ebenezer Baptist Church, and the Southern Christian Leadership Conference (SCLC) was born.

Martin Luther King, Jr. was chosen as the head of the SCLC, but it quickly became evident that someone with organizing skill was desperately needed if their grandiose plans were going to work. Friends pressured King to hire Baker as Executive Director, but King would only bring her on as "acting" director. She quickly got to work mobilizing people in cities across the South for the SCLC's initial Crusade for Citizenship. This was a campaign in the South to hold rallies promoting voter registration. Baker mostly utilized women whose leadership had been honed in local churches. She said, "All the churches depended—in terms of things taking place—on women, not men. Men didn't do the things that had to be done." Baker got those things done for the SCLC and built up the organization, especially with women.

Whether as a staff member at the SCLC or in her later positions, Baker was excellent at tending to the details that kept direct actions going: She kept track of who was in jail following protests; she monitored the needs of people who had been fired from their jobs for joining the protests, ensuring that they got whatever financial support was available.

As student-led sit-in movements spread across the country in 1960, Baker invited the students to meet together. They had been working in isolated circles, encouraged by one another's actions, but there was no coordination or overarching vision. Baker saw the need for these separate movements to come together in a student activist organization. Years earlier Baker had organized a Youth Council for the NAACP. She recommended to King that the SCLC bring the students together for a conference at Shaw University. Though King and the SCLC agreed to sponsor the gathering, Baker persistently urged the students to maintain their independence. Through her inspiration and actions as a catalyst, the Student Nonviolent Coordinating Committee (SNCC) was born—the group that was to provide the most cutting-edge, on-the-ground activism in the major campaigns of the civil rights movement. Baker challenged them to look beyond the lunch counter sit-ins, what she termed "more than a Coke and a hamburger." Rather, they should push to bring about comprehensive change in the whole social structure of the U.S.

Baker resigned from the SCLC to work more closely with the SNCC as an advisor. As arguments swirled throughout the new organization, Baker suggested that the SNCC form two wings with different strategies. One wing would engage in nonviolent direct action. That wing worked alongside the Congress of Racial Equality to engage in the Freedom Rides to challenge the segregated system of interstate bus transportation. The other wing focused on voter registration, leading to the Freedom Summer in Mississippi and the voter registration campaign in Selma, Alabama. These two wings of the SNCC propelled the civil rights agenda through the early to mid-1960s. Throughout that period Baker was the mentor of the young activists. John Lewis called her "our personal Gandhi" and "the spiritual mother of SNCC."

In 1964 as the campaign for voter registration and voting rights was underway in Mississippi, Fannie Lou Hamer and other leaders organized the Mississippi Freedom Democratic Party (MFDP) to challenge the all-white Mississippi delegation to the Democratic National Convention. Baker took charge of organizing efforts to develop support for the MFDP among delegations from the North. She saw the growing strength of this grassroots movement that challenged the entrenched political powers of the Democratic Party. Hamer's testimony to the Credentials Committee, broadcast on national TV, was a riveting story about the violence associated with the segregation system in the South. Millions of viewers saw the passion among African-Americans in Mississippi to achieve the basic rights of citizenships that most Americans took for granted. Although the MFDP delegates failed to be seated at the convention in spite of protest actions on the convention floor, pressure from the MFDP built momentum for permanent changes in national politics. All along, Baker encouraged the delegation to see the bigger picture of what they were doing and not be discouraged by losses along the way: "It is important that you go to the convention whether you are seated or not...This is only the beginning."

Ella Baker never stopped throughout the 86 years of her life. Eventually, she returned to New York, where she participated in the Mass Party Organizing Committee, the Women's International League for Peace and Freedom and the Third World Women's Alliance. She joined in the struggles for freedom in South Africa and Puerto Rico. Baker said, "I believe that the struggle is eternal." In her long-range vision, she saw that each new generation would bring someone to hear the story and pick up the cause. "We who believe in freedom cannot rest," she said.

And now you know her story too.

CHAPTER 33

Bernard Lafayette

(b. 1940)

Nonviolence is how to respond to violence and turn it into a positive force.

—**Bernard Lafayette**

Bernard Lafayette figured prominently in history that unfolded when I was still a schoolboy. I wanted to retell his story and, in the process, I sent a draft of the chapter to Dr. Lafayette. He telephoned me and suddenly history had a voice, a gentle voice that conveyed his astonishing strength and courage in a compelling tone of love. Just his voice expressed so much of the essence of the civil rights movement.

BERNARD LAFAYETTE MOVED TO Selma, Alabama, intent on organizing African-Americans to register to vote in Dallas County. He brought a reputation as a veteran of the Freedom Rides, a reputation that caused many intimidated men and women to steer clear. Even the black principal of the high school threatened to call the sheriff if Lafayette tried to recruit school kids for the cause. But Lafayette kept a low profile. He met people one-on-one, then finally pulled together some small groups to talk about citizenship. He worked slowly and quietly, eventually building up a local movement that was strong enough to become one of the turning points in the civil rights struggle. Quiet organizing by Lafayette made the historic victory possible.

Lafayette was born in Florida, but two years of living in Philadelphia exposed him to life in a racially integrated society. He enrolled in the American Baptist Theological Seminary in Nashville. There he met James Lawson and was recruited into the group of students Lawson was training to desegregate Nashville. He also took classes at the Highlander Folk School, learning Gandhian nonviolence. The success of the Nashville sit-ins was such a watershed that Lafayette and other young leaders moved from there into struggles nationwide. Lafayette joined student leaders from across the South to form the Student Nonviolent Coordinating Committee (SNCC), which became a leading group of civil rights activists.

In 1961 Lafayette was part of the group from Nashville who continued the Freedom Ride to desegregate interstate transportation. The initial Freedom Riders had been beaten and arrested and their bus had been burned. As Lafayette considered his own decision to join the Freedom Ride, he talked things through with his friend and fellow student, Joe Carter, at American Baptist Theological Seminary.

"Are you prepared to die?" Carter, who had already decided to go, asked Lafayette. "There'll be no protection, we'll be on our own."

Lafayette decided to take the risk. Like other riders, he signed a will before heading to Alabama. This second wave of riders, including John Lewis and James Lawson, picked up the buses in Birmingham, Alabama. In Montgomery the riders were attacked. The police gave the Ku Klux Klan 15 minutes between the arrival of the bus and the arrival of the police to severely beat the riders. In Jackson, Mississippi, all the riders were arrested when they tried to desegregate the bus station waiting room. They spent time in the Jackson Jail, and then were sent to the notorious Mississippi penitentiary known as Parcham Farm. It was one of 27 times Lafayette ended up in jail.

After that harrowing experience, Lafayette's skills as an organizer clearly emerged. He and James Bevel left Parchman and began organizing back in Jackson, where they were earlier arrested. They went street by street through the black community trying to recruit young people as activists. Lafayette would make the case for joining, while Bevel would give reasons not to get involved—a tactic that made the idea more appealing for young people eager to try their wings. After evening training sessions, they would require the young people to come back at 6 a.m. to see how serious they really were. Lafayette and Bevel organized a series of protests with 42 young recruits who joined them in an effort to desegregate the Jackson bus terminal. Lafayette said it was the cheapest way to take action because they didn't need to buy bus tickets. They all ended up in jail, but now the young people of Jackson were mobilized for the movement.

Lafayette then went to Selma, Alabama, as an SNCC organizer. It was the heart of the so-called "Black Belt," an area controlled by the powerful White Citizens Council. Even before he and his wife moved into a local hotel, U.S. Justice Department officials were warning them to leave because of threatened violence. Lafayette stayed and studied the politics of the area and the history of lynching in that county. He then went into the small towns around Selma and into Selma's black neighborhoods trying to mobilize voter registration. When people came to the meetings Lafayette organized, he encouraged them to share their own experiences. Soon, people were releasing emotions long bottled up by fear.

When a local African-American leader who had supported their effort died, Lafayette called for a mass meeting to honor the man. Sheriff Jim Clark brought deputized white citizens to intimidate the crowd. Many of Clark's men were armed with bats that had steel rods inserted in the middle for maximum damage. First, Clark's men came into the meeting and listened to the eulogies, then they smashed cars with their bats on the way out. Lafayette knew that this violence would clarify the battle lines and challenge residents to take a stand.

On June 12, 1963, the same night Medgar Evers of the NAACP was assassinated in Mississippi, a white thug severely beat Lafayette. As he was about to lose consciousness, a neighbor came out with a shotgun. Despite the peril he faced, Lafayette pleaded for the man not to shoot the attacker. The FBI later said that the attack was part of a three-state conspiracy to murder civil rights leaders. But Lafayette did not back down. The day after the beating, still wearing his bloody shirt and with his face bruised and swollen, Lafayette went downtown. A black lawyer encouraged him to go home, but Lafayette said, "This is the symbol we need." He made himself visible in the community, shaming local leaders who had been timid to take greater risks themselves.

Lafayette continued organizing and holding mass meetings. In 1965, he was among the civil rights leaders who decided to make Selma a focus for the struggle for voting rights. It was the toughest town in Alabama, but Lafayette's organizing had laid a foundation in the African-American community. In early March, 1965, a march was launched from Selma to Montgomery, although that first march did not reach its goal. The crowd was halted at the Pettus Bridge, where police charged and beat marchers—an event later known as Bloody Sunday. Martin Luther King, Jr. came to Selma for a second march, which voluntarily stopped at the Pettus Bridge to avoid violence. A third march that same month finally reached its goal, riding on a wave of national revulsion at the violence unleashed by Southern whites. A political tide had turned. President Johnson presented what became the Voting Rights Act of 1965 to Congress between the second and third marches. With momentum from the protests, the bill passed and Johnson was able to sign it into law later that year.

In 1966, the scene shifted to Chicago, where Lafayette agreed to help the American Friends Service Committee organize for open housing and to prevent lead poisoning, a campaign called "End Slums." Lafayette also was invited by King to direct a national Poor People's Campaign, which would culminate in a march on Washington in 1968. However, during their organizing efforts, Dr. King visited Memphis and was killed in April, 1968. Stunned and grieving, Lafayette continued his work on the Washington campaign, which ended when 50,000 people set up the Resurrection City shantytown on the Mall. This campaign had failed to achieve its goal: A Bill of Economic Rights.

After the death of King and the dissolution of the Poor People's Campaign, Lafayette left his life of full-time activism to focus on his education. He eventually earned a doctorate from Harvard University with a thesis on the teaching of nonviolence in a regular college curriculum. Lafayette then worked in various schools, including an appointment as principal of Tuskegee High School in Alabama. There, the soft-spoken, nonviolent Lafayette encountered a group of teens who had moved from a tough urban setting in the North and brought gang culture with them into the South. They expected this principal would be easy prey. Instead, Lafayette cleaned up the school's culture. He didn't break up the gangs, recognizing the legitimate need of young people to be together in groups. Instead, he transformed the gangs into social clubs. He gave them tasks like taking toys to hospitalized children and cleaning up yards for elderly widows and taught them how to repair windows—so the gangs began protecting property rather than vandalizing it. He even took students on a re-enactment of the Selma-to-Montgomery march. It was one of his favorite jobs.

Lafayette returned to American Baptist Theological Seminary in Nashville as vice president in 1987 and then in 1992 was installed as president. He also became a Senior Fellow for the Center for Nonviolence and Peace Studies at the University of Rhode Island. There he taught the nonviolent principles and methods he'd hammered out in the civil rights movement.

Lafayette then shifted to Emory University where he is the Distinguished Senior Scholar in Residence, but he has never lived in an ivory tower. He continues to work with students, most recently in the Chicago schools where he is seeking to build the beloved community that King envisioned. He helps older children develop mentoring relationships with younger ones, bringing out what is best in the students. He also has engaged in international peace-making, especially in the delta region of Nigeria, where conflict flares over oil development. Lafayette works with a program that exchanges insurgents' guns for jobs. The training begins with non-violence, and then moves on to job training. Overall, this process brings some of the economic benefits from the oil companies to the local people, which is a key to ending insurgency. Lafayette trains people from the delta to become trainers themselves, which empowers the community, multiplies the impact, and spreads community transformation.

What Bernard Lafayette learned years earlier in Nashville sit-ins, Mississippi bus stations and Selma voter registration drives, he has taught to new generations facing new challenges in new settings. As he links lives around the world, the beloved community becomes more of a reality.

CHAPTER 34

César Chávez

(1927-1993)

The greatest tragedy is not to live and die, as we all must. The greatest tragedy is for a person to live and die without knowing the satisfaction of giving life for others.

—César Chávez

I joined picket lines as part of a national United Farm Workers lettuce boycott. I handed out flyers instructing consumers what to buy and what to boycott. But I never knew the spirit of this amazing man until I read his biography. He transformed fields, dirt roads, picket lines and supermarkets into sacred spaces.

DURING THE FIRST STRIKE by the farm workers in California organized by César Chávez, a commercial grower obtained a court injunction to severely limit picketing at his farm entrances. The injunction gutted a key union strength: numbers. Chávez called a meeting of the workers and told them that he had run out of ideas. As a masterful organizer, he declared that the answers to this challenge were among the people who had gathered. He needed their help. After the meeting, three women approached him hesitant to speak, not wanting to offend him. They suggested that rather than picket or demonstrate, the workers should gather at the entrances to pray. Chávez knew that this was the idea he was seeking. He set up a little shrine on the top of his beat-up station wagon, complete with a picture of Our Lady of Guadalupe, candles and flowers. Hundreds of workers came to pray, some leaving the fields during lunch. For two months the vigil lasted, growing in size day by day. Nobody was arrested, and hundreds of new farm workers signed on with the union.

Violence by growers against laborers, supported by governing authorities, has a long and tragic history. For more than a century, the industry thrived on cheap labor driven by a desperate, destitute, unorganized, fearful and generally migrant workforce. A small, quiet man utterly committed to nonviolence created a movement that revolutionized labor conditions for American agricultural workers. With a breadth and passion unmatched in labor history, he built a union from scratch, and caught America's interest and widespread support along the way.

Chávez's father had a small ranch in Arizona but lost his land during the Depression. The Chávez family joined the thousands of dispossessed families seeking work in the fields of California. As a child and teen, Chávez picked crops as his family moved from one harvest to another. He experienced discrimination against "Mexicans" by the wealthy Anglo growers and their labor contractors who controlled the jobs. He realized justice would not come unless the workers themselves organized and demanded change.

As Chávez began challenging the rules, he met a priest who introduced him to the writings of Gandhi, St. Francis of Assisi and pioneers in the labor movement. As a young man he was discovered by community organizers who got him a job with the Community Service Organization (CSO), a Latino civil rights group founded in 1947. Chávez worked for ten years on various organizing projects, especially voter registration. There he learned how to recruit, educate and mobilize people—and he overcame his shyness about speaking in groups. By 1958, Chávez was national director of the CSO, but he knew that his true vocation lay with farm workers.

In 1962, he left the CSO to accept that challenge. In three months, he traveled nearly 15,000 miles, picked peas, worked in vineyards, and met with more than 2,000 workers in the fields, along dusty roads and in their shacks. He would gather a small group together, often in a tiny home and ask if they had heard of the movement. Besides sharing the vision for a union, he listened to their ideas. His key organizing tool was a simple card he used to collect names and addresses and with a place for the worker to put down what he or she considered a just hourly wage. One worker said others always made the decision about what they deserved, but now they were being allowed to vote on what they thought. Those opinions became the groundwork for the eventual negotiations on fair contracts. But a long struggle was necessary first, something Chávez warned the workers would be brutal.

Chávez quickly replicated his efforts through simple yet effective techniques: In a group, he would ask someone to set up another meeting of a few more people in their own home so Chávez could talk to them. Numbers grew quickly and soon a union was formed, eventually known as the United Farm Workers Union. Members helped support each other and developed a community and a commitment that drew still more members into their movement. Before long they were ready to take on some of the growers, demanding to be recognized as the union for the workers and to negotiate fair contracts. The growers refused on both counts, so the union launched strikes.

A boycott became instrumental in organizing, putting pressure on growers and government agencies and dramatically expanding the power of strikes. Chávez would send workers out to key cities across the country to talk with students, churches, unions and other groups about what was happening in the fields and ask for their participation in the boycott. First there was a boycott of table grapes that lasted five years, then of lettuce, then of Gallo wine. The boycotts turned consumers into allies of the workers, mobilizing far more individuals than a strike. "The whole essence of nonviolent action is getting a lot of people involved, vast numbers doing little things"—like refusing to eat grapes, Chávez argued. The boycotts also brought volunteers, as students arrived to help the movement.

From childhood, Chávez was a spiritual person with values that led directly to his profound commitment to nonviolence. For Chávez, truth, nonviolence and God were all one. "Nonviolence also has one big demand—the need to be creative, to develop strategy," he said. "Gandhi described it as moral *jujitsu*. Always hit the opposition off balance but keep your principles."

As the violence in their first major grape campaign heated up, some leaders of the Farm Workers began talking about striking back with violent force. This internal fermentation prompted Chávez's first fast. Drawing on the deep Mexican-Christian spirituality of penance through self-sacrifice, Chávez sought clarity of commitment through his own fasting. Like Gandhi, Chávez's first fast was directed toward his followers, not toward his opponents in the struggle. That first effort was effective in renewing the union's commitment to nonviolence. Over the years, Chávez continued to use fasts as a method for his own discernment about a situation. He also used fasts as an organizing tool to help his followers become more focused and to maintain their own commitment to self-sacrifice. There were many twists and turns in the history of the movement, many victories and many setbacks. Eventually, the United Farm Workers Union was recognized as the major force representing agricultural workers across the country.

Since Chávez died in 1993, his life and legacy have been honored around the world. His favorite jacket now hangs in the Smithsonian. He received a posthumous Presidential Medal of Freedom. But Chávez's true influence can be seen in fields far beyond the regions where this organizer set foot. The United Farm Workers Union website, as of 2011, is one of those signs that his work continues. It contains news and other helpful materials published in English, Spanish—and Thai.

CHAPTER 35

Adolfo Pérez Esquivel

(b. 1931)

We try to act in truth. This is what gives our movement its security: the truth—respect for the human person. Respect for the human person generates constancy and steadfastness. And constancy and steadfastness generate an attack on evil and the possibility of altering the structures of injustice.

—Adolfo Pérez Esquivel

I don't think I've ever come across another peace activist who challenges me to reach deeper into my core spirituality. Adolfo Pérez Esquivel's writings from prison that appear in Christ in a Poncho still move me. I didn't realize how profoundly his voice had influenced me until I began writing a book, A Peacemaker's Journal, filled with quotes for people to reflect on while working toward peace. As I looked over my draft, I realized the journal was far too heavy with quotes from Pérez Esquivel. He expressed so many truths so eloquently that my own spirituality in peacemaking was transformed.

FOR TWO DAYS IN "the pipe," a solitary cell in an Argentine prison, Adolfo Pérez Esquivel was in complete darkness. On the third day guards came in, and light flooded into the cell. Pérez Esquivel saw graffiti all over the walls, some prayers, some insults. What struck him the most was a huge finger-painted bloodstain that said, "God doesn't kill." Pérez Esquivel later wrote that this bloody message was "engraved somewhere on my insides."

Adolfo Pérez Esquivel was an architect and a sculptor. He taught for 25 years at various levels of the educational system, and then his passion for justice and peace took him on a different path. In 1974, he plunged into full-time coordination of the burgeoning nonviolent movements for justice across Latin America. A loose network had been organized at a conference in 1968, but by 1974 the participants knew they needed a more substantive organization. Pérez Esquivel was appointed Secretary-General of the group *Servicio Paz y Justicia* (Service for Peace and Justice).

In that leadership capacity, he traveled throughout Latin America connecting groups that had previously been isolated from one another. There were mothers of people who had "disappeared" in the so-called "dirty war" in Pérez Esquivel's home country, Argentina. There were tin miners in Bolivia and peasant farmers in Ecuador, Paraguay, Brazil and Honduras. He liked to talk about a battle between an elephant and ants: "True, the elephant is stronger. But the ants...well, there are more of us."

As he traveled to bring the "ants" together, Pérez Esquivel taught about nonviolence, which he saw as the only option to bring deep change. He taught, "We know too that one evil cannot be cured by another. Evils don't cancel each other out. They total up." So the movement for transforming Latin America would have to be based on love and truth. He told stories of other movements, helping people to draw strength and insight from each other's struggles. "We try to bring different groups into contact with one another— to set up a tradeoff of experiences and to get them to support one another." Once they were connected, they could be organized for collective advocacy about some of the root issues plaguing all the poor of Latin America. As Pérez Esquivel puts it, "Once we've laid the foundations, the next thing is to witness—to denounce prophetically the situations of injustice in which peasants, workers, and religious groups have to live." Through *Sevicio Paz y Justicia* craft collectives were organized to provide a sustainable economic base for many of the movements. He also published a magazine called *Paz y Justicia* that shared people's stories, encouraging and educating readers.

In his native Argentina, Pérez Esquivel was immersed in the struggles for peace and human rights. In 1976, the nation's democratic government was overthrown by a military coup, plunging the country into a dark period that eventually turned into the "dirty war." Most of the war was waged by military and police kidnapping people, holding them in prison, often without anyone knowing where they were. The "disappearances" mounted, and it was eventually revealed that some 30,000 people had been murdered. Pérez Esquivel said, "Of course, all 30,000 were not killed at once. They disappeared one or two at a time. Though the number of victims rose to five, ten, one hundred, there was no cry of protest from society. And that is why 30,000 people died."

But Pérez Esquivel and some bold women did raise a protest. Mothers and other relatives of the "disappeared" began silently marching once a week in the Plaza de Mayo in downtown Buenos Aires. They were ignored or ridiculed at first, then the military began repressing them. Some of the women were killed. Pérez Esquivel worked closely with the women as a consultant, teacher and guide. He challenged them to think deeply about the root issues behind the violence that had devastated their families. "Your reflection in the course of this meeting has led you from the purely spontaneous and emotional actions you might undertake to an awareness that there are political and social problems to be faced," he said.

In 1977, Pérez Esquivel was arrested and held in prison for fourteen months though he was never charged with any offense. At times he was in solitary confinement. He was tortured severely including by electric shock. He was initially one of the "disappeared" himself, but international furor over his disappearance probably kept him alive. Amnesty International and U.S. President Jimmy Carter appealed for his release. As political pressure built outside the prison, spiritual discipline kept him alive through the brutal captivity and seemingly endless torture. "In prison, I gained the strength to survive under extreme conditions, the strength to resist," he wrote. "That strength is mental and spiritual strength. In prison, one is denied physical freedom. But the mind is free. The mind cannot be imprisoned."

In 1980, Adolfo Pérez Esquivel was awarded the Nobel Peace Prize. Outside of Latin America, very few people had heard of him. But people had heard of the nonviolent movements he had connected and strengthened and to which he had given visibility. In accepting the prize Pérez Esquivel continued to give visibility to those groups: "I accept this prize in the name of Latin America and its workers, in the name of its *campesinos* and its priests who are working diligently for the peace and rights of all." But even after winning the Nobel Peace Prize he was the target of death threats and harassment. The Argentine military rulers took his award as an insult, and the national press gave no notice to his international recognition. Pérez Esquivel said, "Here we always live in uncertainty, but I cannot let myself be paralyzed by it or I would not do anything." When the military dictatorship in Argentina collapsed in 1983, Pérez Esquivel continued his work for human rights across Latin America.

He was a co-founder of both the Permanent Assembly for Human Rights and the Ecumenical Movement for Human Rights. These organizations linked human rights activists with groups for coordinated efforts. Since the 1970s, they participated in international efforts to create a more effective United Nations Human Rights Council, which finally was established in 2006.

Pérez Esquivel's life and voice weaves together a deep Christian spirituality that resonates in Latin America with the pragmatic teaching of nonviolent action. He writes: "In nonviolent combat what we do is just exactly what nice players aren't supposed to do. We refuse to play by one of the rules the system tries to foist on us: the rule that says you have to counter violence with violence. If your opponents can get you to swallow that idea, then they can unleash still greater violence on you. The essential thing in nonviolent combat is for us to render these tactics inoperative by refusing to play by the rules and by imposing our own conditions instead."

Through such an approach, a tortured prisoner held in solitary confinement and mothers grieving their lost children were together responsible for the collapse of a powerful military dictatorship. Adolfo Pérez Esquivel has enabled many "ants" to bring down Latin American "elephants".

CHAPTER 36

Ken Sehested

(b. 1951)

There are a lot more of us out there than anybody knows, and we need to find more ways to stay connected, to instruct and encourage each other, sometimes to argue with each other, because it's not just the world that refuses to listen—sometimes our churches refuse to listen as well.

—Ken Sehested

Ken is the longtime friend who wrote a preface about me for the opening pages of this book, just before it was published. Ken and I have shared board meetings, negotiations with insurgent leaders, peace conferences and even a bed when our work demands we travel to spots in the world with meager resources. What I love most about him is his poet's soul. He can do all the other stuff—organizing, speaking, writing, protesting—very well. But his poetry moves my heart. Each Christmas, I wait to read his newest way of retelling an old story through his Advent/Christmas poem, and every year I am stunned by the fresh light that breaks forth.

IN 1990, THE INVASION of Kuwait by Iraq caught most of the peace movement off guard—and so did the U.S. military response.

Even though it took months to unfold, the U.S. attack on Iraq to remove the Iraqi army from Kuwait took place with little public action from the peace community. One exception was a network of Baptists across the United States who engaged in fasts to protest the rush to war. Then the Baptists had a large gathering in Washington, D.C. to pray for peace prior to the Congressional authorization for war. As a group, Baptists have not been known for their peace witness in the United States, but Ken Sehested has been a key figure in organizing this unlikely group of religious peacemakers.

Sehested was a Southern Baptist in the tradition of Clarence Jordan and Will Campbell, people who took Jesus seriously about loving enemies and hungering and thirsting for justice. In 1983 some Southern Baptists and American Baptists, branches of Baptists who had split in the 19th Century over the issue of slavery, traveled together to the Soviet Union. They visited Soviet Baptists and made a combined witness against the Cold War and nuclear arms race. In 1984, following the joint trip, some of these Baptist peacemakers decided to form a grassroots peace group cutting across all the streams of the Baptist tradition. Ken Sehested offered to give up his job as editor of a journal about hunger to work full-time organizing the new peace network, including an offer to raise the funds to support his new work.

Sehested had heard about pockets of Baptist peacemakers in various places. He traveled around the U.S. meeting those groups and connecting them to each other. He heard about similar groups in Canada, Puerto Rico and Mexico. Sehested liked to say, "There are a lot more of us out there than anybody knows, and we need to find more ways to stay connected, to instruct and encourage each other, sometimes to argue with each other, because it's not just the world that refuses to listen—sometimes our churches refuse to listen as well." Soon the Baptist Peace Fellowship of North America (BPFNA) was born to empower Baptists for the work of making peace and doing justice.

Through his speaking, writing and countless conversations, Sehested pulled the fellowship together. Some existing groups quickly joined together with their regional networks. Sehested encouraged Baptist activists who were feeling isolated to put out the call to find kindred spirits for specific peace projects. The journal entitled *The Baptist Peacemaker* became the communication link through which Sehested could keep the vision fresh and through which the stories of Baptist peace activists could be told, not only in North America, but also around the world.

He attended various national gatherings, setting up a BPFNA display, and met people who told him they never knew there were other Baptists passionate about peace. "Social change does not happen in general; it always occurs in particular," Sehested said. The implication of this was: "Particular change means change within the context of particular institutions, which means, if we're to be effective in our work, we must tend to the details of particular institutions and communicate within the framework of particular cultures." So he worked within Baptist bodies, some of which differed widely in their theological approaches. Peace issues began to appear on the agendas of more Baptist conventions and unions; presented and pressed onto those agendas by the growing grassroots network Sehested was organizing.

Sehested and the BPFNA also brought issues of justice for women into the lives of Baptist groups. When Nicaraguan Baptists and Cuban Baptists ordained their first women pastors, the BPFNA organized delegations of North American ordained women to attend the ceremonies.

Sehested led the way in forging projects that would shape the movement. Banners were made so that the Baptist presence became visible in peace marches in New York and Washington, D.C. In more than a century of mission work, Baptists had spread around the world. So Sehested urged the fellowship to connect along these existing lines of relationship—with a new message about peace. Friendship Tours were organized to the Soviet Union, to South Africa, to Liberia, to El Salvador and Nicaragua, to the Middle East, to Burma and to striking coal miners in southwest Virginia as well. Baptist peacemakers were discovered at key points of leadership in mediation efforts to end civil wars and in nonviolent struggles for political and social change. This peace work was even carried into the streets of U.S. cities in support of one of the BPFNA members, Carl Upchurch, who you will read about in the Mediators section.

Sehested then developed the idea for an international Baptist peace conference that would connect grassroots activists and official denominational leaders. The first conference was held in Sweden in 1988 with a focus on East-West relationships. The second was held in Nicaragua in 1992 with a focus on conflicts in the "Two-Thirds World." The phrase refers to countries that most people call the Third World, but cleverly emphasizes that these nations actually comprise the majority, roughly two-thirds, of the world's population. Further conferences were held in Thailand in 1996, Australia in 2000 and Italy in 2009. These global connections had tangible results. As Baptists worked together in new ways, they sparked a host of fresh initiatives ranging from mediation in northeast India and Burma to nonviolence training in many other parts of the world.

A key to Sehested's effectiveness was his combination of vision, organizational skills, and personal commitment to action. He could articulate a particularly Baptist vision for peacemaking, rooted in the history of Baptist passions for liberty and human rights. He got to know people and remembered their special skills, interests and resources so that he could call on them at just the right moment.

Sehested also put himself on the line. He prayed at the Nevada nuclear test site, demonstrated in the streets, and was a nonviolent escort to Palestinian children stoned by Israeli settlers as the children tried to go to school. He traveled to Cuba when such visits by U.S. citizens were restricted. Later, when he received a peace award from American Baptists, he publicly sent the cash award to support Cuban Baptist peacemakers—an intentional violation of the U.S. embargo against Cuba. Sehested traveled to Nagaland in northeast India to help initiate a peace process seeking to end a war started in the 1950s. He taught Karen refugees in camps along the Thai-Burma border. Prior to the 2003 U.S. invasion of Iraq, he was with the Christian Peacemaker Teams (CPT) in Baghdad calling for a halt in the drive to war.

During the build-up to the first Gulf War in 1990 and 1991, as the peace movement stalled, Sehested quickly mobilized the network of Baptists throughout North America to initiate a fast for peace at least one day each week. He took the lead with a bread-and-water fast for the duration of the conflict. His personal example stirred others to action and to share the story.

In 2002 Sehested stepped down from directing the BPFNA. He and his wife, Nancy Hastings Sehested, started the Circle of Mercy Church in Asheville, NC. He continued writing both prose and poetry along with his ongoing involvement in direct action for peace.

Through connections with religious peace fellowships, Sehested has gotten to know Rabia Harris, director of the Muslim Peace Fellowship (MPT). Following the terrorist attacks on September 11, 2001, the BPFNA and MPT carried out a number of joint projects, including conflict transformation training. Sehested and Harris co-edited *Peace Primer: Quotes from Christian and Islamic Scripture and Tradition*, a resource that has circled the world.

Other religious groups have well-known peace networks, including *Pax Christi* among Catholics, the American Friends Service Committee among Quakers and the Fellowship of Engaged Buddhists. Through his efforts, Sehested proved that even religious groups that aren't known for peacemaking can make a big difference in the world. He likes to say, "What more valuable task could be done than organizing a largely unorganized constituency?" Peace is endorsed in every major religion, but it takes an organizer to make those religious values tangible in a world of conflict. If Baptist peacemakers can be organized, any religious tradition can be.

But Sehested's work isn't finished and his vision is larger than what we see today. He puts forward this challenge: "Can you imagine this: One day, when the general public hears the word Baptist, they will think immediately of Gospel-inspired justice and peace work? Instead of associating the name with the follies of TV evangelists, wouldn't it be nice if they thought: Oh, those are the folks who care for the poor . . . who resist racial discrimination . . . who speak out against gun-barrel diplomacy . . . who care for the environment? Imagine that!"

CHAPTER 37

Lucius Walker
(1930-2010)

The only way social progress has been made in our country— and this is probably true in other countries—is that people challenge injustice and seek to change unjust and repressive laws...So I think that my Christian responsibility is to break unjust laws—such as the U.S. blockade against Cuba—and to call our country into an accountability for a higher level of morality.

—Lucius Walker

"Dan, can you come to San Diego?" Lucius Walker invited me to join in an action at the U.S.-Mexico border crossing to take medical and educational supplies to Cuba, which was in violation of the U.S. embargo. Just a few days before, customs officials had seized computers headed for use in church-related health clinics. So I traveled to that spot along the border and led a worship service. Then I took my first trip to Mexico, walking with an armload of artificial limbs for people in Cuba. Lucius exhibited a passion and long-term staying power that few possess.

IT WAS AUGUST 2, 1988. A ferry was carrying an educational delegation from the United States across the Rio Escondido on the Atlantic Coast of Nicaragua. Suddenly machine gun fire erupted from the forest-covered bank and raked the boat with deadly fire. Two Nicaraguans were killed. Among the 29 people wounded was the Rev. Lucius Walker from New York City. He was the leader of the delegation, the Executive Director of the Interreligious Foundation for Community Organization (IFCO) that had sponsored the trip. As he was recovering from his wounds, Walker came up with a way to strike back, consistent with his philosophy of non-violent engagement in struggles for justice.

Walker first organized the IFCO in 1967 with a broad agenda of assisting the poor in areas including education, employment, economic development, housing, health care and voter registration. But Walker soon enlarged the group's focus from local concerns to national and international issues ranging from Native American rights to Puerto Rican self-determination. That global expansion eventually led to the Nicaragua study tour that was attacked by the Contra insurgents, a group funded by the U.S. government.

Walker's response to the attack was Pastors for Peace caravans, a new effort encouraging individuals, churches and community groups across the U.S. to aid people in Nicaragua suffering from the Contra campaign. He organized an actual caravan of trucks and buses packed with humanitarian aid. Eighteen vehicles carrying 70 tons of supplies made the first journey. In addition to the supplies, volunteers left the vehicles to help communities in Nicaragua. Shortly after the first caravan arrived, Hurricane Joan devastated Nicaragua's Atlantic Coast. Walker quickly organized another caravan, this time with 25 trucks taking 200 tons of relief supplies. As the caravan made its way south, two trucks were dropped off in El Salvador to provide some relief in war-stricken areas. The real benefit of Walker's idea was that countless Americans became involved in the hands-on effort to collect and transport supplies to Nicaraguans, whose stories they heard and carried back to the U.S. Walker fueled the effort by bringing key figures from Central America to the U.S. to speak at rallies in churches.

Another long-standing issue came to the forefront of the IFCO's attention. The fall of the Soviet Union had a crushing impact on Cuba—Cubans lost some of the buffering that protected them from the harsh impact of the U.S. embargo. Walker led a fact-finding delegation to Cuba and met with various Cuban church leaders to plan solidarity efforts. The Pastors for Peace model quickly came to mind, and the U.S. / Cuba Friendshipment caravan was organized. Through direct people-to-people sharing through religious communities, supplies would be brought to Cuba in violation of the embargo. The purpose was two-fold: To provide substantive assistance; but also to highlight the suffering caused by the embargo. "We refuse to be complicit with a policy of death and starvation," Walker said. 'We need to stop putting a pretty face on this brutal blockade—to admit that Cuban children are being denied access to lifesaving medicines because of our government's policies, and to stop punishing those innocent children."

In November 1992, 100 volunteers brought 15 tons of supplies—powdered milk, medicines, Bibles, bicycles and school materials—to the U.S.-Mexico border for shipment to Cuba. U.S. officials blocked their way, and CNN caught border agents assaulting a Catholic priest carrying Bibles for Cuba. The quick public response to these heavy-handed government actions prompted officials to allow the caravan to cross the border. But that was not the last confrontation.

Walker really wanted to challenge the blockade, so the group decided not to apply for an export license. Walker argued that such a license allowed the U.S. government too much control, in effect acknowledging the blockade. "We choose instead to respond to a higher authority," Walker said. "What the U.S. government calls 'trading with the enemy,' we regard as taking a cup of cold water to a neighbor in need."

The next challenge took place in Laredo, Texas, during the summer of 1993. U.S. Treasury officials seized a yellow school bus, claiming that Castro could use it as a military vehicle. The 13 "caravanistas" on the school bus refused to get off and began a fast until it was released. For 23 days the bus sat in the Texas heat. Walker called upon the extensive network the IFCO had built up through the years of the Pastors for Peace caravans, and Washington was inundated with calls about "the little yellow school bus." Demonstrations were held in 20 cities, and a solidarity fast was held in Havana in front of the U.S. Interests Section. The bus was finally released. It was taken across the border with the rest of the caravan, eventually making it to Cuba where it has been serving the needs of the Martin Luther King Center in Havana ever since.

The sixth caravan to Cuba was stopped at the border crossing in San Diego. Customs officials seized four hundred computers, even though all of the computers were obsolete by U.S. standards. The computers were destined for a United Nations-sponsored string of rural health clinics in a project requested by the Cuban Council of Churches. Again, Walker mobilized the IFCO/Pastors for Peace network, and many supporters came to the border crossing with newly donated computers. Again, the computers were seized, though medical supplies were allowed through. Walker and four others began a "Fast for Life" at the border crossing. After a few weeks they moved the fast to Washington, D.C. across from the U.S. Capitol. Various American church groups got involved in lobbying and international organizations from Europe, Africa and Latin America eventually pledged to send 1,400 computers to Cuba in response to the fast. Finally, the U.S. Treasury agreed to turn the seized computers over to the United Methodist Church for delivery to the Cuban health clinics. Afterward Walker said, "Perhaps our government came to understand the depth and seriousness of our commitment, and decided not to engage us in another long struggle."

As of this writing, 20 Friendshipments have been made to Cuba delivering more than 2,000 tons of aid. Besides "aid caravans" to Nicaragua and El Salvador, similar caravans have traveled to Chiapas, Mexico, and to Haiti. Walker used his vision and organizing skills not only to move supplies around the world, but also to connect lives. As an African-American, he was especially committed to connecting American minorities with marginalized communities in other parts of the world, recognizing that struggles for peace and economic justice are forces that must circle the globe.

While drafting this book, I enjoyed talking with my old friend again. Sadly, he did not see the final publication. At age 80, Walker died of a heart attack at his New Jersey home in the autumn of 2010.

CHAPTER 38

Teresita "Ging" Quintos-Deles

(b. 1948)

It was the task of the citizens' peace movement to pick up the pieces and continue and steer the peace process.

—Teresita "Ging" Quintos-Deles

As I worked with Asian-Pacific leaders to plan a conference on conflict resolution, Filipino members of our planning team insisted that we call on "Ging," the popular nickname for Teresita Quintos-Deles. We invited her to address a plenary session and she was wonderful. For all of her strength and determination, what I remember is her smile. She is beaming in all the photos I've seen of that event. None of the struggles she has weathered has quenched her delight in life. That joy is potent, continuing to win out over the heaviest of oppression.

THE PEACE TALKS BETWEEN the Philippine government and the New People's Army had broken down. So local people took matters into their own hands. In the village of Hungduan, townspeople negotiated with insurgents and secured their agreement to pull back from their community. Immediately after that, the townspeople organized to prevent the army from setting up their own base in Hungduan. They created a protected area, a space sheltered by the expressed will of the grassroots residents to be free from the violence of the conflict that was so destructive around them. This was one of Teresita Quintos-Deles's local projects—to move grassroots communities into a central role in the peace processes in the Philippines.

Since the People Power movement brought down the Macros dictatorship in 1986, Ging has been a leading organizer to keep the peace process alive. She co-founded and led the Coalition for Peace (CfP), the first non-governmental alliance to seek an end to ongoing conflicts in the Philippines, which began with a nearly twenty year war involving the Communist insurgency by the New People's Army. When formal talks stalled, Quintos-Deles launched an effort to reopen the process through involvement of a third-party: the CfP, a people-based organization.

At first, these efforts were rebuffed by warring parties with questions: "Who are you? How many are you?" In response, the CfP shifted its focus toward building a national constituency for peace. Both the government and rebels claimed to speak for the people of the region—there was no other organized voice to challenge those claims. Quintos-Deles and the CfP engaged in marches, educational programs and other efforts to help people understand the root causes of the conflict and mobilize their own responses. One of their innovative responses was called a People's Christmas Cease-Fire, unilaterally declared by a network of groups that the CfP organized. They couldn't enforce a cease-fire, but they could warn both sides about violating the will of the people for this brief oasis from conflict. . Quintos-Deles said, "Healing and reconciliation has to happen on the ground. To make this possible, people have to own the peace process through their participation in it."

The Christmas Cease-Fire sparked people's imaginations, and soon that idea grew into creating peace zones, like the effort in Hungduan. Many communities took up this idea. As Quintos-Deles worked on organizing the local communities, she noticed that to succeed in confronting armed groups, a community needed a strong internal structure, perhaps an indigenous structure, a church or another sturdy social network. She organized gatherings so community leaders could compare experiences and get ideas on what worked best. Soon, local circles were part of a national movement.

As the peace movement grew there was need for more coordination. In 1990, Quintos-Deles became Executive Director of the Gaston Z. Ortigas Peace Institute, which was formed as a secretariat for the CfP. Using this flexible new structure, they soon were encouraging more citizens' initiatives—and were cooperating with other coalitions in the Philippines. A key to success in this work, Quintos-Deles says, is not worrying about organizational names or credit—but continuing to bring more people together in effective ways. "We have different organizations for different purposes," she says. "We will invent more and more of such organizations to bring in more and more citizens who may not feel comfortable with certain groups."

In 2001, Quintos-Deles left the non-governmental side of the struggle to take a government position. She was asked to become Lead Convener of the National Anti-Poverty Commission. Two years later, she became the first woman to be directly engaged in the governmental side of negotiations when she was appointed the Presidential Advisor on the Peace Process. She brought her non-military, pro-victims awareness to the highest level of the government. She challenged generals who engaged in excessive force in their military campaigns, even prompting apologies. She said, "Security policy could not be left to the military—and to the men—to decide. Civilian perspectives—and women's perspectives, in particular, had to be put on the table in deciding the issues of war and peace." Quintos-Deles resigned her position in 2005 in protest over alleged corruption in President Gloria Arroyo's re-election campaign.

Quintos-Deles is now respected as a leading activist for peace and women's issues across much of Asia. She has been a leader in various international gatherings. She has served on the United Nations Committee on the Elimination of Discrimination Against Women.

"Peace is a universal aspiration," she says. "Unfortunately, there is an enormous distance between everybody's dream of peace and the realities of war and violence that threaten people's lives." The struggle is long, she says, and people must organize for enduring action. "We can set the foundation (for peace) in our lifetime and hope that one day our stake in the peace process will take hold. Hope is the lifeblood of peace advocacy."

Mayerly Sánchez
(b. 1984)

Peace begins with yourself, with the way you treat your family, your friends, your communities, your country—but it does not stop there. Peace that begins in the hearts of children can cover the whole world.

—Mayerly Sánchez

During the past 20 years or so, Colombia has been synonymous with violence. For many of us, it has seemed a hopeless place dominated by drug traffickers, right-wing paramilitary groups and corrupt politicians. Add U.S. support with a lot of weaponry and you have the makings of a tragic mess. A biblical prophet spoke of a child leading the people, and in Colombia, children have been among the most courageous of visionaries. They aren't just "the future"—they are the present. Mayerly Sánchez and her friends stunned me with their youthful hope.

IN 1996, GANG MEMBERS in Soacha, a suburban slum of Bogotá, stabbed a 15-year old boy to death. The murder nearly went unnoticed in Colombia, a country with the highest murder rate in the Western Hemisphere where as many as 30,000 people are killed each year. But, one person noticed—the boy's friend, 12-year-old Mayerly Sánchez. She turned her grief into a determination to work for peace.

Sánchez began with a children's peace club. She was a sponsored child under World Vision International, a Christian relief and development agency, and was able to draw on World Vision support. Soon, she gathered a small group of children in a local park beginning with "conversation contests" in which players were disqualified for using insults. They organized soccer games, inviting gang members to join. They put on plays about peace, first for families, and later for entire communities. The club grew, and in 1996, Sánchez was invited to a national UNICEF workshop for child leaders to share peace-building ideas. At that meeting the *Movimiento de los Niños por La Paz* (Children's Movement for Peace) was launched.

The first project was massive: to achieve a nationwide vote by children between 7 and 18 years of age to express their hopes for the future of their nation. This children's mandate was an idea carried out first in Mozambique and then in Ecuador. With help from UNICEF, World Vision, the Red Cross and other organizations, Sánchez and her young colleagues led a national campaign, speaking to children and organizing the vote through churches and schools. The children spoke eloquently about their experiences with violence. The child leaders received death threats, but as Sánchez said, "They can kill some of us, but they can't kill us all." Eventually both the government and guerilla forces pledged not to disrupt the national children's vote. On October 25, 1996, 2.7 million children startled the world by expressing their right to peace and an end to violence in what became known as the Children's Peace and Rights Mandate.

The following year, the Mandate was put to the general population, and 10 million Colombians voted in support of the vision lifted up by the children. Spurred by this groundswell, Colombians elected a president with a peace platform who began peace talks with Colombian guerillas. Although those talks have been on-again, off-again efforts, the peace movement has changed Colombian politics by mobilizing people who had been intimidated by the army, the paramilitaries, the guerillas and the drug gangs. Children forced peace to the top of the political agenda in this violence-plagued nation.

The Children's Movement for Peace has grown to more than 100,000 children with 400 different organizations participating. Sánchez trains small groups of children to be leaders, then each of these children set up their own groups to train both families and communities in the skills of nonviolent action. One 15-year old child reported, "Mayerly taught us that peace needs to be practiced," so it is in the interactions with friends, with neighborhood gangs, with kids at school and in the family that these skills must be honed.

For Sánchez, this is how a culture of peace is shaped. "In our families, which is where we begin, a culture of peace is beginning to be generated—then on the street where we live, then in the neighborhood, and from there it can spread nationally." The Movement calls for peace zones around schools and is taking conflict-resolution programs into schools—realizing that children learn these principles best from other children.

The Children's Movement for Peace is also aimed at pragmatic change in public policy. Colombia's largest employers are armed forces. Children are often are recruited, sometimes forcibly, into the military, guerilla groups or drug militias. Advocacy by the Movement convinced the government to halt recruitment of boys under 18 for military duty.

In 1998 the Children's Movement for Peace was nominated for the Nobel Peace Prize, the first time in history that children had received such an honor. They have received three subsequent nominations. Though they were not selected for the prize, the nomination brought important international exposure. Sanchez and other youth leaders were invited to a meeting at The Hague in the Netherlands to highlight the plight of the children in Colombia. These Colombian children have become role models for children around the world.

Sánchez, now into her 20s, has earned a college degree and continues to participate with the Children's Movement for Peace, teaching and leading workshops. But, the group's goal is to fill leadership positions with teens. At this time, Sánchez is employed by World Vision and the Colombian government on a project to educate children about the dangers of land mines. She supports her family, following the death of her father by a hit-and-run driver. She is one of the most important visionaries pursuing peace in Colombia, expressing what she envisions in words so simple that any child can understand: "We define peace in four words: love, acceptance, forgiveness, and work."

PART 7
Mediators
Midwives of Peace

WHEN A PEACE AGREEMENT is finally sealed, the good news is splashed across front pages, television networks and websites. Political leaders celebrate as they take credit for the success, their faces beaming in the media spotlight. Far behind them, by choice, stands the mediator—usually a figure who intentionally moves into the background after a great deal of hard work. These are the midwives of peace.

Mediators work in so many forms today that levels of international mediation now are categorized. Track One mediation is the domain of presidents and prime ministers, generals and ambassadors, often working with retired heads of state. The United Nations and transnational government-related organizations frequently are involved. Dag Hammarskjöld of Sweden became the second Secretary General of the United Nations in 1953. The U.N. was still a young organization, seeking ways to define itself in the era following World War II. Hammarskjöld dedicated his office to mediation, setting a high standard for his successors. He mediated in conflicts between Israel and the Arab states, particularly during the Suez Crisis of 1956. He mediated between China and the United States to secure the release of prisoners of war from the Korean conflict. Hammarskjöld was killed September 11, 1961, when his plane crashed on a mediation mission in the Congo.

Track Two mediation is undertaken by nongovernmental actors—individuals, teams and organizations. These efforts have dramatically increased in recent decades thanks to growing expertise and widespread training in conflict resolution. Nongovernmental organizations (NGOs) have become key players, often trusted in situations where politicians are viewed with suspicion. Mediators in NGOs can open back channels and help warring parties explore new possibilities for solutions outside the glare of media.

Mediators may come from outside the conflict zone. Some religious and academic institutions have trained staff and ongoing programs that provide neutral perspectives in conflicts. These institutions also may have access to financial resources to carry out a peace process—a critical need in many poor countries. Other mediators may come from inside countries and ethnic groups that are fighting, but can be effective if they are trusted for their personal credibility. These inside mediators have a vested interest in achieving a solution, they know the context intimately and they may be able to rely on crucial relationships with leaders from the warring sides. Often, these inside mediators are religious leaders, respected for their compassion and integrity, or traditional elders, respected for their wisdom and their accountability to their people. Sometimes teams inside a conflict invite outside mediators to join them, drawing on both internal and external strengths.

One of the earliest Track Two initiatives was the "Peace Ship" during World War I. A number of European feminists lead by the Hungarian pacifist Rosika Schwimmer tried to create a traveling conference to explore common ground for a peace agreement between the belligerents. The European powers were stuck in trench warfare that was grinding up a generation of young men, so it seemed to Schwimmer and other pacifists that citizen "peace ambassadors" might offer an alternative to the carnage. The women's delegation came to the U.S. seeking support and met with the American industrialist Henry Ford, who agreed to charter an old steam ship for the group. A cluster of religious leaders, journalists and others interested in peace joined Ford and the feminists. In 1915, the group sailed on the "Peace Ship" to various European neutral ports including Copenhagen and Stockholm to hold consultations. Eventually they drafted a platform for peace, but they were met with disdain by all the warring governments as well as by the United States, which was not yet engaged in the war. The conglomeration of peace mediators also became notorious for their own internal wrangling, to the delight of critics. The initiative collapsed, but their work found new life when their ideas were reflected in President Wilson's Fourteen Points, his manifesto in early 1918 outlining U.S. goals in World War I. His list included a commitment to transparent peace treaties that would not be entangled with private deals on the side.

The conflict between Israel and the Palestinians has seen no end of Track One diplomacy. The way to peace in the Middle East is littered with the wreckage of U.S. initiatives, efforts by various clusters of nations, "roadmaps" and U.N. resolutions. The only process that achieved an agreement between Israel and the Palestinians was a Track Two initiative facilitated by a Norwegian educational NGO. At a time when open formal talks between the government of Israel and the Palestinian Liberation Organization (PLO) would have been too politically risky for either side, members of a research team from the Norwegian Institute of Applied Science approached key figures on both sides with an invitation to meet informally in Norway. In a modest private home in Oslo while a toddler from the host family played at their feet, the Palestinian and Israeli representatives agreed to the framework of a peace accord. That agreement, which allowed the PLO to take control over the West Bank and Gaza as a legitimate governing body, was sealed by a famous handshake on the White House lawn. President Clinton, Prime Minister Yitzak Rabin and Chairman Yasir Arafat were up front. Quietly sitting in the crowd were the Norwegian educators who had made it all possible.

Sometimes governments and diplomats are bypassed altogether by direct people-to-people contacts across lines of conflict—a form of grassroots, Track Two mediation. These occasions may come at joint conferences, friendship tours, city-to-city exchanges, music concerts or athletic events. Through direct exchanges, fears can be expressed, misperceptions cleared up, and hopes shared. Often people find their own reflection in the face of the enemy and hear their own hearts through the voices from the other side.

During the Cold War there were many such encounters between citizens in the East and those in the West. One of the simplest and most eloquent examples of people-to-people mediation was conducted by a 10-year old schoolgirl. In 1982, the Cold War between the United States and the Soviet Union had increased to a frightening intensity. Samantha Smith—a schoolgirl from the small town of Manchester, Maine—asked her mother if she would write to Soviet Premier Yuri Andropov and ask if the Soviet Union intended to start a war. Her mother challenged her to write the letter, so Samantha did. Andropov received the letter and invited Samantha to visit the Soviet Union, meet with Russian people and see that they did not desire a war. Samantha Smith's trip to the Soviet Union received a lot of media coverage. She especially connected with Russian children and became an international advocate for peace, traveling to many countries urging an end to the Cold War. Samantha and her father were killed in a plane crash while returning home from a peace mission, but her efforts rank among the most poignant people-to-people efforts and one of the most effective in lowering fears. Such grassroots mediation helped to provide a political opening between President Reagan and Premier Gorbachev that brought an end to the Cold War.

Northern Ireland reached a peace accord after multiple efforts were put forth over many years—and a key ingredient proved to be long-term grassroots mediation by a number of religious groups in the region. Three communities were particularly noteworthy for their reconciliation work before and after the peace accord. All were ecumenical communities, but each came out of one of the different major religious traditions in the conflict:

The Corrymeela Community was started by Ray Davey, a Presbyterian minister; The Christian Renewal Centre was started by Irish Anglicans; The Columbanus Community of Reconciliation was started by Catholics under the leadership of the Jesuit priest Michael Hurley. These communities were based in different parts of Northern Ireland, but all of them practiced reconciliation within their own circles. Together, they provided safe places for others involved in the conflict to meet. Their witness through years of violence helped others coalesce around them and build a broader constituency for peace.

Sometimes the pain and bitterness in a conflict is just too great for the warring parties to overcome by themselves. Mediators provide the encouragement needed to keep forging ahead. They believe so firmly in a peaceful future that, at times when hope is dim, they generate a vital confidence that peace is still possible. In the end, though, most mediators are like midwives who stand back and allow the beaming parents to bask in the glow of their new birth.

Adam Curle
(1916-2006)

**What's peace?...It recognizes
one humanity in which
all lives are precious and
worthy to be loved and given
help towards fulfillment.**

—Adam Curle

*As a Baptist peacemaker working
both for Baptist mission agencies
and grassroots organizations, I
am inspired and my own work is shaped by the historic
peace churches, especially Quakers and Mennonites. I
never met Quaker scholar and activist, Adam Curle, but
he was a forerunner in international mediation work and
blazed the trail many of us are following to this day.*

IN 1970 THE NIGERIAN army overwhelmed that of the Biafran
rebels, forcing a surrender and ending a 3-year-long civil war that
left half a million people dead. Many feared a bloodbath following the government victory with occupation troops flooding the
rebel region and exacting a harsh revenge. Instead, Nigerian President General Yakubu Gowon was generous toward the defeated
rebels, saying there were "no victors, no vanquished" in the war.
Most people close to the situation believe Gowon's bold steps
toward reconciliation were the fruits of the labor of a quiet back-
door mediation effort of a small team of Quakers including Adam
Curle.

Curle was born with the name Charles Thomas William Curle, but became known by the name of his birthplace in France, *L'Isle-Adam*, outside of Paris. His mother lost three brothers in the quagmire of World War I, and she instilled her abhorrence of war in Adam. Such feelings had not gelled yet when Curle joined the British Army in World War II. Toward the end of the war he took a position rehabilitating returning prisoners of war. He plunged into the study of psychology, eventually becoming a professor and lecturer. Curle's anti-war convictions were refined as he committed himself to pacifism and the Quaker tradition.

Curle became a professor at the Harvard Centre for Studies in Education and Development. Then, he immersed himself in efforts across Africa, Central America and South Asia that would lay groundwork for peace. He was part of a Quaker team that shuttled between India and Pakistan during a war in Kashmir. The Quakers carefully listened to each side, then communicated between the sides, which opened up possible solutions. Although the Quakers didn't succeed in resolving the Kashmir crisis, all parties reported that the process was helpful. Curle soon would have a more significant impact in Nigeria.

In the post-colonial period, Quakers worked in many African countries. Curle and his Quaker colleague, John Volkmar, made 12 trips to Nigeria during the civil war to gather information and look for options that might end the war. They came with no official political status, which helped them to be accepted as politically neutral parties interested only in ending the killing. As the Biafran leader General Emeka Ojukwu later said of them, "Any political actor would be suspect; only a nonpolitical actor would have a chance of bringing the two sides together or giving the necessary type of assurance." Curle and his colleagues had three goals: to open lines of communication; to reduce suspicions, misperceptions and fear; and to support an officially negotiated settlement.

First, they arranged meetings with both sides and were transparent about the process. Both sides knew about their meetings, what they would carry back to the other side and what would remain confidential. The opponents began to rely on these mediators to carry key communications. Flying into the rebel enclave was a risky venture, as the Nigerian army gunners knew planes also might carry supplies and arms. Curle's and Volkmar's willingness to take this risk underscored their trustworthiness. They were more than passive messengers—they also presented their own substantive ideas about ways to move negotiations forward.

In changing the perceptions of each side, Quaker views about humanity and the divine were especially pertinent. As Curle said, "Virtually the sole dogma, if this word is not too emphatic, of Friends concerns: 'That of God in every one'.... One cannot be hostile or violent toward another without being hostile or violent toward oneself...In working for peace I am simply doing what I've sensed is carrying out a normal human function: to realize—make real—the bond between us all."

Deep listening was one way Curle and his team focused on "that of God in every one." As Curle said of listening, "In this way peacemakers may reach the part of the other person that is really able to make peace, outwardly as well as inwardly." The respect built up in these intensive listening sessions allowed the Quaker team to "speak truth to power" in interactions with both sides. When Nigerian bombers hit hospitals and markets in Biafra they spoke to Gowon about how such bombings didn't drive the rebels to lay down their arms, but only fed the charges of genocide. The Quakers helped the government side to see that toward the end of the war the Biafrans were driven more by fear, which helped Gowon take his conciliatory position following the battlefield triumph. As one observer noted, the Quakers "tried to resolve the hardness of the heart."

Many official diplomatic mediation efforts were undertaken during the Nigerian civil war, most notably by the Secretary-General of the Commonwealth of Nations and the Organization of African Unity. Curle and the Quaker team were often present to help clarify messages, deliver messages, defuse tension, and encourage continued commitment to a negotiated settlement. The Quakers encouraged Gowon to bring observers into the battle zone and investigate charges of misconduct and monitor the treatment of prisoners and refugees. Though the efforts of the Quakers and other mediators did not achieve a negotiated settlement, the deep process of building understanding, accurate communication, and even empathy led to an extraordinary postwar peace.

In 1973, Curle was appointed to the first chair in Peace Studies at the University of Bradford in the United Kingdom. Building upon the foundation Curle laid, this program has not only grown into one of the best in the world, but has become a global model. Curle retired from Bradford in 1978, credited with helping define the field of peace studies.

Before his death in 2006 at age 90, Curle continued working in conflict zones ranging from Zimbabwe and South Africa to the Balkans and Sri Lanka. In Croatia, he inspired the creation of the Osijek Peace Centre, which has become a key institution for peace, trauma healing and reconciliation in that region. To this day, mediators draw on his courageous example and pragmatic techniques.

CHAPTER 41

Carl Upchurch

(1950-2003)

Social change has always bubbled up from the bottom. Those on the top—the ones who have attained the power and grabbed the money—appear little inclined to change the status quo voluntarily. Change can't occur until the poor unite to articulate and support each other's struggles for justice—to refuse to tolerate injustice

—Carl Upchurch

Shortly after the Los Angeles uprising Carl called me about an incredible invitation he had received from the LA gangs to help them find a way to peace in the streets. I knew I had to help, so I scrambled to find some of the funds that enabled Carl to spend a month in LA with the gangs. Then I got his report—what a prophetic powerhouse blow and challenge to all of us! Carl wouldn't let us rest with smug progressive stuff; he pushed us to astonishing action. I participated in the gang summit in Minneapolis-St. Paul and helped with the national summit in Kansas City and a follow-up summit in Pittsburgh. Carl died from an illness way too young, leaving a huge hole in the movement, especially for our cities.

A GANG SUMMIT? TO many people that sounded like a meeting to maximize the profits from the drug trade, but it actually was a gang-initiated, grassroots effort to bring peace to the streets of U.S. cities. At the heart of this movement was Carl Upchurch, a child of the slums of Philadelphia, a former federal prisoner and a peace activist who blazed a peacemaking trail where nobody had gone before.

Upchurch described himself as "convicted in the womb," born into a poor, violent setting where the crippling injustices of systemic racism left people in the most desperate and hopeless situations. He saw his grandmother shoot his grandfather when he was three years old. Soon he was running with gangs, beating up other kids, stealing whatever he wanted, and going through the revolving doors of the juvenile criminal justice system. His next stop was adult prison, and following a string of bank robberies, he ended up in the federal prison system with a 10-year sentence.

In a solitary prison cell, Carl Upchurch's life turned around when he discovered a collection of William Shakespeare's sonnets under the leg of a wobbly table. That moment became a key scene in the 2002 made-for-TV movie, *Conviction*, with Omar Epps portraying Upchurch. Poetry opened up a new world. Soon he was devouring books. The experience was so visceral that he actually voiced loud debates with authors he was reading. He discovered the rich academic and activist heritage of black resistance writers. He realized that nobody was going to set him free; he would have to liberate himself. Racism and poverty may have been responsible for the world into which he was born, but he was responsible for what he would be in that moment and in the future he would shape. Upchurch also pursued his formal education while in prison, and continued upon release.

After his release from prison in the mid-80s, Upchurch formed the Progressive Prisoners Movement (PPM), which pushed for prison reform. African-Americans are sentenced to prison, and to death row, at a far higher rate than other Americans accused of crime. Upchurch recognized that systemic racism played a role in that pattern and in the dehumanizing aspects of the prison system.

On the other hand, PPM challenged prisoners not to blame others for their plight but to take responsibility for their own actions and confront within themselves the dynamics of toxic self-hatred, addiction and violence.

In 1992, members of the Bloods and Crips gangs in Los Angeles were struggling to form a peace agreement but failed to obtain any support from the religious or public institutions in the city. Someone saw a PPM brochure and contacted Carl about helping them work on peace in the streets. Drawing upon his religious community for support, Carl spent a month in LA then wrote a report to some of the sponsoring religious and peace organizations. He challenged them to work in directions that no one had dreamed of before. Upchurch discovered indigenous community leaders, some of them gang members or former gang members, others local activists working closely with the young people on the streets. He learned of anti-violence efforts with gangs in Minneapolis-St. Paul, Boston, Chicago, San José and Cleveland. Together, Upchurch and these gang-based peace activists formed the Council for Urban Peace and Justice. Because of Upchurch's own story, he was able to gain the trust and respect of high-level gang leaders in city after city. He heard from voices that no one else could have reached, and then used his skills to shape those voices into a powerful challenge—both to those in decaying urban neighborhoods and those in positions of power.

Upchurch promoted the shocking idea of convening a national gang summit to address common issues and to explore new ways of relating to each other and to the gangs' communities. The first National Urban Peace and Justice Summit, or Gang Summit, was held in Kansas City from April 29–May 2, 1993. Gang members from 26 cities came together and met in two churches under the facilitation of Upchurch and his team of urban peacemakers. They discussed their systemic issues and problems and explored their own feelings and responsibilities. They prayed together—though they came from different religions, some with no religious background at all, they all knew they needed divine help. At the closing worship service, gang members laid their "colors" on the altar and pledged to work for reconciliation.

In spite of media skepticism, the energy from the summit flowed back into many cities. Follow-up local summits were held in Minneapolis-St. Paul, Chicago, Cleveland, Pittsburgh and San Antonio. In many urban areas the murder rate from gang violence plummeted. Cease-fires were established, and local community workers helped calm volatile situations that previously had spun out into cycles of retaliatory violence. In some cities "tables" were set up to bring together gang members, church leaders, city officials, social workers, probation officers and prosecutors to solve problems such as the barriers to employment for young men with long criminal records. Because gang members cited finding legitimate jobs as their number one issue, their discussions centered around this topic.

Upchurch was not content with peacemaking in urban streets. He also wanted to address the underlying issues that fed the violence. He became a national voice by challenging racism in the criminal justice system and the punitive policies regarding incarceration that were especially focused on people of color and the poor. He challenged traditional peace groups who worked against injustice in Central America and apartheid in South Africa, but were afraid to touch the issues of injustice and racism at home. He even challenged African-American leaders from the civil rights movement who he felt were abandoning the poorest people and communities to enjoy the benefits won for the black elite and middle class. He did not seek a platform for himself, but repeatedly would create a space through his connections and personal presence, then allow African-American and Latino voices from poor neighborhoods to speak in settings that had never been accessible before.

Over the years, cycles of violence have come again to these cities, but the movement Upchurch founded has continued past his death in 2003. Urban Peace, Justice and Empowerment Summits continue to be held as the national collective of gang peace organizations continues to work together to address the issues plaguing urban communities. Gang summit veterans continue to strive to reduce violence and secure cease-fires between warring gangs. An ongoing National Council for Urban Peace and Justice continues as a voice against what amounts to the criminalization of entire communities of color. The council also encourages best practices for positive community transformation instead of merely locking away hundreds of thousands of young black, Latino and Native American young men. The ripples of Carl Upchurch's peacemaking work continue to touch some of the most shattered lives in our cities and bring new hope.

CHAPTER 42

Óscar Arias Sánchez

(b. 1940)

**We must trust that dialogue—
so often scorned as too
slow or too simple—is the
only path to peace and
the light that can guide us
through these dark hours.**

—Óscar Arias Sánchez

*I visited the Óscar Arias Peace Park
in San José, Costa Rica. Embedded
in the concrete base all around the central monument
are rusting, shattered guns. Armies and insurgents once
used those guns across Central America. At the top are
statues of two young women. One is holding aloft a gun
snapped in two. The other is playing a violin. It took the
only nation in the Americas without an army to end the
wars that plagued Central America for over a decade.*

AFTER YEARS OF RELATIVE quiet in the global news, Central America once again became a front-page story when a military coup deposed the president of Honduras in June, 2009. The president was picked up in the middle of the night, flown by military plane to Costa Rica where he was dumped in his pajamas on the runway. The military installed a new president, but all the governments in the Americas reacted negatively. The former president tried to return in spite of threats by the Honduran military. Everyone turned to Óscar Arias for a solution. This president of Costa

Rica had mediated an end to civil wars in Central America, so perhaps he could help move the Honduran crisis to an acceptable solution.

Óscar Rafael de Jesús Arias Sánchez grew up in a wealthy Costa Rican family. After receiving his university training in law, economics and political science, he joined the National Liberation Party, a social democratic political party. After serving in various positions and in the national Legislative Assembly, Arias ran for president and won in 1986. He stepped into office at a very volatile time.

During the 1980s, Central America was torn by war—civil wars in Guatemala, El Salvador and Nicaragua cost tens of thousands of lives. The United States supported the military regimes in Guatemala and El Salvador while supporting the Contras, who sought to overturn the leftist Sandanista government, in Nicaragua. Panama was invaded by the United States. Wars were spilling over into Honduras and Costa Rica.

Costa Rica was the only country without a standing army, having abolished the army in 1948. Even before he was sworn in as president, Arias had traveled throughout Central and South America to invite heads of state to his inauguration. When they were gathered together, he suggested an alliance "for the defense of democracy and liberty." He wanted all governments to hold free and fair elections and commit themselves to meeting the people's needs and interests. Arias believed no army or totalitarian regime was entitled to make those decisions for people.

A three-year peace effort initiated by the presidents of Mexico, Panama, Venezuela and Colombia, called the Contradora Process, ultimately failed to win the trust of all the parties to the various conflicts. That's where Óscar Arias stepped in. Based on his discussions with the Central American presidents and leading figures of the resistance movements, Arias drafted a plan that dealt with all the conflicts in Central America, holding all the nations to the same standards. As he met with the Central American leaders, he educated them on what genuine democracy was: "In democratic systems, everything that is not prohibited is permitted, while in totalitarian systems, everything that is not permitted is prohibited." On August 7, 1987, the presidents of Nicaragua, Guatemala, El Salvador, Honduras and Costa Rica signed the Esquipulas II Accord. The Accord called for a simultaneous cease-fire, amnesty for all rebels, and restoration of full press and political freedoms.

Achieving that peace was not easy. Arias had to cajole many of the leaders to keep commitments they had made to the process. The Accord was weak on sanctions to back up the agreements, but Arias' own involvement helped ease the parties through the difficulties. The biggest problem was the political pressure of the United States that sought to shape all decisions in Central America through either military or diplomatic means. They felt the Arias plan gave too much recognition to the Sandinistas in Nicaragua, treating them as a legitimate government. Even though Arias was moving the parties to peace, the Reagan Administration still tried to pump hundreds of millions of dollars of aid to the Contras in a destabilizing way that was not allowed by the Accord. "There are profound differences between what Washington thinks and what Costa Rica thinks," President Arias said. "We both believe that a durable peace in Central America is possible only if there is democracy. But how to achieve that democracy is where we part company." Arias did not give in to the diplomatic pressure from the U.S. but pressed forward in achieving the agreement.

The peace agreement was most unstable in Guatemala, not achieving a genuine resolution to the civil war until 1994. But it did start the dialogue between the government and the opposition forces, something that had not happened in 25 years.

The Nobel Peace Prize was awarded to Óscar Arias in 1987 as the Central American peace process was still being shaped. Following the signing of the Accord, Arias used the monetary part of the award to launch the Arias Foundation for Peace and Human Rights. This foundation has three programs: The Center for Human Progress to foster better opportunities for women in Central America; the Center for Philanthropy to encourage giving for social change; and the Center for Peace and Reconciliation to work on demilitarization and conflict resolution in the developing world.

After he stepped down as president of Costa Rica, Arias became active in many peacemaking institutes and organizations including the Stockholm International Peace Research Institute (SPIRI) and the International Negotiation Network of the Jimmy Carter Center.

In 2003, Arias led a campaign to amend the Costa Rican constitution to allow former presidents to seek re-election. When the campaign succeeded, Arias then ran for another term as president. He won by a narrow margin in 2006. In his second term, he tried to address the global issue of the debt crisis of many poorer countries. His Costa Rica Consensus suggested mechanisms whereby debt forgiveness and international aid from wealthier nations to poorer countries would be tied to both lower military spending and to increases in spending on education, health care, housing and the environment. Most proposals coming from the global economic powers have called for cuts in social services and fail to address growing militarization among poor countries. The model of building peace in Costa Rica, and its extension through Arias' mediation into the surrounding region, provides a constructive challenge to many of the development models operating today.

Arias established an enduring platform for peace. He brought major strengths to all of his endeavors: coming from the only country in the Western Hemisphere with no armed forces and the most viable economy in Central America. The importance of his work now is clear, acknowledged in the Nobel Prize and his greatest accomplishment—a major peace agreement ending some of the worst wars in the region.

But Arias is clear that this work is not finished. "The combination of powerful militaries and fragile democracies creates a terrible risk" that continues to endanger Latin America, he says. He calls the increasing amount of military spending in the region "a ridiculous sum," especially during a time when only Colombia is engaged in armed conflict. "More combat planes, missiles and soldiers won't provide additional bread for our families, desks for our schools or medicine for our clinics. All they can do is destabilize a region that continues to view armed forces as the final arbiter of social conflicts."

This is his clarion call: "The liberating army we need in the Americas today is one of leaders who come together in peace, in the spirit of cooperation."

CHAPTER 43

Jimmy Carter
(b. 1924)

We will not learn how to live together in peace by killing each other's children.

—Jimmy Carter

I once slipped a sword past the Secret Service. It was at the Carter Center where I was to have a short talk with President Carter about peacemaking in Burma. Carter had written us a letter that opened some doors for us in a mediation initiative. One of the insurgent leaders gave us a ceremonial sword to give to Carter. As I sat in the waiting area with the wrapped sword in my lap, the hulking Secret Service agent never checked the long package. I got into the inner office with only Carter and my friend from Burma. I drew out the sword and presented it to him with flowery words about swords being beaten into plowshares someday. That sword must now be stored somewhere amid the vast collection of gifts housed at the Carter Center. I'm just glad I was not searched and arrested!

IT CAME DOWN TO grandchildren. For eight days, negotiators tangled over one of the most complex conflicts on the planet. Israeli Prime Minister Menachim Begin and Egyptian President Anwar Sadat had been hosted by U.S. President Jimmy Carter at the Camp David retreat outside Washington, D.C. Carter had worked one-on-one with each leader, occasionally bringing them together for direct encounters. But after all these efforts, the quest for peace was falling apart yet again. Sadat was packing up to depart, frustrated by the refusal of Begin to yield anything at one key point. Begin had earlier asked Carter for autographed photos to give to his grandchildren. As the leaders prepared to fly out, Carter found the photos and took them to Begin. They talked about their grandchildren and the world they hoped to give to them. Carter quietly brought these beloved little ones into the harsh realities of Middle East politics. There was no sermon, no nuanced diplomatic talk. There were just two parents who had hopes for their families, and they sat for a bit in quiet reflection. Begin signaled a shift in his position. Sadat delayed his departure. Quickly, the final hurdle was overcome and a peace agreement was achieved between Israel and Egypt that would last for decades. The Camp David agreement was a highlight of the presidency of Jimmy Carter.

Carter's life now is largely defined by his many peacemaking efforts—yet his early career did not suggest this path. He graduated from the U.S. Naval Academy and became a submarine officer. At one point he commanded the Navy's second nuclear submarine. When his father died, he resigned his commission and returned to the family peanut farm in Georgia. Soon he was active in local politics. Carter was elected governor of Georgia in 1971, which launched him into national politics.

In 1976, Carter was elected President of the United States. He moved human rights to the forefront of U.S. foreign policy, not just as an oft-stated value, but also as a priority in shaping that policy. Conflicts in the Middle East have been a perennial concern of U.S. leaders, but Carter engaged in peace efforts beyond what any previous president had undertaken. He held private talks with both Begin and Sadat in their countries. When Sadat indicated a willingness to go to Jerusalem for peace, Carter followed up with a discussion with Begin and carried Begin's invitation for Sadat to address the Israeli Knesset. Later, Carter took 13 days to personally and directly participate and acted as an intermediary between the two leaders at Camp David. When the discussions stalled, Carter drew upon his Christian faith, praying that "somewhere we could find peace." After producing 23 versions of the "Framework for Peace" during those 13 days, they had an agreement.

Apart from the Camp David Accords, Carter negotiated a treaty to return the Panama Canal to the government of Panama and established diplomatic relations with the People's Republic of China. In attempting to move toward a resolution of the Cold War, he negotiated the SALT II treaty with the Soviet Union. He had his successes and failures as a president; the most notable failure was the seizure of the U.S. embassy in Iran and the resulting hostage crisis. Carter was defeated by Ronald Reagan in his bid for a second term.

Following the exhausting Camp David process, Carter wrote in his diary, "I resolved to do everything possible to get out of the negotiation business." Fortunately for the world, that idea turned out to be one of Carter's personal failures. After leaving the White House, Carter launched the most noteworthy post-presidential career in U.S. history. In 1982 he founded the Jimmy Carter Center in Atlanta, Georgia, housed in his Presidential Library. The purpose of the Carter Center was to resolve conflict, promote democracy, protect human rights and prevent disease and other afflictions. For example, the center established the International Negotiation Network (INN), more recently reorganized as the Conflict Resolution Program as part of the center's Peace Programs. The INN hosted annual conferences on conflicts around the world, drawing together government officials, opposition leaders and influential nongovernmental organizations.

To strengthen these efforts, Carter enlisted global leaders including many former heads of state and Nobel laureates—a star-studded list that included Desmond Tutu, Eduard Schverdnadze, Lisbet Palme, Andrew Young, Olusegun Obasanjo, Sir Shridath Ramphal and Óscar Arias. Carter and his INN staff engaged in a number of mediation efforts in Liberia, Haiti, Bosnia, Sudan, the Great Lakes region of Africa, Uganda, Venezuela and the Korean peninsula. The Carter Center hosted rounds of talks between the

Ethiopian government and Ethiopian and Eritrean rebel groups, a process that eventually led to the independence of Eritrea.

Carter became a focal point and organizer of many international election-monitoring delegations. His involvement helped certify fair and free electoral processes so that transitions to democracy could be peacefully achieved. The Carter Center has sent teams to more than 70 elections, most notably those in Panama, Nicaragua, Venezuela, Nigeria, Jamaica, Indonesia and East Timor.

Besides his peacemaking work, Jimmy Carter has labored on behalf of the poor, both in the United States and in Africa. He has become a leader in Habitat for Humanity, which builds homes for poor families using "the economics of Jesus" in which no interest is charged. One week each year he will lead a "blitz build" for Habitat and use his presence to mobilize thousands of volunteers to construct new homes. Through the Carter Center he has quietly launched one of the largest public health initiatives in Africa. River blindness, the world's second-leading infectious cause of blindness, has afflicted millions of people in sub-Saharan Africa. The Carter Center's project on river blindness has almost eliminated that dreaded scourge.

The prime motivating force for Carter is his Christian faith. He taught an adult Sunday school class in his local church before running for president and continues to teach as often as he can. Busloads of visitors converge on his church simply to visit those Sunday classes.

Many criticize him for certain policies or choices he made as U.S. president. Others criticize him for involving himself in diplomatic matters that should be left to current administrations. Still others criticize him for supposedly losing his neutrality as a mediator in written and public statements such as his 2007-2008 messages against the Israeli actions in Gaza. Though he decried the Hamas rocket attacks, he saw Israeli intransigence and use of overwhelming force in civilian areas as a major impediment to peace. Sometimes, mediators choose to step aside from their neutral role when they feel the cause of peace is better served by drawing attention to the imbalances of power and persistent actions that block resolution.

Whether he has been wrong or right in each specific case, Jimmy Carter has thrown himself without reservation into some of the thorniest conflicts on the planet, seeking peace in tangled disputes. He has mobilized many others to join in the cause of peace. He has set a standard of committed action by former government leaders and invited other world figures to join the cause as they step down from office. Retirement from office is not the end of peacemaking. For Jimmy Carter, it was just the beginning.

CHAPTER 44

Wati Aier

(b. 1948)

It is creative love which makes the hateful beautiful, brings the false into truth, and transforms evil into good. Such creative love can become the power in Naga politics.

—Wati Aier

I'll never forget embracing Wati in Bangkok, Thailand, tears streaming down our faces. We had just secured the first commitment to an informal cease-fire from a pivotal Naga faction, a key step in ending a war that had lasted as long as Wati could remember. We didn't realize how long and hard the road ahead would be, but at least Wati could see hope where none had been before. A few days earlier I'd told Wati the peace process was dead in the water, but with tenacious hope planted in such thin soil, Wati pressed on. He's one of my biggest heroes.

MIDWAY THROUGH THE SOCCER game the players knew this was a special event that had to be repeated. Participants didn't worry about the score; rather they were moved by who their teammates were. On one side were members of different insurgent groups who had been fighting each other. Facing them were traditional tribal leaders who had also been deeply divided. Now they were playing together, and they knew they had to take these games back home. Soccer, or "football" as most of the world calls it, had become a powerful symbol of reconciliation in a decades-old conflict. The football match was the brainchild of Wati Aier, the leading mediator for a reconciliation process among the Naga people that had been going on for twelve years.

The Nagas are a tribal people living mostly in the hilly country northeast of India and northwest of Burma (also known as Myanmar). They have had few historic ties with India but were put under the administration of the British Raj during the colonial period in India. As independence neared, the Nagas expressed their desire to be separate from India, even declaring their independence one day before India did in 1947. But with the assassination of Gandhi, who had agreed to Naga independence, the new Indian government refused to let the Nagas separate. In 1955 the conflict exploded into war, and as of this writing the Nagaland state is still under Indian army occupation and martial law. Also, a flawed peace agreement in 1975 resulted in a bitter split among the Nagas themselves. Naga insurgent groups began fighting each other, and as many Nagas were dying at the hands of their own as from Indian army action.

Wati Aier was the founder and principal of a seminary in Nagaland. The vast majority of Nagas are Baptist Christians, the fruit of over a century of mission work by American Baptists. As a result there is a strong religious link among the different sub-tribes of Nagas and a deep respect for the Baptists in the U.S. Wati has a great passion for his Naga identity that comes out in the songs he writes. One of them, "By the Blue Streams of Nagaland," has become the informal Naga national anthem.

Wati also has great passion for reconciliation. In early 1997, Wati began making contact with various Naga insurgent leaders in each of the factions. He would meet with those he knew, then work his way up the chain of command, utilizing his stature in the church to gain their respect to proceed with more meetings. He talked about bringing all the Naga factional leaders together to explore reconciliation, along with Baptist mission and peace leaders from the U.S. The Nagas couldn't hope to come to an effective peace agreement with India without coming to some sort of a peace accord among themselves, so the first Naga reconciliation talks since the fractures some twenty years earlier were scheduled to occur in Atlanta.

At the last minute, one of the key groups did not show up. The other three groups met, along with various Naga political and church figures. They were hosted and facilitated by Baptist peacemakers and an American Baptist mission leader. An appeal for reconciliation was agreed to and publicized, and the group commissioned Wati to attempt to bring the last group into the process. That group condemned the Atlanta talks and specifically branded Wati as a "betrayer of the Naga cause." Yet after a few months of persistent appeals, the top leaders of that faction agreed to meet with him in Bangkok. The sessions were rough—angry words were spoken. Wati listened a long time, and then began to push back. That group had made a cease-fire with India, so Wati said, "Why not a cease-fire with your Naga brothers?" The leaders agreed to a very short cease-fire to allow the Nagas to celebrate the 125th anniversary of Christianity coming to the Naga people.

During the anniversary observations more than 100,000 Nagas gathered in a stadium for worship. Wati preached about reconciliation and invited the Nagas to pray for peace, which they did, passionately, using the Naga traditional "mass prayer" where everyone prays aloud simultaneously. The power of 100,000 voices lifted in prayer for peace carried an informal four-day cease-fire into one that lasted for a few years.

As the informal cease-fire stalled with no substantive progress on either a political agreement with India or reconciliation among the Nagas, Wati worked with other Naga civil society leaders and Baptist peacemakers from the U.S. to initiate the "Journey of Conscience." This was a nonviolent campaign to take Naga concerns to the Indian public. A large delegation of Nagas traveled to Delhi to hold a vigil at Gandhi's tomb. They also held a conference with Indian human rights activists, journalists, academics and retired politicians. They engaged in street demonstrations calling for a just peace to end the Indo-Naga conflict. Through their connections with the Indian public during the" Journey of Conscience" activities, the larger political context shifted both in Nagaland and in India as a whole. Support grew for peace talks, and the civil society began pushing the agenda that the political leaders had been setting aside.

During this process Wati could not get the key leaders to meet face-to-face, so the process was long and cumbersome. Not only would he travel to Bangkok at times to meet with one leader, then into the deep jungles to meet another, but he was maintaining his own academic work as well. Eventually, the lack of progress led to a deterioration of the situation on the ground. Each group had a cease-fire with the Indian army, but the lack of a formal agreement between the Naga groups themselves left the Naga public living amidst growing instability. Violence began to escalate resulting in attacks and rising antagonism between some of the Naga tribes.

In the spring of 2008, Wati was able to capitalize on the invitation of a Christian prayer group to bring all the factions together—not the top leaders, but some second-level leaders. They met for a series of extended sessions in Chiang Mai, Thailand, with a team of international peacemakers to help facilitate the process. Throughout the sessions, Wati was holding conversations and working behind the scenes bringing people together and keeping them talking. He would jump into situations that were stalled, with his own example of vulnerability and confession on the one hand, or with a prophetic exhortation based on their common Christian faith on the other. He challenged people: "Today we must, in all sincerity, consciously accept the pain and dismay of our situation, making the cry for freedom out of the depths of the oppressed Nagahood and answering with a call to reconciliation. Nagas can be made free through reconciliation."

During one of those Chiang Mai sessions Wati brought up the idea of a soccer game. Suddenly, talk of unity was no longer an abstract concept as people from different factions were on the same team. Following the close of those sessions, similar soccer games were held in two Naga cities surrounded by other reconciliation events such as days of prayer and music, in which all groups participated. As he spoke about the "good therapy" of the soccer matches, Wati added, "Just their coming together, mingling together and shaking the hands of people who have not seen each other in years, it is progress." During the second match, widows and orphans of some of the victims of factional fighting gave flowers to the players and expressed forgiveness and their hopes for reconciliation. As Wati spoke about the difficult task of reconciliation he said, "Wounds are still fresh, but by the grace of God we are moving in the right direction."

It takes more than sports to make peace, so Wati and the other civil society leaders in the Forum for Naga Reconciliation have mediated between the factions in a series of practical negotiations. They have discussed military disengagement, funding of the factions, moving toward reconciliation, and pursuing political talks with the government of India.

After all this groundwork, Wati was able to accomplish what was only a dream 12 years earlier: bringing the top leaders together for reconciliation. In June 2009, they signed "A Covenant of Reconciliation." The reconciliation process still has a lot of work ahead of it, as of this writing in 2011, but Wati has toiled with patience, determination and humility through years of challenges. He has brought along other leaders, especially a younger generation. The result is a process that has deep roots in Naga society. The reconciliation process has involved Naga institutions and organizations from churches to women's groups, as well as student, business and human rights groups. Wati says, "It is creative love which makes the hateful beautiful, brings the false into truth, and transforms evil into good. Such creative love can become the power in Naga politics."

CHAPTER 45

Hizkias Assefa

(b. 1948)

If one is allowed to work with the parties step-by-step and layer-by-layer, it is possible to get them to meet at a deep level when they recognize the humanity of each other and recognize that their commonalities are much greater than their differences. And based on that they can have the vision, fortitude and mutual tolerance to work towards peace and reconciliation.

—Hizkias Assefa

I first learned of Hizkias Assefa 20 years ago through his writings about the Sudan peace process. I thought he was an academic since he was also on the faculty of the Summer Peacebuilding Institute at Eastern Mennonite University. Then I discovered how much he was doing as an activist in mediation throughout Africa. Assefa is that wonderful combination of activist-academic who puts his depth of intellect and experience into practice.

IN DECEMBER 2007, A hotly contested election in Kenya spilled over into violence. Many deeper simmering divisions were revealed as the fighting spun out of control. Kofi Annan, former Secretary General of the United Nations, brought a team from the African Union to try to mediate. Annan invited Hizkias Assefa to join them as an expert advisor on mediation. Assefa helped the team structure the mediation process, think about the root issues, overcome the obstacles to an agreement, and draw the civil society into the peace-building process. Together, they secured a political solution to a violent crisis that established a power-sharing government.

Hizkias Assefa is a hidden presence behind many of the peace processes that make the news. The warring political leaders are seen shaking hands, but Assefa's mediating role remains humbly behind the scenes. He is an academician, teaching conflict studies at Eastern Mennonite University and earlier at George Mason University, but he regularly leaves the ivory tower for the hot zones of conflict. Often, this pushes him beyond the neatly worded conclusions in academic papers. He writes, "I know all the theories, and in fact I have even written about them. But they feel different when you are in the middle of these problems and are expected to do something about them. Then, all the theoretical answers that you felt you knew sound strange and are unable to help you with the problems."

Assefa began his career as a lawyer, working with the government and in private practice in his homeland of Ethiopia and in the United States. As he studied some of the mediation efforts in Sudan, his vocation shifted. He began teaching—both at universities and in grassroots training workshops—in more than 50 countries. He has also engaged in second-track (nongovernmental) mediation efforts from the community level to the national level in places such as Sudan, Nigeria, Rwanda, Burundi, Ethiopia, Mozambique, Uganda, Sri Lanka, Afghanistan, Colombia and Guatemala. He established the African Peacebuilding and Reconciliation Network (APRN) based in Nairobi, Kenya as the center for his mediation and training work.

In the 2007-2008 Kenya crisis and in other conflicts, Assefa's goal is not merely to halt the fighting. There are always deeper reasons that a conflict erupts into violence, and these issues must be addressed if a conflict is to be truly transformed.

"Regrettably, addressing root causes is very complicated. It is a long-term process," Assefa says. "Once there is no immediate pressure of turmoil, it seems that the pressure is off of everyone—the politicians, the negotiators, the population, even the mediators and sponsors of the process. So people lose focus on the long-term underlying issues, and things slowly begin to return to business as usual." That's not Assefa's goal—as such seeds, if ignored, will sprout in conflict once again. Neither is he interested in merely moving a conflict from a battlefield to a negotiating table. Such bargaining is not as important as making fundamental changes to prevent future violence, he believes. Parties must move from their roles as antagonists to become collaborators in solving a shared problem.

Assefa also brings a concern for self-reflection into peace processes. In most conflicts, even while people are engaged in peace negotiations, they tend to see the problem as embodied in the other side. Deeper peace, even reconciliation, requires people to look at themselves as well: "Since responsibility for conflict is usually not entirely on one side, reconciliation encourages the parties to look within themselves as well as at the other to explain the cause of the conflict and possible ways for resolving it."

This inner work, especially, calls for religious responses—often there is so much chaos in a complex conflict that religious leaders can provide a moral compass. As Assefa says, "Religious leaders and institutions have a unique opportunity to become the conscience of humanity and help reestablish sanity and healing in this broken world by giving us insight into how to deal with the more deep-rooted sources of human conflict than politicians, soldiers or merchants can do."

In Nigeria, Assefa focused for years on grassroots peace-building involving problems like land disputes that had prompted violence. Through his efforts, community leaders learned to work together to resolve these problems peacefully. The wisdom of his approach was obvious when conflict broke out again across a larger region and these smaller communities became islands of peace, refusing to get sucked into the violence around them.

Assefa hopes to see a worldwide linking of such community-based efforts.

Assefa is able to continue his mediation in very thorny conflicts because of hope. "What my experience has taught me is that regardless of how complicated the problems might appear, it is possible to work through them and find solutions that are mutually satisfactory to every stakeholder in the problem," he says. "Most of our problems on this earth are created by us and therefore we have the capacity and the obligation to unmake them."

PART 8

Nonviolent Activists
On the Front Line

THE CHINESE TANKS RUMBLED in columns down the avenues leading to Beijing's Tiananmen Square. For a month, student activists had occupied the square in a protest that was growing in size and global attention. On June 4, 1989, the Chinese government ordered the army to clear the square and re-establish order. As various citizens fled the on-coming tanks, one man moved toward this military might. He placed himself in the center of the broad avenue. A small man carrying a simple satchel; he was everyman—an ordinary person, unidentified and unnamed, going about his daily business. Yet he was also unique. He was willing to interrupt his affairs to act upon what he believed. He stood alone while others ran. What he felt we don't know; what he did was captured on film for the entire world to see.

The column of tanks approached him. He didn't move. They came right up to him and stopped. The lead tank ground its treads to turn and go around him, but the man shifted over to block the tank's new approach. The tank turned the other way, and the man shifted once more. Suddenly two people ran into the street, seized him and moved him back toward anonymity. His action, standing calmly alone to block overwhelming military might, became a global symbol for nonviolent action.

Nonviolent activists are risk-takers, but they also know that, ultimately, they do not stand alone. That figure in Tiananmen Square looked isolated—but he took action like the crowds, including nuns and priests, who blocked tanks in a 1986 peaceful revolution in the Philippines. To this day in the Philippines, people remember their 1986 slogan: "I stopped a tank with my heart."

Nonviolent action has a long but sporadic history. The ancient Greek poet Aristophanes told of Athenian women who refused to have sexual relations with their husbands until they stopped their warfare. Popular British accounts from the 11th century say that Lady Godiva rode nude in protest of oppressive taxation. A century later, Hugh of Lincoln, later known as St. Hugh, interposed himself between mobs seeking to attack Jewish ghettos, halting acts of anti-Semitic violence. He also engaged in tax resistance against King Richard I, refusing to allow church property to be taxed to support the Crusades. Richard seized some of the church-owned lands in Lincoln, but Hugh would not relent. Eventually his tax resistance forced Richard to give in. In the 20th century, large crowds of Germans engaged in nonviolent resistance and halted a military coup that tried to overturn the democratic Weimar Republic. The nonviolent resistance to the Soviet invasion of Czechoslovakia in 1968 could not be crushed by the tanks for nine months. The Czechoslovak resistance lasted far longer, with far less loss of life than was experienced in the violent resistance to Soviet military might in Hungary in 1956.

The idea of nonviolent action crossed the Atlantic early in American history. Before the Revolutionary War, Americans resisted taxation. Benjamin Lay engaged in early guerilla theater to prod Philadelphia Quakers to take an anti-slavery position in the 1750s. He stood outside an American Quaker meeting house with a bare leg in deep snow, and smashed tea-cups that held slave-grown sugar. He even took his actions of objection to the extreme—almost beyond nonviolence—when he kidnapped a slave owner's son for a few hours to illustrate the evils of kidnapping human beings. In other nonviolent actions, American Quakers resisted war taxes—and abolitionists boycotted slave-related products. The strategy wasn't limited to North America. In 1944, nonviolent resistance movements brought down the military dictatorships of Maximiliano Hernández Martinez in El Salvador and Jorge Ubico in Guatemala.

The watershed in modern nonviolent activism was Gandhi's campaign to drive the British out of India, followed by the civil rights movement that took hold in the U.S. Through the writing of Gandhi and many others in that era, nonviolent activism rose from its roots to become a philosophy and coherent strategy that attracted millions. People Power brought down repressive governments in the Philippines in 1986 and in 2001 and in Chile in 1988. The Soviet empire collapsed largely through nonviolent movements in Poland, East Germany, Czechoslovakia, Romania, Estonia, Latvia and Lithuania, as well as the nonviolent resistance that prevented a military coup from seizing power in Russia in 1991. The Shah of Iran was deposed by a nonviolent Islamic revolution, though the post-revolutionary period was anything but nonviolent. Unsuccessful nonviolent movements deeply shook the governments of Burma in 1988, China in 1989 and Belarus in 2006. The Rose Revolution brought democracy to the Republic of Georgia in 2003. The Orange Revolution succeeded in Ukraine in 2004. The Cedar Revolution drove the occupying Syrian army out of Lebanon in 2005. Slobodan Milosovic, the dictator of Serbia, was driven from power, not by NATO bombs, but by a nonviolent campaign led by Serbian students in 2000. Shock waves of political protest spread throughout the Arab world in early 2011, ignited by nonviolent protests that brought down authoritarian regimes in Tunisia and Egypt.

The freedom struggle in South Africa began with nonviolent activism. The Zulu Chief Albert Luthuli became the head of the African National Congress (ANC) and led in nonviolent strikes, boycotts and other acts of civil disobedience. He led campaigns against the passbooks that blacks were forced to carry to allow them to travel within the country. He acted out of a deep Christian faith, and though he did not expect churches to be involved in organizing political movements, he did call for the churches to "be with people, in their lives," especially in the struggle against the apartheid system. Luthuli was the first South African to receive the Nobel Peace Prize. Even though much of the ANC's struggle shifted to violent action after his death, his accomplishments laid the foundation for the nonviolent struggles that eventually helped bring the apartheid regime to the point of collapse.

As Gandhi understood, sometimes one person may act in a way that triggers a broad response from others. Rosa Parks refused to give up her seat for a white person as she sat on a segregated bus in Montgomery, Alabama. Her intentional action sparked the first major campaign in the American civil rights movement. In Burma, Aung San Suu Kyi walked alone through a line of soldiers barring her way during an election campaign, facing down the guns with her moral courage. Gandhi's simple march to the sea to make salt inspired tens of thousands to join him.

Even in large movements there are many individual acts of courage, which taken together and multiplied, generate a force more powerful than violent repression. In the late 1980s, a breakthrough moment for democracy in Chile occurred on a night when people were urged to bang pots and pans at a certain hour if they supported an end to the Pinochet dictatorship. The cacophony helped to drive away the fear that gripped so many Chileans after years of government-backed murder and torture to suppress democracy. While the din fueled the spirit of many—some brave soul was the first to strike a pot on that silent evening.

As in Tiananmen Square, nonviolent activists can't always fade into the cacophony, but sometimes must put their own bodies on the line to stop the machinery of violence and injustice.

Brian Willson, the decorated Vietnam veteran turned peace activist, literally put his body in the way of a train taking arms to the armies of Central American dictatorships. The train, which had plenty of time and distance to stop, ran over him as he sat on the tracks, severing his legs. Rachel Corrie sat in front of an Israeli military bulldozer that was preparing to demolish a Palestinian home in Gaza. She was part of a nonviolent organization protesting the Israeli occupation of the Gaza Strip and West Bank and the illegal destruction of homes. The bulldozer ran over her, not once, but twice, killing her.

Nonviolent activists move from their homes and workplaces, from classrooms and houses of worship, from the relative safety of friends—to engage in front line struggles against injustice. They confront, expose and challenge. They may risk imprisonment, injury and even death. These are shock troops. Their power lies, not in violence, but in the courageous offering of their lives.

CHAPTER 46

Abdul Ghaffar Khan
(1890-1988)

One learns a good deal in the school of suffering. I wonder what would have happened to me if I had had an easy life, and had not had the privilege of tasting the joys of jail and all it means.

—Abdul Ghaffar Khan

*I stumbled across **A Man to Match His Mountains**, a biography of Abdul Ghaffar Khan that appears in some editions as **Nonviolent Soldier of Islam**, in a Christian mission library while researching my earlier book, **Christian Peacemaking**. I was immediately swept up in the story. Later in Jerusalem, I saw the book on the desk of the Director of the Palestinian Center for the Study of Nonviolence. That sparked a great conversation. I've become convinced that Ghaffar Khan is one of the lights we need to shine on the path of interreligious peacemaking.*

JAILED BY THE BRITISH because he was starting schools among the Pathan people of the North-West Frontier Province (today's northwest Pakistan), Abdul Ghaffar Khan was asked by the skeptical warden about his professed belief in nonviolence. Such a practice among the Pathans was incongruous, for the Pathans were noted for their violence and for being a culture that celebrated revenge and blood feuds. Khan told the jailer that he had embraced nonviolence because of Gandhi. The jailer asked what he would have done if he had not heard of Gandhi. The six-foot-three-inch Khan seized two of the jail bars in his hands and slowly pulled them apart. "That is what I would have done to you."

Abdul Ghaffar Khan was called Badshah Khan, "King of the Khans" by his Pathan people. In India he was known as the Frontier Gandhi. He transformed the warrior culture of the Pathans through a nonviolent interpretation of Islam, creating a massive nonviolent army that played a key role in expelling the British from India. He opened the bars of the British colonial prison through nonviolent direct action.

In 1910, Khan began his work as an educator. The British did not permit schools that were not under their control, preferring uneducated masses, as they would supposedly be easier to control. Khan traveled to villages throughout the mountainous frontier, starting schools and encouraging quality independent education. He talked to people everywhere he went, presenting a vision for the renewal of the Pathan people.

As Khan passed through the village of Zagai he was stranded for a number of days. He went to the local mosque and fasted and prayed. Though Khan did not share much of his inner spirituality, he emerged from that time in Zagai a changed man with a depth and power that others immediately noticed. He had given himself completely to God; but he explained that serving God is done by serving God's children. That passion of nonviolent service drove him for the rest of his life.

Ghaffar Khan joined the movement for independence and was taken with the calm, strong demeanor of the Hindu Mahatma Gandhi. He quickly grasped the inner meaning of Gandhi's teaching. Then Khan forged an Islamic teaching of nonviolence based on the Muslim values of *amal* (selfless service), *yakeen* (faith) and *muhabat* (love). For Khan, love was not sentiment, but a powerful spiritual force that could turn anger into transformative action to overcome exploitation and injustice. Regarding the union of Islam and nonviolence, Khan said, "There is nothing surprising in a Muslim or a Pathan like me subscribing to the creed of nonviolence. It is not a new creed. It was followed 1400 years ago by the Prophet all the time he was in Mecca, and it has since been followed by all those who wanted to throw off an oppressor's yoke. But we had so far forgotten it that when Gandhiji placed it before us, we thought he was sponsoring a novel creed."

Khan was first arrested for speaking at a political meeting during the first *hartal* called by Gandhi. A *hartal* is a period of prayer and fasting that is also effectively a strike, a nonviolent tool to shut down a society. During the *hartal,* Khan led the meeting in the Frontier region. He was sentenced to six months in prison, wearing shackles during the entire time, which left him permanently scarred. Shortly after being freed, he was re-arrested for starting schools and sentenced to three years hard labor since he would not show submission to the British authorities or apologize and stop his activity.

When Khan got out of prison in 1924, the first big push for independence had fizzled. Violence had begun to erupt among the freedom movement but Gandhi halted it. Gandhi was then jailed, as Khan was being released. Khan returned to his home and began the hard work of reshaping the Pathan's cultural view of violence. He taught, in the words of his son Ghani, "that love can create more in a second than bombs can destroy in a century; that the kindest strength is the greatest strength; that the only way to be truly brave is to be in the right; that a clear dream is dearer than life itself." Khan challenged people to a revolution that would build through nonviolence and service rather than destroy through a flood of violence.

Khan also called for the freedom of Muslim women, rejecting the traditional system of *purdah* that kept women isolated. He urged women to come out from behind the veil and join in the nonviolent movement for their own freedom. In a Pathan journal Kahn started reading, one writer exclaimed, "O Pathan, when you demand your freedom, why do you deny it to women?"

Through his leadership in teaching and organizing, Khan developed a nonviolent army called the *Khudai Khidmatgar* (Servants of God), or "Red Shirts," to resist the British—an army of trained, professional, nonviolent soldiers had never been developed. Khan knew that nobody other than a Pathan would be recklessly brave enough to face an enemy for a righteous cause without a weapon. He knew they wouldn't retreat or retaliate. Khan challenged his people with the new concept and more than 100,000 Pathans responded. They joined this red-shirted army by swearing an oath that included these pledges: "I promise to refrain from violence and from taking revenge. I promise to forgive those who oppress me or treat me with cruelty. I promise to refrain from taking part in feuds and quarrels and from creating enmity... I promise to devote at least two hours a day to social work." The army was completely voluntary and comprised of women as well as men. Ghaffar Khan spoke of this form of struggle as *jihad*, with only the enemy holding swords.

Ghaffar Khan's *Khudai Khidmatgar* became one of the most potent forces of resistance against British colonial rule through protests and strikes. In the city of Peshawar the British arrested key *Khudai Khidmatgar* leaders. Quickly, a spontaneous strike was organized and hundreds of unarmed Red Shirts gathered to protest the arrests. British armored cars arrived and began firing at the people. As people fell, new ranks of the Red Shirts would boldly step forward to nonviolently risk being shot, even baring their chests at the British troops. Hundreds of people were killed and thousands injured as the carnage continued for six hours without one violent action from the disciplined protesters. One unit of British soldiers were so moved by the courage of the Red Shirts that they refused to follow orders *en masse*. The British soldiers involved in that massacre were later severely punished for their action, but the damage was done to the credibility of British colonial rule. Thousands of volunteers continued to rush to join the *Khudai Khidmatgars*, replacing those who had fallen. It was later said that the British feared a nonviolent Pathan more than a violent one as their nonviolent resistance made the North-West Frontier Province ungovernable.

As the struggle continued, there was renewed violence as British soldiers hunted down Red Shirts who continued their nonviolent resistance, unbowed. Khan was frequently imprisoned, and then banned from the North-West Frontier Province. He moved into Gandhi's *ashram*, and the two apostles of nonviolence became very close friends. As the moment of independence for India approached, violence between Hindus and Muslims exploded. Gandhi and Ghaffar Khan worked alongside each other with a vision of an India in which Hindus and Muslims could live together in peace—but the partition of India into two countries, India and Pakistan, happened in spite of their efforts. Ironically, they would both suffer from their own co-religionists for promoting a multi-religious nation—Gandhi was killed by a Hindu extremist for urging peace with Muslims, and Ghaffar Khan was imprisoned by an Islamic government in Pakistan for being "pro-Hindu."

Abdul Ghaffar Khan died in 1988 at age of 98 under house arrest, a life-long witness for the compatibility of nonviolence and Islam. He once said, "My religion is truth, love and service to God and humanity. Every religion that has come into the world has brought the message of love and brotherhood. Those who are indifferent to the welfare of their fellowmen, whose hearts are empty of love, they do not know the meaning of religion."

CHAPTER 47

Diane Nash

(b. 1938)

**We can't let them stop us
with violence. If we do that,
the movement is dead.**

—Diane Nash

*Why are women so often overlooked
as we tell our truly important
stories? Diane Nash was someone
I considered for inclusion in this
book for a while, but I just couldn't
find enough reliable information about her life, beyond
a Nashville sit-in campaign. Then I talked to James
Lawson who told me that I must include her. He shared
some stories and guided me to a rich mine of information
about her, which inspired me to complete this chapter.
In reading this profile, you are helping to heal the sexist
blindness that robs us of the wisdom we can glean from
so many bold and courageous women like Nash.*

DIANE NASH CONFRONTED MAYOR Ben West of Nashville on
the steps of City Hall. She stood at the head of a silent march of
more than a thousand African-Americans who had been pushing for desegregation of Nashville's downtown stores and lunch
counters. One of the clergy leaders and the mayor were about to
get into a debate when Nash stepped in with a simple question:
"Mayor West, do you feel it is wrong to discriminate against a person solely on the basis of their race or color?" Aside from all the

political and economic debates, this question cut to the heart of the matter. As West later recalled, "They asked me some pretty soul-searching questions—and one that was addressed to me as a man. And I found that I had to answer it frankly and honestly—that I did not agree that it was morally right for someone to sell them merchandise and refuse them service. And I had to answer it just exactly like that." The gathered marchers erupted in applause. The next day's headline read: "Integrate Counters—Mayor." This breakthrough culminated in a student movement that changed Nashville and honed key leaders for the U.S. civil rights movement. At the center was Diane Nash.

Nash had been raised in a black middle-class home in Chicago. She experienced little of the impact of racism and even was runner-up in a local beauty contest, a precursor to the Miss Illinois pageant. But when she enrolled at Fisk University in Nashville, Tennessee, she was confronted with the harsh realities of Southern segregation, including separate restrooms for "white women" and "colored women." She began to feel "stifled and boxed in," and resented the inferiority that was being pressed on black people by the white-dominated society. A white exchange student at Fisk invited her to attend the workshops led by James Lawson, a black minister who taught nonviolent strategies for attacking the system of segregation.

Nash was skeptical at first, but Lawson's teaching about overcoming self-hatred and centering on loving oneself to develop a basis for nonviolent action began to change her views. "We came to a realization of our own worth," she said. As the workshops continued, her clarity and intense commitment to nonviolence propelled her into the emerging movement's leadership. She was elected chair of the Student Central Committee of the Nashville movement. Nash often honestly expressed her feelings of fear and inadequacy: "We are going to be coming up against…white Southern men who are 40 and 50 and 60 years old, who are politicians and judges and owners of businesses, and I am twenty-two years old. What am I doing? And how is this little group of students my age going to stand up to these powerful people?" Then, despite those fears, she went out and took action.

Nash and the other students launched teams who sat down at lunch counters, where they were refused service. Eventually, the stores were forced to close the counters. When they reopened, the students came back. The police arrested protesters, and more students took their places at the counters. Hundreds of students came again and again, much to the consternation of the police. Then the police allowed young white toughs access to the demonstrators, and the protesting students had food and drinks dumped on them and cigarettes ground out on their heads. Some were dragged off stools and beaten. The police arrested the nonviolent activists but not a single one of their attackers.

As a child, Nash had been terrified of jail since that was where "bad people" went. Now she found herself in jail with other demonstrators, and as they were being processed before a judge and fined, Nash changed the tactics. She told the judge that she and some of the other students were refusing to pay the fines, willing to stay in jail. She said, "We feel that if we pay these fines we would be contributing to and supporting injustice and immoral practices that have been performed in the arrest and conviction of the defendants." The commitment of the students to stay in jail and be seen in the city on work details only gave the movement more positive attention in the black community, increasing support for the activists.

After her release, Nash and a few students went almost immediately to a bus terminal and seated themselves at a lunch counter for whites, where for a change, they were served. But the movement intensified as the city refused to integrate downtown facilities. A boycott of the downtown stores was launched, complete with picketing. As the boycott gathered support, the home of the movement's lawyer was bombed. Nobody was injured, but the damage was severe. In anger, the students marched silently to City Hall—their numbers swelled as neighbors joined them. There, on the steps of City Hall, Nash confronted the mayor, and the tide turned in Nashville.

During the middle of the Nashville campaign, Nash had participated in the founding meeting of the Student Nonviolent Coordinating Committee (SNCC). She was seriously considered as the SNCC's first chair, but a man was chosen instead. Nash later said, "Before the women's movement, men and women tended to see the males as naturally in leadership positions." But Nash exercised leadership in spite of such assumptions. Her leadership reached the national level when the Freedom Ride organized by the Congress on Racial Equality (CORE) was halted following violent attacks in Anniston and Birmingham, Alabama. Nash called James Farmer of CORE to see if he would object to Nashville students going to Birmingham to continue the ride. Farmer tried to dissuade her, calling it suicide. Nash responded, "We're not stupid. But we can't let them stop us with violence. If we do that the movement is dead."

Nash organized the riders, including some of her closest friends from Nashville. She felt trepidation because of the risk that they might be killed. Nash was asked to stay off the buses and recruit more riders, coordinate the overall action and deal with the press and the U.S. government. She refused to give in to the pressure from President John Kennedy and his brother Robert who was the Attorney General when they appealed for a suspension of the Freedom Ride. She challenged them: "Here are people acting within their constitutional and moral rights…. but they have been confined and imprisoned for it. And somehow the Attorney General and the President of the United States…can do nothing about such a gross injustice."

When the riders got to Montgomery they were attacked and beaten. Nash kept track of all the riders who had been scattered, some ending up in hospitals. By the evening of the Montgomery attacks, male clergy and civil rights leaders had gathered, including Martin Luther King, and Nash was pushed to the side. Robert Kennedy and King were on the phone to each other, and King tried to call off the ride. James Farmer of CORE was the only one who supported Nash, and at her refusal to call off the ride, Farmer passed the message on to Kennedy, "We have been cooling off for three hundred and fifty years. If we cool off any more, we will be in a deep freeze. The Freedom Ride will go on." Nash later appealed directly to King to try to get him to join the ride, but King refused. Farmer, however, did board a bus for the next leg of the journey. Again in Jackson, Mississippi, Nash quietly hustled around town keeping track of arrested activists to make sure nobody disappeared by falling through the cracks of the white prison system.

Following the Freedom Ride, the SNCC reorganized itself with a twin thrust of nonviolent direct action and voter registration. Nash was chosen to head up the SNCC's direct action wing. She married James Bevel, another Nashville student activist who had become a national leader. In a campaign in McComb, Mississippi, Nash, along with Bevel and Bernard Lafayette, were arrested for "contributing to the delinquency of minors," the segregationist legal interpretation of their efforts to recruit teenagers to join in protests. They were sentenced to two years in prison. Nash, though she was five months pregnant, chose not to appeal, comparing segregated Mississippi to prison. She released a statement from jail, "I believe that if I go to jail now, it may help hasten that day when my child and all children will be free—not only on the day of their birth but for all their lives." The judge who imposed the original sentence of two years let her go after she served ten days.

Nash and Bevel then moved to Selma, Alabama, to join with Bernard Lafayette and his wife in organizing African-Americans to register to vote. Bevel moved further into the public spotlight, while Nash did the less glamorous work of door-to-door canvassing. She was also caring for two small children by this time. Selma turned out to be the pivotal moment in the civil rights movement, culminating in the passage of the 1965 Voting Rights Act. This time, Nash was not at the head of the marchers, but she had helped build and mobilize the constituency in Selma that made that city the prime point for breakthrough action.

In 1968 Nash and Bevel were divorced. The SNCC was disintegrating from fatigue and internal clashes. For some years, Nash took low-paying jobs to support her children, but she remained active in various causes. She continued to support civil rights and human rights groups. She joined in the anti-war movement. She put her children through college, though her own activism had short-circuited her college degree. She eventually became a real estate agent in Chicago.

Diane Nash expresses no regrets about her choices. "My living has made a difference on the planet," she says.

She certainly made a difference. Her image still stirs our courage as we recall her standing bravely before racist thugs, police, a mayor, judges, the U.S. Attorney General and even the president himself. Nothing would dissuade her from the course of justice.

CHAPTER 48

John Lewis

(b. 1940)

We were determined not to let any act of violence keep us from our goal... We knew our lives could be threatened, but we had made up our minds not to turn back.

—John Lewis

I'm wonderfully haunted by an image of John Lewis stepping off the Freedom Rider's bus—but not in Rock Hill, South Carolina, the first time he was attacked as he left the bus. I think of him in Montgomery, Alabama, as he rode into town with his head and ribs still aching from Rock Hill. This time, another white mob was waiting with the full intention of drawing blood. He knew precisely what would happen; yet he stepped off that bus and soon absorbed a beating that left him unconscious. Nonviolence sounds great as an ideal philosophy, but Lewis embodied it in a way that I will never forget. If I ever I have to face such a moment, I pray his example will guide me.

IN ROCK HILL, JOHN Lewis calmly stepped off a bus and into a savage beating. Lewis was one of the Freedom Riders, an integrated team of civil rights activists who were challenging the laws in the American South that segregated interstate buses and bus terminal waiting rooms. A crowd of about 20 or 30 young white men was waiting at the Rock Hill bus station in South Carolina. Lewis was the first to exit the bus, and he went down almost immediately under a hail of blows. He was bleeding and his ribs were racked with stabbing pain.

Born to a sharecropping family in Alabama, Lewis left the family farm to study at Fisk University in Nashville. He had listened to Martin Luther King, Jr. on the radio during the days of the Montgomery bus boycott, so he quickly gravitated to the student activists pulled together by James Lawson. The students in Nashville launched a movement of lunch counter sit-ins. Black and white students would sit together at the counters of the downtown stores where they were first ignored, then harassed, beaten and arrested. Lewis had been afraid of jail, but he was prepared for the experience by the extensive role-plays Lawson used in pre-action training. Lewis said of his experience going to jail to confront injustice, "I had never had that much dignity before… It was exhilarating—it was something I had earned, the sense of the independence that comes to a free person." After months of sit-ins, marches and a boycott, the mayor and business leaders gave in, and the lunch counters were desegregated.

The Nashville movement provided leadership for the broader civil rights movement as many of the student activists became the well-trained, focused and committed leaders who could do the hard work of organizing and the risky work of serving on the front lines of the struggle. The next call to action came when the Congress of Racial Equality organized the Freedom Ride. Lewis joined the ride at the beginning, and was the first casualty when he was beaten in Rock Hill, South Carolina. At that point, he needed to recover, so the Freedom Riders went on without him. Then the action stalled in Anniston and Birmingham, Alabama, when one bus was burned and riders were so badly beaten that many were hospitalized. Lewis, still bandaged from his first beating, was determined that the Freedom Ride must continue. He called his friends from the Nashville movement. The cost of their involvement was evident from photos in newspapers—but they knew that this was the moment in the struggle when nonviolence was crucial in order to confront the violence of bigotry and legalized injustice.

Lewis led the next stage of the Freedom Ride, leaving out of Birmingham. When the bus got to Montgomery, Lewis was again first off the bus. This time, there were reporters to greet him, but moments later a mob of more than 200 people surged around the corner of the bus station attacking Freedom Riders and the media with clubs and bats. Lewis and his white bus-mate Jim Zwerg were beaten unconscious. Four days later, Lewis was on another bus crossing into Mississippi. There, the Freedom Riders were arrested and held for six weeks in sweltering jail cells full of bugs and rodents and with open toilets. Lewis and some of the other riders were sent to the maximum-security wing of the notorious Mississippi prison known as Parchman Farm. The courage and sacrifice of Lewis and other Freedom Riders brought pressure on the federal government to finally enforce desegregated interstate travel for all people.

To coordinate the organizing of young people for the civil rights movement, Lewis helped form the Student Nonviolent Coordinating Committee (SNCC). He was named the first chairman. Even though he was only 23 years old, he joined the other top leaders as a major shaper of the movement. He helped organize the 1963 March on Washington and was a keynote speaker along with Dr. King.

In 1964, Lewis helped Robert Moses lead the SNCC voter registration campaign in Mississippi during the "Freedom Summer" that brought students from around the country to register black voters. The next year, he was in the front row as one of the leaders of 600 marchers heading from Selma, Alabama to Montgomery to campaign for voting rights. The marchers were attacked by state troopers at the Edmund Pettus Bridge in an action that became known as "Bloody Sunday." Lewis and the marchers had just begun to kneel and pray in front of the lines of police, when the police charged. Lewis was again savagely beaten with a police baton. He lost consciousness and suffered a fractured skull. A photo of his beating was published around the nation. The next day Lewis checked himself out of the hospital, and with his head swathed in bandages, gave a press conference saying the march would continue. The courage of the nonviolent activists who suffered under the brutality of the police propelled the nation to pass the Voting Rights Act of 1965. Lewis stood in the Oval Office as President Lyndon Johnson signed the bill into law.

Though he was arrested more than 40 times and severely beaten again and again, Lewis remained a proponent of nonviolence. As a faction of the SNCC turned from nonviolence to an angry philosophy of "black power," Lewis was forced out of SNCC leadership. He left the organization to work in voter registration and education, believing that the empowerment of African-Americans through political enfranchisement was the way to permanently change the structures of racial injustice.

In 1981, Lewis ran for office and won a seat on the Atlanta City Council. Then in 1986, he was elected to the U.S. House of Representatives, where he has served for over 20 years. Lewis continues as a voice of conscience for economic and racial justice.

CHAPTER 49

Bolivian Women Hunger Strikers

Nellie Paniagua, Angélica Flores, Aurora Lora and Luzmila Pimentel

When a people discovers its own force and its own truth, it is able to forge its own history.

—Permanent Assembly for Human Rights

I was in Bolivia shortly after the election of Evo Morales, who describes himself as the first Amerindian president of a South American country. This was as profound a historical moment for Bolivia as the election of Barak Obama was for us in the U.S. Morales wouldn't have been elected without the movement of pride and courage ignited by hunger-striking Bolivian women. I saw the continued marginalization of the indigenous women, but I also saw them bursting through again and again to express their desires and even their demands for justice.

BOLIVIA HAS BEEN THE poorest country in South America, and Bolivian tin miners have been among the most oppressed in that long-suffering land. A string of military dictatorships had ruled the land, including a seven-year reign by General Hugo Banzer in the 1970s. The tin mines were the focus of struggles for justice, both because of the hardship and poverty endured by the miners and their families, and because of the potential for labor organizing in the mines. The government and mining companies responded to the miners' hopes for justice with troops, arrests, firings and other forms of repression.

Then, in late 1977, four Aymara Indian women—wives of miners—engaged in a nonviolent action that mobilized the Bolivian people and forced a military dictator to accede to their demands. For seven years, Banzer had ruled Bolivia for the benefit of the wealthy, freely using arrest, exile, torture and even "disappearance" to maintain his firm hand. The general suspended all unions and political parties. In 1977, he was feeling international pressure about his human rights abuses, so he announced an amnesty. The move was a farce, because only 14 of the country's 348 imprisoned or exiled political dissidents were covered by the amnesty. The husbands of Nellie Paniagua and Angélica Flores had been arrested and fired. Aurora Lora's husband was in hiding while Luzmila Pimentel's husband was in jail for his union activities. Banzer's amnesty did not include their husbands, so in desperation, they decided to act.

The women launched a hunger strike. They traveled from the mining district to La Paz, the Bolivian capital. There they met with the Catholic Archbishop Jorge Manrique, who was respected by the common people and also was part Aymara. Their idea for a hunger strike had the blessing of the archbishop who even offered his own residence as a site, which provided high visibility for the action due to its short distance from the presidential palace.

They began the strike with readings from Jesus' Sermon on the Mount from the Gospel of St. Matthew. This was selected because the women knew that Martin Luther King, Jr. drew most of his inspiration from this text. But another biblical story led them in a more controversial direction. The story of King Herod massacring the innocent children prompted the women to invite their children to share in the hunger strike. The women presented four demands related to their strike: amnesty for political prisoners and exiles; restoration of jobs to the workers who had been fired for union organizing; reinstatement of labor unions; and the removal of the Bolivian army from the mines.

Eventually, they won. At that time, it appeared the toppling of the Banzer regime would usher in a new era of justice and democracy. As it turned out, a cycle of coups, dictatorships and death squads continued to send waves of bloodshed across Bolivia. But these courageous women proved the catalytic power of personal action. More hunger strikes would follow. Their original action energized mass movements across Bolivia in a way nothing had before.

In a celebration mass after the strike, one woman said, "I want all of you to realize that it was the women who did this, and that we are good for something more than cooking, cleaning and looking after children." The action of the four women also proved the political potential of long-oppressed groups like laborers and indigenous people. Evo Morales was an Aymara teenager when these courageous women carried out their hunger strike. In 1982, democratically elected, civilian government finally came to power. Then in 2006, Evo Morales became the first indigenous Bolivian ever elected president. Capturing the power of that first Bolivian hunger strike, the Permanent Assembly for Human Rights said, "When a people discovers its own force and its own truth, it is able to forge its own history."

CHAPTER 50

Daniel Berrigan and Philip Berrigan

(b. 1921) (1923-2002)

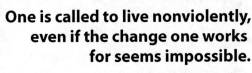

One is called to live nonviolently, even if the change one works for seems impossible.

—Daniel Berrigan

Peacemaking is not only a central characteristic of the Gospel, peacemaking is the greatest need of the world today. We are the daughters and sons of God, and that means we are called to be peacemakers.

—Phillip Berrigan

I worked for nine years in King of Prussia, Pennsylvania, where a massive factory assembled components for nuclear weapons systems. It was owned by a group of corporations including General Electric and Lockheed Martin-Marietta. That is where the Berrigans engaged in the first Plowshares action—a protest for which they both spent time in jail. Their trial took place in Norristown, across the river from our home. At times I joined the on-going vigils at the plant led by the Brandywine Peace Community. One Good Friday we marched the Stations of the Cross by walking meditatively from building to building—benign-looking structures designed to manufacture mass destruction.

IT WAS MAY 17, 1968. Philip and Daniel Berrigan, along with seven other anti-war activists walked into the draft board's office in Catonsville, Maryland. They opened filing cabinets and took out 378 files of young men to be drafted. They dumped the files into two garbage cans in the parking lot and then poured home-made napalm over the documents and incinerated them. They were all arrested and eventually put on trial as a group. They became known as the Catonsville Nine.

The burning of the draft records in Catonsville was one of the signature protest actions of the Berrigans. They moved beyond the protests of street marches and tried to actually disrupt the machinery of war, whether it was the war in Vietnam or the future preparations for nuclear war. They were nonviolent against people, but they were destructive of property, which resulted in many years in prison. They argued, however, that their acts of destruction were moral acts that sought to halt the far greater destruction of human life by these instruments of violence.

The Berrigans were born into a second-generation, working-class, Irish-Catholic family. Daniel, the older brother, joined the Jesuit order and was ordained a priest in 1952. While Daniel was in school, World War II broke out and Philip was drafted. He served in the artillery and was later promoted to Second Lieutenant in the infantry. He said of himself that he became "a skilled and remorseless killer." He was deeply affected by the violence of combat, including the Battle of the Bulge, as well as the racism he experienced in the boot camps. His conscience was so stirred that he committed himself to total resistance to war itself. After the war, Philip too, studied for the priesthood and was ordained in 1955.

Philip challenged Daniel's way of thinking about faith, calling his pacifist brother to a greater engagement with the injustice and violence of the world. Later, a friendship with Thomas Merton helped further Daniel's radicalization. The brothers participated in the civil rights movement. They marched in Selma and Montgomery for voting rights. They participated in sit-ins and boycotted segregated buses.

Their dramatic actions in protest against the war in Vietnam catapulted them to national attention. Philip Berrigan was the first to engage in the more dramatic direct action protests. He was one of the "Baltimore Four" who entered the Baltimore Customs House in October 1967 and poured blood on U.S. Selective Service draft records. They had drawn their own blood and supplemented it with poultry blood. Philip Berrigan wrote, "This sacrificial and constructive act is meant to protest the pitiful waste of American and Vietnamese blood in Indochina." He was sentenced to six years in prison for this act, becoming the first Roman Catholic priest in the U.S. to be imprisoned for political reasons.

Meanwhile, Daniel and the historian-activist Howard Zinn went to North Vietnam during the Tet holiday in 1968 during which the historic Tet Offensive erupted. They facilitated the first release of American prisoners of war: three pilots who had been shot down while bombing the north. Tet is a time for family reunions, so Berrigan and Zinn felt this peace gesture was appropriate, even as the war continued to escalate.

Philip was released from jail on bail in 1968 but immediately began planning a way to continue his protests in modified form. He invited Daniel, who was teaching at Cornell University, to join him along with other anti-war activists for a protest in Catonsville, Maryland. A local high school physics teacher helped them make the napalm that they used to destroy the Catonsville draft files. Philip was sentenced to three and a half years in prison. Daniel was sentenced to three years but chose to go underground instead. He was a fugitive for four months until he was captured by the FBI and imprisoned, then released in 1972.

The Berrigans' action inspired many activists, including other priests and nuns, to take similar actions against draft boards, always risking significant jail time. Following the pattern of the Berrigans, the activists engaged in spiritual disciplines both in preparation for the action and also to sustain themselves through the long jail sentences. Daniel said, "It is very rare to sustain a movement in recognizable form without a spiritual base," so retreats were part of the preparation for action. These religious activists would resist what they saw as "lawless laws" but submit to the punishment meted out. Philip helped in planning many of these events. In some cases the activists served significant jail time, and in other cases the courts dropped the charges or dismissed the cases. At one point, Philip was arrested along with others for conspiracy—for discussing the idea of placing Henry Kissinger under citizens' arrest for waging an illegal war.

After the war in Vietnam ended, the Berrigans turned their attention to the Cold War and the nuclear arms race. Along with six other activists they began the Plowshares Movement in 1980. The name was a reminder of words from the prophet Isaiah, "They shall beat their swords into plowshares and their spears into pruning hooks." In a literal enactment of this prophetic verse on September 9, 1980, six Plowshares activists slipped into the General Electric plant at King of Prussia, Pennsylvania. This was the Nuclear Missile Re-Entry Division that made nose cones for Mark 12A warheads, a first-strike nuclear weapon. The activists found two nose cones and beat them with hammers, cracking them. Then they poured blood on documents and prayed for peace in the place where nuclear warheads were assembled. Their trial and case was long and complex with appeals that lasted 10 years. Eventually they were sentenced to the time they had already spent in jail.

Their action launched a movement around the world that resulted in more than 70 Plowshares actions. Philip Berrigan's last Plowshares action was in December 1999 when he hammered on an A-10 Warthog attack plane. He was convicted of malicious destruction of property and sentenced to 30 months in prison. Though he was released a few months early, he totaled 11 years in prison for his actions of civil disobedience. Daniel called the Plowshares actions "Theatre of the Absurd."

Both the Berrigans were writers. Daniel was the most prolific, writing poetry as well as prose. He wrote a prize-winning play, *The Trial of the Catonsville Nine*, based on the action against the draft board. The play ran for years on Broadway. Daniel briefly appeared in the role of a Jesuit priest in the hit movie *The Mission*, starring Robert DeNiro. He also served as a consultant for the film, which explored the options of violent and nonviolent resistance to oppression—neither of which "succeed" in the movie. For the Berrigans, success wasn't the issue. Daniel said: "The good is to be done because it is good, not because it goes somewhere. I believe if it is done in that spirit it will go somewhere, but I don't know where. I don't think the Bible grants us to know where goodness goes, what direction, what force. I have never been seriously interested in the outcome. I was interested in trying to do it humanly and carefully and nonviolently and let it go."

In 1973 Philip married Elizabeth McAlister, who was also a peace activist. Philip once viewed marriage as a hindrance to full commitment to peace action because of family concerns, but he found a perfect partner in Liz McAlister. She also engaged in Plowshares actions, such as entering the Rome Air Force Base in New York and hammering a B-52 loaded with nuclear weapons. That action brought Liz a 3-year sentence. Philip and Liz shared in acts of civil disobedience and the separations of jail time. Together they helped found Jonah House, a Christian community in Baltimore to support the work of peace, serve the poor and resist unjust government actions.

Daniel joined the faculty of Fordham University and became Fordham's Poet-in-Residence. He worked with victims of AIDS, especially terminal patients. Daniel once said, "There is no peace because the making of peace is at least as costly as the making of war—at least as exigent, at least as disruptive, at least as liable to bring disgrace and prison and death in its wake."

As Philip neared his death from cancer in 2002, he said, "The greatest need of humankind today is peace. Unless peace can become a reality from which all persons inevitably will benefit, humanity itself will flounder, will gasp and will die out..."

Both Berrigan brothers worked throughout their lives for the cause of peace and were willing to pay that very high cost. Their actions and their words inspired many others to follow their risky example, hoping to halt the work of war.

CHAPTER 51

Mothers of the Plaza de Mayo

Azucena de Vicenti, Sister Alicia Domont, Hebe Bonafini, Nora Cortinas, Adela Antokoletz, Juanita Pargament, Enriqueta Maroni, Matilde Saidler de Mellibovsky, et al.

It is as if lions grew inside of me, and I am not afraid.

—Hebe Bonafini

One of my favorite Bible stories to use in training sessions is the story of Rizpah in 2 Samuel 21. She was a mother who watched as her two sons were executed for crimes of their father. She began a nonviolent action that ended up changing the heart of King David and healing a long-standing division in the land. I think of the Mothers of the Plaza de Mayo as daughters of Rizpah. They turned trauma into creative courageous action that challenged rulers and eventually healed their land. I tell their story almost every time I tell Rizpah's.

"*LAS LOCAS DE PLAZA de Mayo*" they were called—"the mad-women of the Plaza de Mayo" or "the crazy ones." They must have been crazy to challenge the Argentine military, which had seized power in a 1976 coup. They must have been crazy because their own children had been seized by the military or police and "disappeared." They must have been crazy because some of them were arrested and never seen again. But they kept coming to the central square in Buenos Aires in silent vigil to protest the systemic violence of the military regime. Eventually the madwomen became the conscience of a nation seared by violence and fear, leading the way out of one of the darkest chapters of Argentina's history.

The Argentine military overthrew a stumbling democratic government and launched a "national security" policy that sought the extermination of all "subversives." A "subversive" was not just a member of the small leftist insurgency, but "anyone who opposes the Argentine way of life"—as defined by the nation's generals. General Ibérico Saint Jean said, "First we will kill all the subversives; then we will kill their collaborators; then…their sympathizers, then…those who remain indifferent; and finally we will kill the timid."

The generals cast a wide net of repression in what was to be called the "Dirty War." First in night raids, then in broad daylight, soldiers or police seized students, academics, journalists, artists, union leaders, and anyone who raised any kind of a voice of protest as well as people who seemed completely apolitical. Those seized were subjected to torture: beatings, electric shock, near drowning, faces smashed with hammers, dislocated bones, rape and being hung upside down. Babies born to pregnant prisoners were stolen. An estimated 30,000 of those detained "disappeared." After the regime was overthrown, it was revealed that many of those who disappeared were taken in helicopters and dropped into the ocean. A mother said, "Nothing can do more human harm than the pain of such long years of uncertainty—of simply not knowing. The passing days with their alternations of feeble, fading hope and hopeless depression cause a grave deterioration of spirit and body." All of Argentina was paralyzed with terror.

A few women began to recognize each other in the lines at the police stations of those seeking information about missing relatives. One of the hurdles they had to overcome was the shame and suspicion that came from the government-promoted notion that anyone arrested was guilty and deserved harsh treatment. As these women talked together, they realized that their loved ones did not deserve this. Provoked by their grief and anger, they decided to act. On Saturday, April 30, 1977 fourteen women gathered at the Plaza de Mayo in the center of Buenos Aires to protest the disappearance of their children. Then they realized that Saturday was not a good day to confront officials since government offices were closed, so they switched their upcoming actions to Thursday.

The next Thursday twenty women gathered—the numbers swelled each succeeding week. The women wore white scarves. Sometimes they carried photographs of their children. They filed a collective petition of habeas corpus in the courts. The police drove them away with guns. When that did not keep them away, the police arrested them. Eventually some of the women disappeared themselves—but more stepped forward.

In spite of the heavy censorship, the Mothers published a paid advertisement in the *La Prensa* newspaper. Boldly resisting the fear that the military repression had instilled in the general population, 237 women signed the advertisement demanding to know where their relatives were. It was the first message of resistance to the policy of the generals that went out in the press.

Then the Mothers developed a national petition that listed 571 people who had disappeared and 61 people detained without charges, demanding an investigation and due process of law in these cases. They gathered more than 24,000 signatures from supporters. During a demonstration of 800 Mothers, they presented the petition to the government.

Initially, the Mothers had been ignored. Then they were called madwomen, "*las Locas*." As their resistance expanded and grew in boldness, the military knew they had a serious challenge on their hands. A high-level military officer infiltrated the group and called in a police raid. A dozen people were arrested. Then in a follow-up raid Azucena De Vicenti was kidnapped. She had been one of the founders of the Mothers and a leader. None of those arrested were ever seen again.

Surviving members of the group continued their actions. They appealed to the world press. When international dignitaries visited, they set up demonstrations at the statue of San Martin, the liberator of Argentina, a traditional stop for foreign visitors. During the 1978 World Cup soccer championships the women exposed their vigils to the international press, prompting the military to engage in a strong propaganda campaign against them. Though the repression continued, the women found a variety of creative ways to continue their protests at places of relative safety where their voices could be heard by larger audiences. Matilde Saidler de Millibovsky, whose 29-year old daughter had "disappeared" said, "We were showing our countrymen the dreadful truth the dictatorship took pains to hide in thousands of ways."

At one point, the women, who had seemed to be in a slight decline under the military pressure, mobilized a major demonstration when the Organization of American States met. From that point on, there was a discernable shift in power as the women were never again forced out of the plaza. The resistance spread, and in 1981 a general strike was launched to protest the dictatorship.

In 1983 the military regime collapsed and democracy was restored to Argentina. The Mothers of the Plaza de Mayo continued to advocate for an accounting of the "disappeared" and to bring perpetrators to justice. They searched for the children born in prison to women who were pregnant when arrested. Eventually they found more than 80 grandchildren who were reunited with families.

The Mothers also extended their work for human rights beyond Argentina. They joined in solidarity with other movements against disappearances, torture, and extra-judicial killing throughout Latin America. As one Mother said, "I don't want another mother, in this country or in any other, to have to live through what I have. Beyond my personal case is the basic principle of the systematic use of repression and state terrorism as a method of government, which I must denounce and combat."

In the face of one of the most vicious military dictatorships in the world, grieving women made a nonviolent stand. Enriqueta Maroni who lost two children and a son-in-law said, "Our love for our children made us defy their whole repressive apparatus."

Their courage eventually cracked the powerful structures of repression and brought the regime down. It was a poignant victory because so many loved ones were never found. One of the Mothers wrote: "We had always been at home, busy only with the family... When we went to look for our children we found a new world where everything was rotten...We learned to put aside our self-centeredness, always being concerned with ourselves and our families... Now we began to really understand many things, which our sons and daughters had told us and which, in those times, we did not want to accept and we could not imagine. The 'disappeared' represented everyone and the struggle had to be everyone's struggle."

CHAPTER 52

Lech Wałęsa
(b. 1943)

Victory can be achieved by various means. It can be gained with tanks and missiles, but I think that one wins better with truth, honesty and logic... This is a new weapon.

—Lech Wałęsa

I'm not Polish, but I've sometimes lived in largely Polish communities, including Hamtramck, Michigan, where my wife and I now reside. Poland has often been carved up by the powers around it, never united enough to stand against others. But a united movement wondrously called **Solidarność** *(Solidarity) cracked apart one of the most powerful empires in history. It was led by ordinary Poles, working-class people like my neighbors—who are so proud of what was accomplished in their homeland.*

ONE OF THE GREATEST ironies in history is that the Communist empire was undone by a genuine national workers' revolution. The workers' nonviolent revolution that began in Poland was the key blow that eventually led to the collapse of the Soviet Union and its iron grip over Eastern Europe. At the head of the revolt was an unemployed electrician named Lech Wałęsa.

Wałęsa was born to a peasant family during World War II. When he was older he joined the flow of workers to the cities of

Poland, which was engaged in massive industrialization under the new Communist regime. In 1967, he landed a job as an electrician at the shipyard in the coastal city of Gdańsk.

The first clash between the shipyard workers and the government erupted in December 1970. Wałęsa was a member of the illegal strike committee. When the government succeeded in crushing the strike, Wałęsa was briefly jailed. Then in 1976, he was fired from the shipyard for his organizing efforts as a shop steward. He supported his family by various temporary jobs, but he continued to make contact with union activists, joining the illegal and underground Free Trade Unions of the Coast. Meanwhile the state security apparatus kept Wałęsa under surveillance and periodically detained him.

In August 1980, the 17,000 workers at the Gdańsk shipyard went on strike. In the 1970 clash, they had taken their protest into the streets where the workers were easy targets for the police, but this time they decided to occupy the shipyard. They locked the gates and refused to leave. The government couldn't risk destroying the shipyard with an assault on the workers. Wałęsa raced to the shipyard, dramatically climbed the fence and was enthusiastically received by the striking workers. During the strike, families passed food over the fence for the workers. Many of the workers, including Wałęsa, were devout Catholics, so priests joined the workers to say mass.

Wałęsa became the leader of the Strike Coordination Committee at the shipyard. Initially the strike was about higher wages, but Wałęsa urged them toward the more visionary and political demand for free trade unions. The strike at the shipyard inspired other workers throughout Poland to join with them, and an Inter-Factory Strike Committee was formed to coordinate the strikes. The Polish government finally entered into negotiations with the strikers, led by Wałęsa. On August 31, 1980, the Gdańsk Agreement was signed giving workers across Poland the right to strike and to organize their own independent trade union.

After the successful strike in Gdańsk, representatives gathered from the various unions across Poland, and they established

The Solidarity Free Trade Union (*Solidarność* in Polish, Solidarity in English). The union grew to about 10 million members, representing most of the industrial workers in Poland. A related agricultural union also was also established called Rural Solidarity. In September 1981, Wałęsa was elected chairman at the First National Solidarity Congress, held in Gdańsk.

With growing fear that the Soviet Union might invade to suppress the increasing strength of Solidarity, General Wojciech Jaruzelski declared martial law in Poland. Solidarity was "suspended," and many of its leaders arrested. Wałęsa was arrested and detained for 11 months in a house at a remote location to keep him in isolation. After his release he was allowed to return to his old job in the shipyard, but only under intense surveillance. However, he still managed to keep up secret contacts with other underground union activists, while remaining above the law.

In 1983 the Nobel Peace Prize was awarded to Wałęsa, an action criticized by the Jaruzelski regime. Fearing that the government would not let him return if he left Poland, Wałęsa sent his wife to receive the prize on his behalf. The international attention helped Solidarity continue its struggle during the height of the martial law period.

When Mikhail Gorbachev began launching reforms from Moscow, the pressure from Solidarity began building again in Poland. In 1988, Wałęsa and Solidarity struck with renewed confidence, occupying the Gdańsk shipyard once more. Jaruzelski was forced to negotiate with Wałęsa and Solidarity. Solidarity was legalized, and the Polish government reached an agreement with the union to hold semi-free parliamentary elections that for the first time allowed the participation of non-Communists. In June 1989, the Solidarity-endorsed candidates won overwhelmingly, taking all but one of the seats in the national assembly not reserved by law for the Communist Party. The first non-Communist Prime Minister was chosen: Tadeusz Mazowiecki, an advisor to Solidarity.

The political pressure for change became unstoppable. In December 1990 the first free general election was held in Poland since World War II. The electrician who had led the strike that began the revolution became the first president of Poland in the post-Communist era. Poland's successful rejection of Communism opened the floodgates of change in Eastern Europe. In short order, the East German regime collapsed and the Berlin Wall came down. The Czechs held their "Velvet Revolution," and Eastern Europe crumbled as a Communist bloc. The Cold War ended, and in 1991 the Soviet Union broke up. One of the greatest empires in history crumbled in large part from nonviolent resistance launched by the union Wałęsa led.

Though Wałęsa was a brilliant union activist and leader of the resistance to Communist Party rule, his presidency was erratic. He fought with many of his old Solidarity colleagues, including Mazowiecki. In 1995 when Wałęsa ran for a second term as president, he was narrowly defeated. He has since alternated between speaking engagements around the world and venturing again into Polish politics, each time with less success than earlier forays. He will be remembered not for his political career but for his activism at the shipyard and at the negotiation table. There he won a true workers' revolution, using nonviolence, tenacity and faith.

CHAPTER 53

Maha Ghosananda

(1929-2007)

**We must remove the landmines
in our hearts which prevent
us from making peace. The
landmines in the heart are
greed, hatred and delusion.
We can overcome greed with
the weapon of generosity;
we can overcome hatred
with the weapon of loving
kindness; we can overcome delusion with the
weapon of wisdom. Peace-making starts with us.**

—Maha Ghosananda

*I stumbled across reports about the prayer marches of
Maha Ghosananda while researching someone else for
this book. Until that discovery, I knew of nothing hopeful
that came from the Cambodian killing fields. Yet here was
a monk who inspired a movement that faced down one of
the worst horrors of humanity with prayer and a centered
spirit. I was awed by this witness and knew it had to be
brought from the jungles of Cambodia to global awareness.*

THE PEACE WALKS IN Cambodia led by Maha Ghosananda
were often accompanied by the sound of weapons firing and
explosions. Instead of heading toward safety the walkers headed
directly to the battlefields. Cambodia had suffered through more
than 20 years of bombing, invasion, genocide and civil war. This

Buddhist monk led a series of yearly walks throughout Cambodia that challenged the armed groups and ignited hope among a population who had despaired of peace being possible. The people were challenged directly by Maha Ghosananda whose motto was "Peace is possible!"

Born in rural Cambodia, he entered a Buddhist temple at 8 years old and began his education as a monk. His name became Maha Ghosananda, which means "great joyful proclaimer." When he completed his university education, he left for India. There he met the Japanese monk, Nichidatsu Fujii, who had studied under Ghandi. Nichidatsu introduced Ghosananda to the principles and practices of nonviolence through a Buddhist framework.

While he was studying meditation in Thailand, the United States started bombing Cambodia during the Vietnam War. In 1970 the U.S. invaded Cambodia and, through a coup, installed a military regime. The Khmer Rouge insurgency (Communists) grew in response and marched into the capital city, Phnom Penh, in 1975. They immediately drove the population out of the city in a genocidal program to remake Cambodia. Part of the policy of the Khmer Rouge was to eliminate Buddhist monks and temples. Every one of Maha Ghosananda's family members and Buddhist colleagues were murdered. The only monks who survived the killing fields (death camps), were those in exile such as Ghosananda. Only 3,000 of the original 65,000 Cambodian monks remained when the Khmer Rouge came to power.

As reports of the horrors filtered into Thailand, Ghosananda was torn with anguish. His meditation master challenged him to foster peace in his own heart and wait for the right time to return home. "Don't weep," his master told him, "Be mindful."

In a clash with Vietnam in 1978, the Khmer Rouge leadership was toppled from power and retreated into a rebel force that fought on for another decade. Ghosananda saw this as an opening through which he could move. He went into the growing refugee camps at the Thai border as the survivors of the genocide came streaming out with stories of horror beyond imagining. When they saw Ghosananda, the expatriates rejoiced and wept, falling on their knees at the sight of a Buddhist monk publicly ministering to people once again. The saffron-robed monk moved gently among them, bowing with respect and teaching about non-retaliation, reconciliation and love. He opened up his *wat*, (his temple), for refugees.

Throughout the 1980s, as the Vietnamese-supported government and the Khmer Rouge continued to fight, Maha Ghosananda traveled the world, teaching Buddhist peace principles in the Cambodian exile communities and meeting with various world religious leaders. He began talking about raising an "army of peace" whose ammunition would be "bullets of loving kindness." He participated in the peace negotiations, often opening sessions with prayer and meditation. In 1991, the Paris Agreement was signed which closed the refugee camps and repatriated the refugees—even though fighting continued.

In 1992, Ghosananda began the first peace walk. It was called the *Dhammayietra*, a walking meditative "pilgrimage of truth" in the tradition of the Buddha who often walked as part of his spiritual discipline. Ghosananda said that they needed to journey to the places of human suffering—from refugee camps to battlefields—and make them their temples. The walkers sought the transformation of the Cambodian people and society. "Wars of the heart always take longer to cool than the barrel of a gun...we must heal through love... and we must go slowly, step by step." The walk began in the refugee camps, crossed the border, passed through some of the conflict zones, and ended up in Phnom Penh, a 125-mile route. Along the way, thousands of people would come out to encourage the walkers and receive traditional Buddhist blessings. In each village Ghosananda would teach about peace and reconciliation. Even soldiers from all factions would lay down their weapons to pray and be blessed.

A second *Dhammayietra* in 1993 was even more risky. It was held just before the first elections, and violence was being used to intimidate voters. Before the march had even begun, a battle raged outside the temple where marchers had gathered. Shots were fired at the temple and three marchers were wounded. A grenade was thrown into the group mere feet from Ghosananda, but it failed to explode. Ghosananda assured people, "Sometimes we are in fear but later the fear is no longer with us. We have to walk and spread our message with compassion, loving kindness and respect for the human rights of all who are victims of war."

They walked for days again, going through zones where the U.N. peacekeepers were afraid to patrol. Soldiers would plead, "Please bless us in a way that our bullets don't hit anyone, and so that no one else's bullets hurt us." Townspeople said, "We were told not to come, but they cannot stop us. This is our religion. We hunger for peace so much." The marchers were joined by thousands of others along the route, especially when they came into the capital. Their witness challenged the intimidation by the armed groups and gave courage to the Cambodian people. The populace responded, and there was a 90 percent turnout of voters at the election.

The third march went into western Cambodia where the fighting was still intense. Pre-walk training covered issues of non-violence, landmine awareness and first aid. They appealed to both sides for negotiations without pre-conditions. As they neared the fighting, their way was blocked by troops. They joined the refugees fleeing the area and then searched for another way to get to their destination. They were passing near government troops when the Khmer Rouge attacked them. Three monks and a nun were killed in the crossfire. The surviving marchers were taken prisoner and taken to the Khmer Rouge camp. They noticed how frightened the young fighters were. The commander apologized to them, assured them he wanted peace, and urged them to remain non-partisan in their work for reconciliation. They were then released with the admonition, "We, too, are tired of fighting for 20 years."

Three more annual *Dhammayietras* were held. The 1995 walk focused on banning landmines. Cambodia had more than 10 million landmines—more mines than people. The marchers collected more than 20,000 signatures to ban landmines globally. The 1996 walk focused on deforestation, especially linked to militarism and illegal logging that thrived during the civil war. The walkers traveled through the most damaged regions in the country and planted 2,000 trees along the pilgrimage route. The final march in 1997 focused on reconciliation between the Khmer Rouge and government forces. They called for forgiveness. They walked the same route as the third march, meeting the commander of the unit who had killed the earlier marchers. They also met Ieng Sary who had been second in command of the Khmer Rouge after Pol Pot. Ieng Sary asked for forgiveness and pledged to work for peace, so Maha Ghosananda offered him a simple blessing. Ghosananda was criticized for this action, since Sary had been among the leadership carrying out the earlier campaign of mass murder. But the monk replied, "In Buddhism, when people know their crimes and they ask for pardon, then the Buddha pardons them. We do not know if [Ieng Sary] is lying or not, but the Dhamma forgives people who return to the light and give up fighting."

Through his bold, nonviolent work, especially through the peace walks, Maha Ghosananda helped Cambodia emerge from the grim years of war and genocide. He enabled ordinary people to begin to believe in the possibility of peace and to make public stands for peace. He connected people to what was best in their own besieged religious tradition. That faith became fuel for national renewal and reconciliation. The monk said, "Peacemaking is like breathing. We cannot stop. If we stop, there is fighting again, we die. If we continue, peace will prevail."

CHAPTER 54

Women in Black

Perhaps the Intifada spoke to women in a way that other wars had not. This was not only husbands and sons making war, not armies, but a rebellion of women and children. Perhaps this spoke to the hearts of women.

—Galia Golan

While in Jerusalem once, I visited a Women in Black vigil. I stood near them in solidarity with their silent protest and heard the abuse hurled at them. I've also seen their impact in inspiring women to witness against war and injustice in my own community. I met some of my best friends through the Women in Black network in Detroit where they allowed this man to stand or march silently with them as war was developing in Iraq.

THE WOMEN STOOD SILENTLY around the square. They held signs in Hebrew and English that said, "Stop the Occupation." Some passing drivers yelled sexual insults and profanities at them and passengers in buses spat on them. They were called "whores" and "Arafat lovers." Occasionally, tomatoes, oranges and eggs were hurled at them. They all dressed in black. They had been there the week before, and they were coming again the next week.

Women in Black was launched by Israeli women in 1988 as a protest against the Israeli occupation of the West Bank and Gaza.

Palestinians began the first *Intifada* (uprising) late in 1987. As Israeli armed forces responded to Palestinian protests with harsh force and Palestinian deaths mounted, the dormant Israeli peace movement stirred to life. The Jerusalem branch of *Dai LaKibush*, made up of men and women who supported a peaceful solution to the Israeli-Palestinian conflict, held vigils but received little attention. As they thought of how to increase the drama of their protest, one of the men suggested that the women gather in black and the men in white. The women came dressed for the occasion, but the men failed to dress in white. The black-garbed women garnered a lot of attention from the passers-by, looking like a Greek chorus or as if they were at a funeral.

So the Jewish women from *Dai LaKibush* began weekly Friday vigils. Their theme was as simple as the group's name, which means: "end the occupation." The women wore black to create a clear, visible presence. At first some of the women were aggressive, shouting back insults and even becoming physically forceful. But after deep discussion they committed themselves to the practice of nonviolence, believing this was far more effective than responding in kind to their harassers. They determined to be disciplined and dignified, usually maintaining their vigils in silence. They soon expanded, independent of the parent organization. Women in Black had no formal leadership, choosing to act as a collective and make their decisions as a group. They chose Paris Square in Jerusalem as their central gathering point, which gave them strong visibility, but also some separation from the threats and abuse hurled at them by those who drove by. Eventually the square was referred to by the public as the Women in Black Square, an indication of how broadly their witness was noticed.

The movement spread throughout the country, holding vigils at various public places and intersections across Israel. Soon they were joined by Palestinian women who were Israeli citizens. The movement spread further as women in other countries began vigils against the Israeli occupation in solidarity with the Women in Black. Groups were formed in the U.S., Canada, Australia, Mexico, India, Japan and many European countries. There was no formal organization, just a network of women committed to peace and justice. The formula for the vigils and organization was simple enough so that even a small group in a small community could make their presence known, adding to the wider public awareness of their message.

As the movement grew, the focus expanded beyond the Israeli occupation of the West Bank and Gaza. Local groups would bear witness against war, militarism and other forms of violence. They recognized that women experienced war differently than men.

Feminist and peace activist Naomi Chazan is a prominent Israeli scholar of political science and writes about the importance of such movements, "This is not a struggle of tanks but a people's struggle. And the issues of self-determination and equality have special meaning for women." In conflicts around the world, women fear the possibility of rape; and women make up the majority of refugees from conflicts. Women's voices usually are drowned out in mixed groups, even groups committed to peace and justice. Another Israeli feminist, Erella Shadmi, writes, "The unconventional combination of being a woman, being in the public realm, and engaging in a struggle undermines the conventional perception of what is a woman and what is a political struggle, and redefines them."

The followers of the radical rabbi Meir Kahane issued death threats to some of the women. Kahane once sent some of his followers to attack the women during a vigil. It took police armed with clubs and tear gas to drive the attackers away from the peaceful, demonstrating women. They responded to these attacks by deepening their commitment to (and holding workshops on) the practice of nonviolence in the face of attacks and refining their organizational structure and processes. Following Kahane's assassination in the U.S. and funeral in Israel, the police urged them to halt their next Friday vigil. When the women began to enter King George's Street, they found Kahane's supporters lined up in force in yellow shirts with their clenched-fist signs. The women were afraid, but they were not intimidated. They gathered at their usual time, but this time, more women than usual showed up.

"How did we get this way?" Gila Svirsky wondered. "How had we grown from ordinary teachers, social workers, secretaries, executives, and housewives into such brave women? We had clearly taken more courage from this vigil than it was taking out of us in weariness."

Women in Black groups in different countries began developing projects in their own regions, sometimes shifting their efforts to focus on more local conflicts. Italian women began a project called "Women Visiting Difficult Places," in which women engaged with other women on different sides of conflicts to enter into dialogue. Part of this effort included visits to Israel and Palestine. During one such visit, the European women joined Israeli and Palestinian women to form a human chain of 30,000 people around the walls of Old Jerusalem in an event called "A Time for Peace." Following the September 11, 2001 terrorist attacks in the United States, women's groups made an appeal for "justice, not vengeance." When the U.S. prepared to invade Iraq in 2003, Women in Black in the United States and many other countries began vigils in protest of this new war.

In Serbia the Women in Black group (*Zene u Crnom*) held weekly vigils in Belgrade against a growing nationalism and militarism in that area. They drew support from Women in Black in Spain, Belgium and Britain especially. Solidarity visits and vigils were held in various Balkan capitals: Belgrade, Zagreb and Sarajevo.

Meanwhile, in Israel and Palestine, the Women in Black faced new challenges. The Gulf War made it difficult to sustain their vigils because Yassir Arafat and the Palestinian Authority publicly sided with Saddam Hussein and Iraq. This caused many Israeli women who were opposed to the occupation to shy away from expressions of solidarity with the Palestinians. Then in 1994, the Oslo peace process seemed to be moving toward achieving their goals, making protest unnecessary. The number of locations for vigils in Israel shrank to four.

The outbreak of the second *Intifada* in late 2000 and the dramatic escalation of violence brought renewed intensity to the work of Women in Black. More women stepped forward to vigil, and the number of vigil sites increased to fifteen. Women in Black joined with other women's peace organizations to form the Coalition of Women for a Just Peace. Besides maintaining the Women in Black vigils, they have engaged in nonviolent direct actions such as a blockade of traffic around the Israeli Defense Ministry.

What began as a few women in one country has spread to over 10,000 women in many countries, addressing many conflicts besides the Israeli occupation. Through dignity, symbolism and faithful persistence, Women in Black in Israel and around the world have given increased power and clarity to women's voices against militarism and violence. As Gila Svirsky put it, "We, the great army of nurturers, now served up politics with your dinner."

PART 9

Artists

Imagine!

ARTISTS ENVISION OUR FUTURE. They stir imagination and emotion. They rouse us with striking images and spirited songs. Among the last memories Alzheimer's patients retain are songs they learned early in life. The late poet Joseph Brodsky, who eventually won the Nobel Prize and served as America's Poet Laureate, never forgot the despair he felt while imprisoned during the Soviet era—he had challenged the government with his verse. He survived to teach students: "If you are sent to a prison camp—the poetry you carry in your memory may be your entire world. So, we must choose well what world we will carry, no?" Artists equip us with icons and refrains that never can be wrested from us, even in illness, injury or prison.

John Lennon's song, "Imagine," captures the vocation of the peacemaking artist: Imagine a world beyond the divisions we have established. Such artists remind us, in Lennon's words, "I'm not the only one." At times, their artistry commands a global stage with an audience of billions like Lennon, and more recently, Bono of U2. When Bono urges young people to discover the transformative power of the Psalms—telling them that the Psalms are really the Blues sung thousands of years ago—he is moving an audience that other peace activists could never reach.

The arts include visual media, literature, drama and music. The arts can express beauty, but they also express passion, memorialize martyrs, challenge great powers, and stoke courage in millions of lives. A talented comedian might work for laughs, but that same comedian can rip the deceptive mask off propaganda to restore truth in a troubled culture.

I was in the Soviet Union in 1988 as Gorbachev's policies of *perestroika* and *glasnost* were challenging Soviet citizens and Communist Party leaders to re-envision their society. On Arbat Street, the famous pedestrian thoroughfare in the center of Moscow, my friends and I gathered with a large cluster of Soviet citizens to discuss what was happening in their country. We asked how they had maintained their capacity to discuss controversial, social and political issues in the midst of harsh repression. Their answer: "Jokes." Humor was a sharp-edged tool in dismantling the official party line—yet a word-of-mouth bit of humor is difficult to repress and impossible to imprison.

In the 1960s, Dick Gregory was in the first wave of black comedians to break out of the stereotypical minstrel tradition. He was a top-shelf entertainer who even managed to win over white audiences during the days of Southern segregation, through his blend of humor and pride: "Last time I was down south I walked into this restaurant and this white waitress came up to me and said, 'We don't serve colored people here.' I said, 'That's all right. I don't eat colored people. Bring me a whole fried chicken.'" He joined the front lines of the civil rights movement, marching, getting arrested and going to jail. His activism cost him many bookings, but his commitment never wavered. He became an anti-war activist and engaged in many hunger strikes. He traveled to Iran during the hostage crisis to appeal for the release of the hostages while undertaking a hunger strike. Gregory regularly traveled to shattered urban areas where he lent his support to tough causes like negotiations toward a truce among gangs. His comedy helped millions to see what was happening around them with greater clarity.

Sometimes artists stand far from the rest of us—perhaps to preserve their own freedom or sometimes simply because their talent is so astonishing that we realize no one else could paint or compose or write as they do. We might find ourselves standing in awe at a respectful distance. Other artists dive into the heart of a community and draw people around them. Much of the civil rights movement was undergirded by the work of artists giving activists songs to sing. "We Shall Overcome" became an anthem in streets and jail cells thanks to the deliberate work of artists during that time.

Art is healing. Asking children to draw pictures of peace encourages their capacity to envision a new world. From the Holocaust to contemporary urban violence, the arts give men and women a voice beyond words. Anyone who has seen paintings by survivors of Hiroshima understands this power. As we experience these artistic expressions, we are drawn into the community of those who have been wounded and yet are dreaming of change.

Participatory art can be visionary, prophetic and empowering. "We need artists to help explain what is happening in this country, to tell the truth and reveal the lies, to be willing to say the emperor has no clothes, to create moral indignation, to envision alternatives, to reinvent language." So says Natasha Mayers, an artist-activist from Maine who connects art to conditions in her local community and the wider world. Mayers has drawn others into her art, teaching in schools, involving immigrants, refugees, prisoners, the homeless and those in mental health facilities whom she refers to as "psychiatrically labeled." She supervises community murals that bring people together to express their unity. She organized a traveling exhibition, "Warflowers: From Swords to Plowshares," that challenged observers to envision moving toward a peace-based rather than a defense-based economy.

One of the greatest peacemaking artists was the cellist Pablo Cassals. He said, "The love of one's country is a splendid thing. But why should love stop at the border?" Artists can help us discover and unleash love by seeing our common humanity across lines of division. When the Czech playwright Vaclav Havel turned to the peaceful transformation of his long-oppressed homeland, his first campaign poster didn't mention any specific political issue. It proclaimed: "Truth and love must conquer lies and hate." Soon, that iconic poster blanketed Prague.

Mark Johnson used that same passion to launch "Playing for Change," a global project in which he videotapes various musicians in locations around the world performing common songs, such as Bob Marley's "One Love." In editing, he weaves the melody from country to country. His short videos of these internationally blended performances spread virally across the Internet, attracting millions of viewers. A feature-length documentary, "Peace Through Music," finally was produced, but in keeping with the grassroots nature of this movement, the movie is mainly screened at local house parties. Discussions follow. Music flows.

Artists can penetrate every barrier that malevolent forces can devise. Artists can connect us with a common vision of peace, despite geographic distance, injury or even imprisonment. At their best, artists can help us glimpse a better future—and equip us with powerful tools for the difficult journey toward realizing our dreams.

CHAPTER 55

Pete Seeger
(b. 1919)

**Songs, songs kept them
going and going**

**They didn't realize the millions
of seeds they were sowing**

**They were singing in marches,
even singing in jail**

**Songs gave them the courage
to believe they would not fail.**

—Pete Seeger

*I grew up singing Pete Seeger's songs, not always knowing
where they originated. So many singers echo Pete's music!
But that's what he intended. I've sung his songs while
marching in protests. I once sang "If I Had a Hammer" in
a karaoke contest with Asian students in a democracy
movement. Pete is happy when he sees people not
only singing, but also carrying his songs into action.*

THE POWER OF A song.

As the war in Vietnam was building, CBS television censored a
song Pete Seeger sang on "The Smothers Brothers Comedy Hour".
The song did not mention Vietnam or President Johnson. It was
not overtly political. It was a song about an army training exercise
during World War II in which troops were trying to cross a stream
in a swamp. "Waist Deep in the Big Muddy" tells about the soldiers
complaining, but the captain insisting they push on. Each verse
finds the soldiers deeper—knee deep, waist deep, neck deep—"We

were neck deep in the Big Muddy and the big fool said to push on." Finally the captain drowns, and the soldiers turn around feeling lucky to get out alive. Seeger then sang, "But every time I read the papers, that old feeling comes on: We're waist deep in the Big Muddy, and the big fool says to push on." After the song was cut by network censors, the Smothers Brothers went public, generating more attention for the issue than CBS had expected. The network relented, and the song was aired with 7 million people viewing it. "Waist Deep in the Big Muddy" conveyed a powerful image to Americans who were getting frustrated and disillusioned by their nation's growing involvement in the swamp of the Vietnam War.

Yes, the power of a song! All around the world, whenever there is a people's movement for justice, the words arise: "We Shall Overcome." Seeger was active in the South during the civil rights movement of the 1950s and 1960s. He chronicled the songs that were such a significant part of the movement and spread the stories of the civil rights activists around the country through his concerts. "I'll Be All Right" was a gospel hymn sung in black churches throughout the South. In a 1946 strike at a South Carolina tobacco factory, the song-leader, Lucille Simmons, slowed down the tempo and pluralized the last verse: "We will overcome." When some of the strikers attended the Highlander Folk School later in the year, Highlander's music director Zilphia Horton picked it up and later taught it to Seeger, who added a verse or two. Along the way "will" was changed to "shall," perhaps by Septima Clark. At the 25th anniversary celebration of Highlander, the Rev. Dr. Martin Luther King, Jr. was one of the participants. When Seeger led the singing, King said, "We Shall Overcome—that song really sticks with you, doesn't it?" Guy Carawan had learned the song from Horton and in 1959 followed her as music director at Highlander. He taught it at a "Singing in the Movement" workshop and then at the organizing meeting of the Student Nonviolent Coordinating Committee (SNCC). The tradition of holding hands with crossed arms and swaying as people sang was started at the SNCC meeting. In 1963, Seeger recorded the song at his Carnegie Hall concert, and the anthem quickly circled the world. The creation and spread of "We

Shall Overcome" was a typical Pete Seeger experience: a bit of tradition; a contribution from this person and that; and an adaptation for a contemporary setting so anyone could sing it.

Seeger was born to professional musician parents trained in European classical traditions. His mother left musical instruments around the house for him to pick up and explore. He learned by feel and ear before he knew technical terms. As a college student, he fell in love with the 5-string banjo, and eventually wrote the classic guidebook on how to play it. One of his first jobs was with the Archives of American Folk Music, which led him to find and learn from legendary musicians like Leadbelly.

In 1940, at a migrant-worker benefit concert, he met Woody Guthrie, one of the most prolific American folk-song writers. Seeger, Lee Hayes and, later, Guthrie formed the Almanac Singers with some other musicians. The Almanac Singers played for union rallies and in support of strikes. In 1948, Seeger and three friends formed the Weavers, the group that helped to launch the folk music revival nationwide—but Seeger never left his activist roots. A year later, in 1949, he sang with Paul Robeson at a union concert as an "inoculation against fascism." The Ku Klux Klan targeted the concert and stoned thousands of cars. As Seeger drove away from the concert with his wife and children, anti-union vigilantes attacked their car as well. Large rocks shattered the windows, sending glass shards into their hair and clothes.

Seeger had joined the Communist Party in the 1940s in support of workers' rights and the Communist vision of an equitable world. At the same time, he served a stint in the U.S. Army during World War II, mostly entertaining the troops. He left the Communist Party after a few years, but his involvement became a national issue when the House Un-American Activities Committee (HUAC) launched its investigation in 1955. Seeger appeared before the committee and defended his rights from the First Amendment—freedom of speech and association. He recalled the old German song, "*Die Gedanken Sind Frei*," ("My thoughts are free.") and he refused to directly answer the committee's questions. This led to a citation of contempt and a sentence to a year in prison. His conviction was later overturned, but the HUAC hearings left Seeger blacklisted. As a result, he turned to what he called "guerrilla cultural tactics." He would show up in a town with no advance publicity for a concert. First, he would play on a local radio station, then he would invite people to a concert that night. He would be on the road again before protests could be mobilized against him. During the civil rights movement and the growing anti-war movement in the 1960s, he became a popular singer. He had earned the respect of many for standing up for his principles in the face of threats of imprisonment and violence. While marching alongside them, he also challenged the generational divisiveness of young radicals, even recording a song, "Be Kind to Your Parents." By the 1970s, Seeger had become a beloved musical figure from coast to coast.

Seeger and his wife Toshi had purchased land and built a log house on a bluff overlooking the Hudson River in New York. In 1969 they helped start an organization that built a replica of an old sailing sloop, which the organization voted to call "Clearwater." Using the "Clearwater" as a platform, Seeger took the lead in a movement of environmental cleanup of the Hudson. Environmentalism became a frequent theme in his concerts.

The soundtrack to so many memories of this era includes Seeger's music. In 1940 he wrote "If I Had a Hammer" with Lee Hayes of the Almanac Singers—over 20 years before Peter, Paul and Mary turned it into a big hit. "Where Have All the Flowers Gone" didn't begin as a peace song. Seeger got the first three verses from a Ukrainian "short" song. Joe Hickerson took it to a children's camp where the kids and Hickerson played with it, adding verses about soldiers and graveyards. Kids took the song home from camp and shared it with friends. Eventually Peter, Paul and Mary and the Kingston Trio picked it up, assuming it was a traditional folk song. "Turn, Turn, Turn" was Seeger's musical rendering of a passage from the Book of Ecclesiastes, with the added ending "...a time of peace, I swear it's not too late." He popularized the poetry of the Cuban visionary José Martí, setting it to the music of Fernandez Diaz's "Guantanamera." Seeger also put music to "Estadio Chile," the poem written by Victor Jara just before he was executed.

Everyone who attended a Pete Seeger concert was expected to sing. Most of his songs, whether written by him or passed on through him, were not meant for performance, but for participation. "My basic philosophy in life is that I'm a teacher, trying to teach people to participate," Seeger said, "whether it's banjos or guitars or politics or whatever." His songs were not just for concert halls, coffee houses and record players. They were for streets, union halls and jail cells. He didn't expect his songs to be played on the radio: "If it's a real good song, it will get spread around anyway."

Seeger said in an interview, "When newspaper reporters ask me what effect my songs have, I try and make a brave reply—but I am really not so certain."

Anyone who has marched in the streets for peace knows the effect. Seeger's songs have been on the lips of people who have never heard his name, yet still draw from his music the courage to march and to hope for a brighter future. As he approached his 80th birthday, Seeger wrote these words:

> *And I'm still searching*
> *Yes, I'm still searching*
> *For a way we all can learn*
> *To build a world*
> *Where we all can share.*

CHAPTER 56

Arnold Ap
(1945-1984)

The only thing I desire and am waiting for is nothing else but freedom.

—Arnold Ap

I knew nothing about West Papua until I was in a George Lakey training session with two Papuan activists. One was a musician with the band Black Paradise, and I bought his CD. The Papuans wore Arnold Ap T-shirts, so I first heard his story from them. Later I learned to sing Ap's song "West Papua" that is featured on the CD. After doing conflict transformation training in West Papua, I feel some of the pain and passion Ap poured into his music.

WEST PAPUA IS THE western half of the island of New Guinea. It was colonized by the Dutch, and in 1963 it was handed over by the United Nations to Indonesia as part of a decolonialization process. The Indonesian government claimed that the region was part of the Indonesian archipelago, but Papuans insisted on their own cultural and geographic independence. In 1961 the Papuans had established their own national legislature, anthem and flag, the latter with their Morning Star symbol.

In spite of the clearly stated desire of the Papuans for independence, the United Nations, with the support of global and regional powers, let Indonesia become the temporary caretaker. Indonesia organized "The Act of Free Choice" in 1969, where a consultation group of Papuan leaders agreed to remain in Indonesia. The act was ratified by the United Nations. However, Papuans protested that it was an "Act of No Choice" because their leaders were surrounded by the Indonesian military during the consultation, their families were under threat, and few international or media observers were allowed to be present.

Throughout the years of colonial rule there had been various resistance movements. In the 1930s and 1940s, a woman named Angganitha Menufandu led a large unarmed resistance movement against Dutch and then Japanese rule during World War II on Biak Island. They defied bans on traditional singing and dancing, refused to pay taxes, and refused to cooperate with forced labor. The Japanese beheaded Menufandu in 1943. West Papuans have continued to strive for freedom under Indonesian rule. A small, armed insurgency began in 1965, but most of the Papuan resistance has been nonviolent. Even some of the factions in the armed struggle have supported the nonviolent campaign for independence.

Indonesia has engaged in a massive effort to stamp out Papuan identity and culture and introduce a homogeneous Javanese culture. Papuan cultural artifacts were burned in a massive public bonfire the day after the Indonesian "caretakers" took over. Political activities were suspended. The name of the region was changed to *Irian Jaya*, an Indonesian term. Language referring to Papuan identity was banned. The Indonesian government encouraged mass migration of Javanese people to the region. International corporations took over vast mining and logging enterprises that devastated the environment. Indigenous businesses were squeezed out in favor of Indonesian entrepreneurs. Meanwhile, a stifling military presence was built up in West Papua, and many Papuans were assassinated or imprisoned, sometimes for crimes as simple as raising the Morning Star flag.

Arnold Ap was an anthropologist and musician. He used music as a way to celebrate Papuan culture and express the Papuan desire for freedom. Ap founded a music group named Mambesak. He also promoted Papuan culture as curator of the *Cenderawasih*

(Bird of Paradise) University Museum in Jayapura and on his popular weekly radio show. Music and dancing were forms of cultural expression that transcended the hundreds of indigenous Papuan languages, so Ap's music helped to shape a feeling of unity for people from the various tribes. The music of Mambesak drew from the diversity of local melodies and musical themes to forge a regional Papuan style. As one Papuan activist said about Ap, "He helped transform our consciousness from the tribal to the national." Mambasak sang of freedom. Their tapes were played by radio stations in towns across West Papua and on battery-powered boom-boxes deep in forest villages.

Because Indonesian officials were trying to crush Papuan identity itself, music and dance became key weapons in the nonviolent struggle for cultural survival. Ap and Mambesak sang of the beauty of their land and their bond to it. They sang about the destruction of their people and their land at the hands of the Indonesian army and outside corporations. With a dynamic tune and rhythm, they sang, "Times are changing rapidly, and the signs of the heritage left to us by our ancestors are disappearing from view. Remaining only are the ruins of our settlement, the villages no longer maintained, abandoned like orphaned children."

"Travel safely" was the refrain in some songs, expressing the anguish of having so many leaders and friends assassinated. Arnold Ap knew that he, too, was a target. The Papuan nationalism expressed in Ap's music quickly came to the attention of the Indonesian authorities. In November 1983 he was imprisoned and tortured by *Kopassus*, the Indonesian Special Forces, though no charges were ever filed against him. An officer in the police special forces later testified that the military authorities saw Ap as "extremely dangerous because of the activities of his Mambesak players and wanted him sentenced to death or given a life sentence but could not find evidence for a charge in court." Then, on April 26, 1984, Arnold Ap was shot and stabbed while trying to escape from prison, according to the Indonesian officials. Eddie Mofu, another musician imprisoned with Ap, was also killed along with two other prisoners. The story later emerged from a survivor that the police had taken them out of their prison cells to a coastal base, where the prisoners were told to go. They were killed along the beach or in the water.

The music of Arnold Ap continues to speak to Papuans about their culture, the pride in their heritage, and their passion for freedom. Recordings cannot be found in the market places for fear of the Indonesian police, but the music is everywhere, passed from hand to hand. Ap's face adorns T-shirts of activists, and his words are sung by musicians who carry on his tradition. Ap's last song was smuggled out of his cell. Titled "The Mystery of Life," it said, "The only thing I desire and am waiting for is nothing else but freedom."

Ap once said, "Maybe you think what I am doing is stupid, but it is what I think I should do for my people before I die." Though he died in 1984, the power of Ap's music has continued to grow, a gift he has given to the Papuan people that is still vibrantly alive.

CHAPTER 57

Václav Havel

(b. 1936)

It is a very clear understanding that the only kind of politics that truly makes sense is one that is guided by conscience.

—Václav Havel

I love Prague—such a beautiful and culturally rich city. How could this wonderful land have fallen into the grip of one of the coldest regimes in Eastern Europe? It took a man with an artist's soul to bring down this soul-less system.

IN 1968, RUSSIAN TANKS crushed a nonviolent revolution in Czechoslovakia, destroying a reform period known as the Prague Spring. In 1989, a nonviolent revolution toppled the government in a mere twelve days. Known as the Velvet Revolution, this revolt ended Communist power in Czechoslovakia and was part of the wave of revolts that quickly brought the collapse of the Soviet Union. At the head of the Velvet Revolution was a playwright— Václav Havel.

Havel was born into a wealthy, intellectual family, but follow- ing World War II and the Communist takeover of Czechoslovakia, he was branded a *bourgeois*. Instead of getting an artist's education as he desired, he was restricted to technical schools and the study of economics. Stimulated by the intellectual tradition of Prague, he eventually found his way into the theater as a stagehand in the 1960s. In 1963 he wrote his first play, "The Garden Party," a satire about modern bureaucracy. He continued writing plays and was finally able to enroll in the Academy of Dramatic Arts.

Havel participated in the Prague Spring, during which he wrote an article calling for the end of one-party rule. The reform movement was then crushed by the invasion of the Warsaw Pact nations. Havel joined in writing a "Ten Points" manifesto that condemned the invasion and provided commentary on Radio Free Czechoslovakia during the nonviolent resistance against the Soviets. As a result, and as the Communists regained control, Havel's writings and plays were banned and his passport confiscated.

In 1975, Havel penned an open letter to the president, who had been installed following the Warsaw Pact invasion. Havel called for an end to the "normalization" process that was instilling fear in people. The Communist regime was offering material improvements in life in exchange for quiet obedience. "For fear of losing his job, the schoolteacher teaches things he does not believe," wrote Havel. "Fearing for his future, the pupil repeats them after him; for fear of not being allowed to continue his studies, the young man joins the Youth League and participates in whatever of its activities are necessary; fear that under a monstrous system of political credits, his son or daughter will not acquire the necessary total points for enrollment at a school, leads the father to take on all manner of responsibilities and 'voluntarily' to do everything required." Instead, Havel called people to reject fear and stand up to those in power: "So far you and your government have chosen the easy way out for yourselves, and the most dangerous road for society: the path of inner decay for the sake of outward appearances...and ceaselessly degrading human dignity, for the puny sake of protecting your own power." Hand-typed copies of Havel's challenge were passed around the country, and the letter was broadcast over Radio Free Europe. People were shocked and then energized by what he said. Later, Havel said this about the letter, "I felt the need to stir things up, to confront others for a change and force them to deal with a situation that I myself had created."

Rock music had become a key vehicle for social, political and artistic dissent—especially stimulated by the band The Velvet

Underground, from which the 1989 revolution took its name. As Havel said, the rock culture created "a temperament, a nonconformist state of the spirit, an anti-establishment orientation, an aversion to philistines, and an interest in the wretched and humiliated." In 1976, a Czech psychedelic band, The Plastic People of the Universe, was put on trial in a Kafkaesque farce that made for ripe responses from artists. Havel's political and legal response was the formation of the dissident human rights group, Charter 77. Its *Charter 77 Manifesto* was a collaborative effort led by Havel with 242 signatories, calling on the government to live up to the International Covenant on Civil and Political Rights in the Helsinki Agreement, signed by Czechoslovakia. The dissidents could claim they were not opposing the regime, merely asking it to live up to its own legislative commitments.

Havel was imprisoned for his protest with Charter 77, later released and then imprisoned again. In 1979, he co-founded the Committee for the Defense of the Unjustly Oppressed to help dissidents and their families cope with the stresses of the multiple layers of repression they were experiencing. All around Europe, Havel's plays were performed in solidarity with the dissident community, but they remained banned in his own country. Havel was imprisoned again for subversion, this time for four difficult years. A later play with clear autobiographical elements dealt with the problems of "post-prison psychosis."

In his essays, Havel wrote about nonviolence as a way to resist the political order that forced people to "live within a lie." He often discussed the power of language to interfere with clear thought, which drew many comparisons to George Orwell. He said in a speech about Cuba, "When more and more people learn to speak their own language and reject the hollow, mendacious language of the powers that be, it means that freedom is remarkably close, if not directly within reach." He sought language that could clarify reality, "calling things by their proper names," and also liberate.

In the 1980s Havel spent less time writing and more involved with politics. He participated in writing *Democracy for All*, a manifesto that called for the end of the leading role for the Communist

Party, which again prompted his arrest. But the Communist officials were feeling the pressure for change. His release from prison was timely, for he was then able to speak to thousands of Czechs at the first officially allowed demonstration. But, he was then arrested for watching from a distance as dissidents lay flowers in Wenceslas Square to remember Jan Palach who burned himself in protest in 1969. Havel wrote, "I hope that the state apparatus will soon stop behaving like one of the ugly sisters, who breaks the mirror because she blames it for what she sees."

Again, shortly after he was released, Havel led the writing of another manifesto, this time one that was signed by over 30,000 restive citizens. On November 17, 1989, a protest was brutally suppressed by police, and the Velvet Revolution was underway. Waves of protest followed. On the 19th, the Civic Forum was established with Havel chosen as its leader and as negotiator with the government. Within days the government conceded to the Civic Forum, and on December 29th, Havel was voted in as president of the newly freed, multi-party democratic nation.

Havel generally remained a popular political figure as president. He worked to dissolve the Warsaw Pact, though it took two years to finally get the Soviet troops to leave Czechoslovak soil. He released prisoners from the jails, but he also sought to reconcile the old Communist Party members into the new Czechoslovakia rather than to prosecute them for their repressive acts. He issued an apology for the expulsion of the Sudeten Germans following Germany's defeat in World War II, something many citizens opposed but that was consistent with Havel's concern for reconciliation following conflicts. He also closed the arms factories tha had shipped weapons around the world.

The division between the Czechs and the Slovaks grew in i sity, even though Havel passionately urged maintaining one When separatist leaders from both sides won in the / Havel resigned as president, refusing to participate in ' tion of the country in 1993. He then was elected the f of the newly formed Czech Republic.

As President of the Czech Republic, Havel supported the invasion of Iraq, citing the example of Neville Chamberlain's sell out of Czechoslovakia to Hitler in 1938 as a failure to stop tyranny early. Yet he also pointed out that the same rationale was used to justify the 1968 Russian invasion of Czechoslovakia.

Whether as dissident or president, Havel remains his own person, acting boldly according to his conscience. He is also remarkably approachable, frequenting pubs in Prague, taking foreign dignitaries to his favorite local watering holes. As his political career came to an end, he was glad to see a generation emerging that wasn't stunted by the "destruction the Communist regime wreaked upon our souls." He enjoyed seeing people live with simple freedom, a freedom he did so much to achieve.

CHAPTER 58

Vedran Smajlović
(b. 1956)

You ask me am I crazy for playing the cello? Why do you not ask if they are not crazy for shelling Sarajevo?

—Vedran Smajlović

I've been to countless Bosnian memorials: Srebrenica where Serb militiamen massacred more than 8,000 Muslim men; the bridge in Sarajevo were snipers gunned down two students who were the first victims of the war; the square in Tuzla where dozens of Croat, Serbian and Muslim youths were partying together when a mortar shell erased their lives. When I heard of Smajlović's musical memorial—an elegy played as sniper bullets whizzed around—I knew I had come to the heart of sorrow as well as a healing courage. I can't read his story without weeping for all my Bosnian friends.

THE MUSICIAN TOOK HIS place, dressed in the customary formal black tails and white shirt. He sat on the stool with his cello between his legs. He took the bow and began to play Albinoni's Adagio in G Minor. He was not in a concert hall. Instead he sat in a crater where the day before, 22 people had died.

Vedran Smajlović (sometimes spelled Smailovic) was the principal cellist of the Sarajevo Opera. He also played in the Sarajevo Philharmonic Orchestra, the Symphony Orchestra RTV Sarajevo and the National Theatre of Sarajevo. In the early 1990s, though, life was difficult for everyone in Sarajevo as war broke out. Yugoslavia was splintering into various nations, including what would become Bosnia and Herzegovina. Serb nationalists surrounded Sarajevo and laid siege. For Smajlović and the other residents of the city, life was a daily ordeal of trying to find food and water amid the shelling and sniper fire that claimed many innocent lives.

On May 27, 1992, a long line of people had queued up at one of the still-functioning bakeries. A mortar shell fell into the middle of the line, killing 22 people and creating a bloody mess of body parts and rubble. Smajlović lived close to the bakery and was appalled by what he saw as he helped the wounded. He felt powerless as he was neither a politician nor a soldier—he was a musician, who could speak truth to the heart beyond any language.

Smajlović took his cello to the spot where those waiting for bread had been butchered and began to plaintively play. He played in a daze but in an incredibly evocative way. In spite of the risk, people gathered to listen. When he was finished he packed up his cello and went to a coffee shop. Quickly people came up to him expressing their appreciation, "This is what we needed." Smajlović went back the next day and the next 22 days, one for each person killed. Sniper fire continued around him and mortars still rained down in the neighborhood, but Smajlović never stopped playing.

Then he went to other sites where shells had taken the lives of Sarajevo's citizens. He played there, and he played in graveyards. He played at funerals at no charge, even though the Serbian gunners would target such gatherings. His music was a gift to all hiding in their basements with rubble above their heads, a voice for peace for those daily dodging the bullets of the snipers. As the reports of Smajlović's performances on the shattered streets spread, he became a symbol for peace. A reporter questioned whether he was crazy to play his cello outside in the midst of a war zone. He countered, "You ask me am I crazy for playing the cello, why do you not ask if they are not crazy for shelling Sarajevo?"

His courageous performances inspired other musicians. Composer David Wilde wrote "The Cellist of Sarajevo" for cello in his honor, and Yo-Yo Ma, perhaps the world's most famous cellist, recorded it and later embraced Smajlović following a performance of the piece. Various folk songs and even a children's book have been written about his action.

In late 1993, Smajlović left Sarajevo. He has continued his musical career as a cellist, and still composes and conducts. He moved to Northern Ireland where he collaborated with Tommy Sands, an Irish folk musician with a large peace repertoire. Their "Sarajevo to Belfast" album celebrates perseverance, peace and healing through situations of violence.

CHAPTER 59

Yuri Shevchuk

(b. 1957)

He implored that boy for one thing: Don't shoot! Don't shoot!

—Yuri Shevchuk

As I shared the concept of this book with a Ukrainian friend, he said that I surely had to include Yuri Shevchuk. Who is Yuri Shevchuk? He popped a CD into his player, and I first heard a voice as distinctive as Dylan's. Later, another Ukrainian friend translated Shevchuk's poetry for me from the Internet. I was hooked. Not only was this someone who sang the message, but he lived it out boldly.

IN 1980, AN ART teacher co-founded a rock band that would launch him toward becoming one of the best-known personalities in Russia. The art teacher was Yuri Shevchuk. The rock band was called DDT. They originated in the city of Ufa, a conservative center in the Ural Mountains of the Soviet Union. They began recording and distributing cassette tapes of their music as part of the underground music scene. Occasionally they performed in officially sanctioned venues.

One of the early songs Shevchuk wrote was "Don't Shoot" in protest of the Soviet war in Afghanistan. The song tells of a boy growing up shooting birds and little animals and winning prizes in shooting galleries. Then, as a soldier, he is sent to a hot spot. The song ends with the veteran coming home:

And when someone remembered the war,
His conscience was buried in heavy guilt.
Before him, as if alive, that boy stood.
He implored that boy for one thing:
Don't shoot! Don't shoot!
Don't shoot! Don't shoot!

DDT entered a major music competition. They included "Don't Shoot" among their submissions and made it to the finals in Moscow. However, a message like "Don't Shoot", while Soviet troops were in Afghanistan, caught the attention of the Soviet KGB. Soon the band members were followed and monitored. Their music was banned, making them even more popular to the young people who passed bootlegged tapes to each other. DDT participated in a "Rock for Peace" festival, but their music was cut out of the televised production because of their illegal status.

Shevchuk, the lead singer and songwriter for the group, moved to Leningrad, now Saint Petersburg, in 1986 to get closer to the heartbeat of Russian culture. The band went through cycles, breaking up and reorganizing with Shevchuk remaining the one constant. As the winds of freedom began to blow through the Soviet Union, DDT traveled across the Soviet empire. In 1988, the band traveled to the U.S. and played for MTV. In 1994, DDT was named Rock Band of the Year and played in front of more than 120,000 fans at a free concert in Saint Petersburg. They continue to be the most popular group in Russia, increasing their following in Europe and the United States.

Shevchuk has a distinct gravelly voice, and his lyrics take a humorous look at life in Russia, sometimes with pointed thrusts at injustice and war. He despises the triviality of pop music, yet has become more popular than any pop musician in Russia. DDT concerts are known for the thousands of people in the audience joining in to sing the familiar lyrics. Shevchuk also includes poetry readings within the set list. Their recordings are a mix of rock and blues, flavored with influences from Russian folk, classical and even religious music.

Shevchuk doesn't consider himself a political activist, but he honestly addresses the problems of life in his homeland—so effectively that he was branded a dissident. "The country is falling into a chasm, and we are laughing as loud as we can, lying about in rusty Jacuzzis like the ancient Romans, observing the end of the empire." Speaking of one of his songs about war, he says, "It's a battle for an enlightened understanding of life, where the colonel is spirit, and the soldiers are poets." He says, "Rock music is freedom, it is internal freedom," so he refuses to play for politicians or businesses, but he will play countless benefit concerts for community organizations.

Besides their lyrics, Shevchuk and the band have made their performance sites and programs into powerful and provocative statements. During the war in Chechnya, he performed more than 50 concerts on a mission of peace, playing for both Russian troops and Chechen civilians.

When the Russian election was held in 2008 in which Vladimir Putin stepped down and put forward his specially groomed successor Dmitry Medvedev, Shevchuk and DDT performed at the Dissenters March that claimed the election was a sham—any opposing candidates were blocked from running. Shevchuk saw this as just one more way that the hopes of a genuinely democratic and just society were being undermined. His participation in the Dissenters March led to the Russian Kultura TV channel banning the airing of his songs. "A bunch of good-for-nothings want to turn our country into a banana republic and our people into a herd of sheep," he says. Yet, as an artist he connects to the great ones of Russia's past: "But the soul spreads its wings above Russia. Pushkin and Dostoevsky, Pasternak and Tolstoy, Visotsky and Bashlashev are watching us."

During the war between Russia and Georgia in 2008, Shevchuk organized two peace concerts in Moscow and Saint Petersburg. Harkening back to the days of the war in Afghanistan and one of their earlier hits, he called the concerts "Don't Shoot." He brought together Georgian and Ossetian musicians (South Ossetians wanting to break away from Georgia were supported by Russia) and

Ukrainians, and together they were called "Peacekeepers." Profits from the concerts were sent to relieve the suffering of both Ossetian and Georgian victims.

Using the platform of his popularity, Shevchuk calls Russia to constructive relationships with its neighbors. "What is patriotism and love for Russia? It's no good idea that patriotism should be bred on antagonism: alternately we get at war-like relations with Ukraine, Georgia or Baltic states. That's no patriotism, that's chauvinism." DDT went to western Ukraine, where anti-Russian feeling has been strongest, and played a series of concerts for tens of thousands of people. They sang in Russian and Ukrainian affirming to cheering crowds that the two nations are brothers and sisters. Shevchuk says if Russia would meet others with a smile, the world would breathe so much easier.

For more than 25 years, throughout all the political changes and the reorganization within his band, Yuri Shevchuk has remained in the forefront as one who artistically speaks the truth in Russia. His music has created a space for people to talk about what is happening around them and to them. He sings with love and earthiness, and calls people to higher dreams.

CHAPTER 60

Zargana
(b. 1961)

The soldiers have guns. The people have only mouths.

—Zargana

*I'd been teaching about nonviolent symbolic actions in Burma using stories from the Bible. At the break one woman told me about a man walking around the city with a fancy silk shirt over a tattered dirty **longyi**, the long skirt-like garment Burmese men and women wear around their legs. I asked what that garb might mean, and she gave me a social analysis about the wealth of the military elites being supported by the suffering of the poor. I asked, "Have you seen this man yourself?" She said, "No." Nevertheless, people were buzzing about this man's clothes as a social statement. I said, "That's the power of symbolic action."*

AS THE MAN HUNG upside down in the notorious Insein Prison, guards asked what he thought of the government. "I don't know," he said, "Everything is upside down." In Burma, formally known as Myanmar, one of the leading voices for peace and justice is a comedian known by his stage name of Zargana (or Zarganar). Finding him on stage or in the street is difficult because he spends so much time in prison.

Born Maung Thura, he adopted the name Zargana, which literally means "hair puller" or "tweezers." He revived the ancient Burmese role of court jester to poke fun at the military dictators who have ruled the country with a brutal hand since the coup of General Ne Win in 1962. "The soldiers have guns. The people have only mouths," he said, so he has used his mouth with his deep warm voice and even silent symbolic actions to make powerful statements in a country known for fearful silence.

In 1982, the young dentist-turned-comedian joined a troupe of actors at the University of Rangoon. The group traveled to villages, giving performances to poor rural families. That exposure gave rise to his reputation as an entertainer, but Zargana developed as a prominent activist during the 1988 democracy uprising. He addressed crowds through his comedy routines. Sometimes just his clothing was a statement, as he would come on stage with the traditional hat of the elites, but with a scarf hanging on the right side. The word in Burmese for "right side" also means "liar." When the military cracked down on the uprising, killing hundreds if not thousands of people and sending thousands more into exile, Zargana was among those arrested. He spent seven months in solitary confinement at Insein Prison, suffering torture. He was forbidden to speak, as the guards feared the power of his jokes might undo their own loyalty to the regime.

Between his stints in prison, including a four-and-a-half-year term in the early 1990s, Zargana continued to mock the government. Though his performances had been banned and censored, he found ways to get his message to the Burmese public. When a stilted National Convention was held to write a new constitution that followed the dictates of the military, Zargana hosted a National Beggars' Convention. He was seen walking around the capital dressed in a fancy dress shirt with gold chains, while wearing a torn and dirty *longyi* and going barefoot. His silent commentary about the wealthy being supported by the poor masses sparked much discussion among the general population.

Cyclone Nargis tore through the Irrawaddy delta region in 2008, killing over 80,000 people. The military sealed off the area and refused to let aid get through, blocking international relief efforts. Zargana, who had just been released from prison for his involvement in the September 2007 protests by Buddhist monks, organized an effort with hundreds of volunteers from within Burma to get food, water and other supplies to the struggling survivors of Nargis. Then he spoke to the world media about the plight of the millions left homeless by the storm, too sorrowful for humor. For these crimes he was arrested yet again and sentenced to 59 years in prison. He was sent to a prison in a distant province where reports have emerged of his declining health. International human rights organizations have called repeatedly for his release.

His Buddhist practice has sustained his courage in the face of on-going repression and personal suffering. Traditionally known for puzzling twists of logic, Buddhist tradition also shapes his verbal repartee. When a reporter asked if his jokes had the power to change things, Zargana replied: "I don't think so, not directly anyway." Then he added: "All they can do is ignite the brains of the people."

CHAPTER 61

Banksy

(b. 1974)

Think outside the box, collapse the box, and take a sharp knife to it.

—Banksy

My artist son, Jon, gave me a coffee table art book of Banksy's graffiti. It was riveting—but am I supposed to relish such vandalism? What I saw disturbed me because Banksy so often speaks truth with alarming clarity and delightful humor, perhaps like a jester mocking a king. There is rebellion in so much of the youth culture today that echoes the rebellion during my youth in the 1960s. Rebellion can be without cause, yet so much of Banksy's rebellion challenges the forces that dehumanize us. My rebellious act is to put Banksy's book on my coffee table and Banksy's chapter in my book.

THE "SEPARATION BARRIER," BETWEEN Israel and Palestine is a grim, grey concrete wall 20 feet high in places, all built by Israel on Palestinian land. Randomly, graffiti art has appeared: a girl holding balloons floating up over the wall; a ladder painted to the top; a hole with a beautiful beach scene seeming to emerge through the wall. Children grace many of the pictures forcing, the viewer to think about the impact of this massive wall on the young ones trapped inside. The wall has become a canvas for the notorious graffiti artist known as Banksy.

Who is Banksy? Nobody knows for sure, although he seemed to be peeking out from beneath his trademark dark sweatshirt hood in 2011, in light of an Oscar nomination for Best Documentary. Banksy directed and appears in, concealed by his sweatshirt hood, the feature film "Exit Through the Gift Shop." In 87 minutes, the film introduces viewers to a host of graffiti artists, including Banksy himself, and takes us to the wall in Israel and Palestine. As a result of the Oscar nod, Banksy is listed as Robert Banks from Bristol, England, born in 1974. But Banksy is internationally famous for toying with the truth.

What we do know is that Banksy rose to prominence during the Bristol underground scene that exploded with graffiti, a format known to its practitioners as "street art," in the late1980s. Banksy says he wasn't good with an aerosol can and was too slow to avoid detection, so he began to paint with stencils. His work has appeared on walls and streets in Bristol and London as well as France, Australia, Palestine, New Orleans and Los Angeles. He has smuggled work into art museums, some of which was removed immediately, while other works were left on exhibition walls, undetected for weeks. He has slipped into animal enclosures in zoos, painting messages "from" the animals. He said, allegedly, "Think outside the box, collapse the box, and take a sharp knife to it."

Some of Banksy's work is humorous and silly, while some is subversive. Banksy's most pointed work exhibits an anarchistic philosophy—skewering huge corporations, authority and the materialism of Western culture. One of his trademark characters is an anarchist rat that is involved in all sorts of mischief challenging the assumptions and views of the establishment. His own identity is perhaps revealed in the masked figure seeming to hurl a Molotov cocktail—except that it's actually a bouquet of flowers in his hand.

Banksy has especially targeted superpower militarism with his artistic wit. He often reverses power roles, such as in a scene he painted of a soldier, gun set aside, being frisked by a girl in a pink pinafore. He juxtaposes pastoral scenes with menacing military machinery. In London, he painted a huge picture of Samuel L. Jackson and John Travolta from a famous scene in the movie, "Pulp Fiction," holding bananas instead of guns. One of his frequently used stencils shows a helicopter armed with bombs. The stencil has appeared on "Wrong War" signs and on street signs that say "Americans Working Overhead." Another scene shows one soldier protecting another as he paints a large peace symbol.

Banksy is also an advocate for the hungry. As a family sits around a feast at their dining room table, in one of his paintings, they are watched by a starving child. Another picture depicts a squatting, starving child with an empty bowl and a "Burger King" crown.

Many critics complain that his street art is vandalism, but Banksy challenges the very assumptions undergirding private property. His wit and social commentary have brought him many supporters. When the city of Bristol planned to remove one humorous painting of a naked man clinging to the windowsill of a bedroom while an angry man confronts a woman inside, neighbors banded together to get the city to let it remain as community art. As vexing as his works are to many governments and businesses, the paintings have become so popular that major art exhibitions have been organized—occasionally with Banksy's legitimate help. Most of his works were freely abandoned in urban settings as he fled police, yet some now sell at auction for huge sums.

Banksy seems pleased to make people laugh, make people think—and make people squirm. He can poke holes in the pride, arrogance and hypocrisy of world culture, even as he draws holes in the walls that separate us.

CHAPTER 62

Bono

(b. 1960)

**When you are trapped by
poverty, you are not free.
When trade laws prevent you
from selling the food you
grew, you are not free. When
you are a monk in Burma
this very week, barred from
entering a temple because
of your gospel of peace...
well, then none of us are truly free.**

—Bono

*U2 is my favorite band. When I watch the video of them
playing "Sunday Bloody Sunday" in Dublin I think of
Bono: Here is a modern prophet communicating in the
language of his generation. There is a depth to their music
that comes from Bono throwing himself as fully into the
suffering corners of the world as he has thrown himself into
the uplifted arms of audiences. Besides that: U2 rocks!*

FANS BOOED THE WORLD'S greatest rock band. U2 is often
called the greatest, partly because of its 22 Grammy awards and
sales topping 150 million albums—and partly because of the
band's courageous peacemaking efforts. But in 1993, European
fans booed the live, on-stage satellite connections that lead singer
Bono made with people caught in the siege of Sarajevo during the
Bosnian war. Even Bono's band members later described the calls

as stinging like "cold water." Bono was forcing Europeans, who wished that the Bosnian war would just fade away, to pay attention to what was happening nearby in Europe. Many fans hated those chilling splashes of reality interrupting their enjoyment of an otherwise red-hot band.

These satellite connections were made after the band became aware of how many people in Sarajevo kept their sanity by listening to U2's music in basements during the siege. The band offered to slip into the city and do a special concert, but their Bosnian hosts didn't want to put them at risk. So Bono paid to set up special satellite connections and used these live calls during concerts to stir the conscience of the people of Europe. The band's song, "Miss Sarajevo," joined by opera star Luciano Pavarotti, recalled a beauty pageant Bosnians held in the middle of the siege to keep up morale. When the war was finally over, U2 was the first major band invited to play in Sarajevo, warmly received by the people who had deeply appreciated their solidarity.

The four members of U2 grew up in the gritty neighborhoods of Dublin and formed their band in 1978 when they were teenagers. Paul Hewson is the band's lead singer, though he is known by his stage name, Bono. Thus began his decades-long journey which transformed him into a person of influence in the highest political circles. As a band, U2's global explosion came in the 1985 televised Live Aid concert. Their set at Live Aid was electrifying—and Bono followed that by making more than music. He and his wife Ali made a trip to Ethiopia, where they worked for several months in a refugee camp. On their last day in Ethiopia, a man offered Bono his son to take home, hoping for a better life for him. Bono didn't take the child, but he held the poignant offer as a motivating image. He said, "Ethiopia not just blew my mind, it opened my mind."

Bono didn't stop there. In the mid-1980s, he and his wife visited poor communities in El Salvador and Nicaragua during the wars in Central America. At one point they were caught in a crossfire, then witnessed a bombing on a nearby hillside that shook the ground beneath them. Bono wrote "Bullet the Blue Sky" from that experience, a searing song in which he takes on the weapons trade. He wrote "Mothers of the Disappeared" about the human rights violations in Chile, then later performed the song in Chile as part of the Conspiracy of Hope human rights music tour with Amnesty International. Many of the mothers joined the band on stage.

Some of his most powerful activism was close to home. In 1983, U2's third album, *War*, reached No. 1 on the British charts. One of the songs, "Sunday Bloody Sunday," commemorates the bloody incidents of 1920 and 1972 when British soldiers massacred Irish civilians—but it's not a cry for vengeance. It's a powerful anti-war song, which includes the line, "But I won't heed the battle call." Bono pleads, "wipe your tears away," and in a renunciation of violence recalls the "victory Jesus won on Sunday, bloody Sunday," a hint of redemption and resurrection of hope. At concerts, Bono would often perform the song while parading with a white flag. The Provisional IRA threatened to kidnap Bono, and IRA supporters once attacked the band's van. After years of singing "Sunday, Bloody Sunday" ("How long, how long must we sing this song?," the chorus asks)—and after the Good Friday Peace Accord finally was signed—U2 performed the song before tens of thousands at a huge outdoor concert in Dublin. Bono led the crowd in a chant that included, "No more petrol bombs, no more Saracens (the British armored cars), we're not going back there."

Bono did more than sing. He publicly put himself in service of the peace process. In May 1998, the recently signed Good Friday Peace Accord was getting so much contentious publicity that many feared it would be rejected in an upcoming public referendum. At an unrehearsed U2 concert in Belfast, along with the band Ash, the Protestant and Catholic factional leaders David Trimble and John Hume were invited on stage to shake hands. Bono then stepped between them, grasping their hands and lifting them high like victorious prizefighters. Bono praised them as men "who have taken a leap of faith, out of the past and into the future." The swelling emotion at that event, enhanced by a somber remembrance of the victims of all sides, changed the political momentum. As affirmative votes finally carried the Peace Accord, everyone agreed that the iconic image was the photo of Trimble, Hume and Bono.

Through the years, Bono went where no rock musician had gone before. Many had dabbled in political activism before him, but Bono became an expert on the economic and political injustices plaguing the planet. He did such extensive homework that other economic and political experts recognized his valuable contributions. There's not another rock musician who appears regularly in the *New York Times'* influential *Sunday Week in Review* section next to other prize-winning political columnists. Bono also became a regular participant at the global forum at Davos, Switzerland, where he kept pressing for a serious and sustained response from the more developed nations. The U2 "front man" transformed himself into a "front man" for invisible millions caught in the grip of global poverty, disease and conflict.

To date, Bono's most successful effort was his advocacy with the Clinton administration during the Jubilee Campaign to cancel debts held by developed nations of the poorest countries in Africa. Bono met with various world leaders on the issue and helped to achieve key agreements. Because the follow-through on those agreements has been disappointing, Bono continues to lobby for debt forgiveness.

Bono teamed with Bill and Melinda Gates to found DATA (Debt, AIDS, Trade, Africa) to advocate with the developed nations for fighting poverty and AIDS in Africa. He also co-founded—along with a host of anti-poverty and anti-hunger non-profits—the ONE campaign, named after the U2 song "One." That effort mobilizes grassroots individuals around the world to help overcome extreme poverty and preventable disease. Millions have joined with ONE to help. In 2008, DATA and ONE merged under the name ONE.

Rock stars live in an exotic universe of fame, glamour and celebrity privilege—a lavish lifestyle Bono could have enjoyed like so many other performers. Instead, he is charting a unique path toward peacemaking. While he has achieved historic successes,

Bono also has been booed—more than once. Some of his campaigns have not reached their goals. But Bono—and all of the artists in this final section of this book—have an influence even larger than any nonprofit they may form or temporal campaign they may launch. They are creators of images and music that rattle around in millions of minds—potent carriers of the peacemaking message that will continue to shape new ideas around the world.

Why risk his popularity, fame and fortune? Bono puts it this way: "I would have felt culpable if I hadn't done what I could see needed doing. Love thy neighbor is a command, not a piece of advice."

Those are eloquent words, yet they pale when compared with U2's lyrics. Two simple words, "Walk On," now form a signature for Bono's life and work. The song, composed to honor the imprisoned Nobel laureate from Burma, Aung San Suu Kyi, a democratic politician supporting democracy and human rights through peaceful means, appeared on a 2000 album. "Walk On" lives on more than a decade later. For years, to keep Aung San Suu Kyi from being forgotten, the band performed the song at nearly every concert—and passed out masks of her face so people in the audience would keep her iconic image alive as well. As her visage rose in a crowd, the band would sing:

What you've got, they can't deny it.
Can't sell it, can't buy it.
Walk on, walk on.

Epilogue: "Hope, with its eyes wide open!"

HOW CAN WE DARE to hope? How can we keep pushing against the tide of violence? When one war is finally brought to a weary end, another breaks out with horrifying ferocity. When long labors establish a new legal framework for justice, critics soon arise and erode hard-won achievements. There is no end to the work of making peace.

Prophets and visionaries rekindle hope in each new generation. Isaiah's vision of beating swords into plowshares and Martin Luther King, Jr.'s dream still stir millions. But that's not the entire solution. Moving from hope to substance requires commitment. The Catholic mystic and peacemaker, Thomas Merton, wrote, "To hope is to risk frustration, so make up your mind to risk frustration."

One source of strength is the long-range vision that we have explored in these pages. As Martin Luther King, Jr. said, "The arc of the universe is long, but it bends toward justice." That wisdom stretches back through the centuries. The Great Law of the Six Nations Iroquois Confederacy exhorts, "In our every deliberation, we must consider the impact of our decisions on the next seven generations."

So we must open our eyes, risk frustration, look into the future and summon courage for commitment now. Then what is that next step we take? No, it won't be as bold as King standing at the Lincoln Memorial. The power to change the world lies in each small, mindful act we make. Jesus said, "The Kingdom of Heaven is like a mustard seed"—so tiny, yet its impact can be huge.

Joanna Rogers Macy spoke of the pivotal change of one person or one act through this image: "Before water turns to ice, it looks just the same as before. Then a few crystals form, and suddenly the whole system undergoes cataclysmic change."

With all of the grand visions and great hopes pushing at our back, our responsibility is to ultimately take that next small step. We must act faithfully, not someday—but today. The Irish poet Seamus Heaney insists that even the grandest achievements in the realm of justice depend on individuals standing on the shore of history and daring to "believe that a further shore is reachable from here."

Long before Martin Luther King, Jr. stood at the Lincoln Memorial, he struggled alone through a night of doubt in the kitchen of his modest home. Waking that next morning and setting out to work another day may have been his most courageous achievement. Our future begins in each new day, the singer-songwriter Jan Krist proclaims, as we arise and dare to hope:

> Hope, with its eyes wide open,
> Hope, with its will unbroken,
> Hope.

Take Action!

Ideas for Peacemakers

WHAT SHOULD WE DO next? Here are some ideas for peace-making actions related to each section of this book. Consider these ideas a brainstorming list—suggestions rather than instructions. The list is far from complete, so creatively adapt and add to what you'll find on these pages. The most important thing is—take a next step!

Part 1: "I Have a Dream"
Prophets and Visionaries

- Set up a peace pole with a local congregation, city hall, library, school or similar institution. To order a peace pole, contact: The Official Gift Shop of The World Peace Prayer Society at: www.shoppeace.org (also at 26 Benton Road, Amenia, NY 12592, phone: 845-877-6093). They can handle international shipments. You can also contact them via email at info@worldpeace.org.
- Help to plan the next Martin Luther King, Jr. Day in your area. Most communities in the U.S. have some

sort of public event, so check with your local city hall or congregations to learn who is planning such an event. Most groups are delighted to have additional help.

- Do inspirational peace readings on video and upload them to YouTube.
- Pray daily for peace and for peacemakers.
- Subscribe to *Sojourners* magazine: www.sojo.net/index.cfm?action=magazine.subscribe

Part 2: *"Presente!"*
Litany of Martyrs

- Christians can celebrate All Saints Day (November 1st) with a special educational focus on peacemakers who have devoted their lives to the cause. Talk with leaders in a local congregation.
- Visit memorials or museums that call us to peace: Such memorials could include the Martin Luther King Center, Atlanta, GA (www.thekingcenter.org), the U.S. Holocaust Memorial Museum in Washington, D.C. (www.ushmm.org) and the National Japanese American Memorial, also in Washington (www.njamf.com).
- Plan your international travel to include memorials or museums. Consider places such as Auschwitz or the Hiroshima Peace Park. These destinations can become major pilgrimages for peacemakers.
- As you visit a memorial or museum, reflect on these questions: What values are honored? What feelings or actions are evoked? Does the memorial move toward support for war or support for peace? Does the memorial support healing or division? Write

an editorial in a local paper about what you have observed, or write a blog and publicize it on your network.

Part 3: Gaining Ground on Military Science
Peace Theorists

- Go to the Albert Einstein Institution website and download materials on topics related to nonviolent struggle: www.aeinstein.org/.
- Read some of the works about "liberation theologies" related to the religious traditions or oppressed groups closest to you. Form a study and reflection group in your local religious community to share in this exploration.
- Read some of the books recommended throughout this book, especially titles such as Gene Sharp's, *The Politics of Nonviolent Action*, William Ury and Roger Fisher's, *Getting to YES* and John Paul Lederach's, *The Journey Toward Reconciliation* or *Building Peace: Sustainable Reconciliation in Divided Societies*. Discuss these with friends or your small group. Talking about such books with friends will enhance your experience and expand your own imagination.
- Enroll in a peace studies or conflict transformation course at a local college or university. These programs have multiplied over recent years. Degrees are available at all academic levels.

Part 4: Pulling Levers of Change
Advocates

- Join Amnesty International and write monthly letters in support of prisoners of conscience. For information go to: www.amnestyusa.org.

- Join Human Rights Watch, obtain their reports, and support their advocacy efforts. For information go to: www.hrw.org.

- For those in the United States, write your Senators or Representatives about a peace issue of special concern to you and of timely significance. Always write courteous letters, and you may wish to ask for a response. Almost all members of Congress have e-mail and can be contacted through their websites. You can find a listing of all the U.S. Senators and their contact information at: www.senate.gov. A similar listing for the U.S. House of Representatives is: www.house.gov. Letters can be more effective than e-mails and can be posted to the following addresses:

- Become active in local political organizations, and advocate about peace and justice issues.

- During election campaigns, host a candidates' night at your house, community center or religious community. Invite all candidates for a particular office to participate. Present them with specific questions related to pressing peace and justice issues. Publicize their responses in a post-event communication.

- Organize a home or group viewing of: *Pray the Devil Back to Hell*. The DVD can be obtained at: www.praythedevilbacktohell.com/v3/

Part 5: Opening New Toolboxes
Trainers and Teachers

- Get involved in basic training through Training for Change: www.trainingforchange.org. Or, if you are deeply involved in peace and justice activism, you might want to attend the "Super-T," a series of four workshops lasting about 3 weeks.
- Invite Training for Change or some other organization that does training in peacemaking or social activism to your community. You can host a training session, which would include doing local advertising and recruiting of participants, finding a suitable facility for the training, and handling the logistics of holding such an event, including possible meals.
- Begin a "peace book club." Contact your local library or bookstore about this to invite their support, sponsorship and publicity.

Part 6: Making the Muscles Move
Organizers

- Begin a local peace group. Talk with your circle of friends to see if someone would be interested in connecting with you about a specific concern or issue. One simple first step is to gather for a weekly study or discussion. Do research about regional and national groups to develop affiliation support. You might find a group already organized nearby that you can join and help to expand—or you might organize a new chapter of a nearby group.

- Start a Facebook group to focus on an issue—the more specific, the better, so you are not duplicating other major causes.
- Begin a peace study group in your religious community. Study the teachings of the scriptures and your traditions that speak on themes of peace, justice, reconciliation, etc. Invite members of your local congregation to join in the study. Find a way to share what you have learned in a larger context.

Part 7: Midwives of Peace
Mediators

- Volunteer at a community mediation or restorative justice program. This could be in conjunction with a local court system for alternative dispute settlement, or it could be in a peace mediation program of a local school. Contact your local court or school system to see what programs (if any) are going on. Training is required for mediation facilitation, but the programs usually provide for the training of community facilitators.

Part 8: On the Front Line
Nonviolent Activists

- Join a local peace group, such as Women in Black at: http://www.womeninblack.org/en/vigil
- If you are a person of faith you could join a religious peace fellowship related to your faith tradition. You might start by considering these organizations:

- Subscribe to the newsletter "This Week in History": www.peacebuttons.info/index.htm. This newsletter is packed with the history of actions taken by activists throughout many struggles. You can also order many peace buttons and give them away. Wear one, and if someone comments, take it off and give it to the person.
- Wear a "peace" T-shirt. This may seem like a very small thing to do, but it gives visibility to people who are concerned about peace.
- Organize a group to watch "A Force More Powerful" together (perhaps in a series of sessions): http://www.aforcemorepowerful.org/ This documentary is made up of six half-hour segments that examine historical nonviolent movements: Gandhi's Salt March, the Nashville sit-ins during the U.S. civil rights movement, the Port Elizabeth struggle against apartheid in South Africa, Solidarity in Poland, the people of Denmark against the Nazis in World War II, and the movement in Chile to bring down the Pinochet dictatorship.

Part 9: Imagine!
Artists

- Organize a children's art or poetry fair on themes of peace. Contact your local library, public school, academic institution, city hall or religious community about hosting the fair and displaying the submissions.
- Organize an interreligious children's art fair on themes of peace and diversity. Set up a traveling exhibit of submissions that can be taken to the various participating religious congregations. Children could be given quilt squares on which to paint a peace

theme. The assembled quilt could then be taken to various public sites.

- Hold a community sing event at your home using the *Rise Up Singing* songbook: http://www.singout.org/rus.html.
- Hold a "Playing for Change" open house. Instructions for hosting an open house and resources can be found at: http://www.playingforchange.com/
- Make your own art inspired by a peacemaking theme or a story of one of these peacemakers. Write a story or poem, paint a picture, do a photo essay to their words or post something on YouTube.
- Work with a local theater group to host a peace-themed play or drama about peacemakers.

Acknowledgements

THE WRITING AND PUBLICATION of any book always involves far more people than just the author. I am especially grateful to David Crumm and John Hile of Read the Spirit Books for their work in editing, publishing and encouraging me in this project. This is now the third book we've done together, and I don't grow weary of working with such an affirming and competent team. Thanks also to copy editors Stephanie Fenton and Celeste Dykas, and graphic artists Rick Nease for the cover design and Brad Schreiber for his advice on page layout. Thanks also for the extra "eyes" in proofreading the final manuscript from cousins Jan Ackerson and Louise Eddington.

Ideas for peacemakers came from Fyodor Raychynets, Ken Sehested, and my son, Jon Buttry. Special thanks also to Richard Deats, Anatole Denisenko, Raymond Ker, Joan Jara, Liz MacAllister of Jonah House, Dwayne Shank of *Sojourners*, Fumi Johns Stewart of The World Peace Prayer Society, and Lucia Bruno of Pastors for Peace. I also profoundly appreciate the affirmations, clarifications and permissions of some of the peacemakers included here: James Lawson, Bernard Lafayette, Pete Seeger, John Paul Lederach, Mubarak Awad, George Lakey, Ouyporn Khuankaew, William Ury, Gila Svirsky, Erella Shadmi, Galla Golan, Ken Sehested, Wati Aier, Hizkias Assefa, Jan Krist and the late Lucius Walker before his death in 2010. They all provided invaluable help, and any errors that remain are my responsibility.

None of my writing projects would be possible without the constant love and encouragement of my wife, Sharon Buttry. She has shared many of my peacemaking experiences and the relationships with these fine people. She believes in what I am doing and is willing to pay the price of such peacemaking herself.

Sources

MANY SOURCES OF INFORMATION used in researching *Blessed Are the Peacemakers* are listed on the following pages. We are listing these sources partly to acknowledge our appreciation for other writers and online resources—and partly to guide readers to ways they can learn more about the peacemakers whom they find most interesting. Unless other permissions and sources are noted, photos used in the book are generally available in public domain.

Introduction

- King, Martin Luther, Jr. (1964). *Why We Can't Wait.* Penguin Books
- Ross, Will. Healing scars of Kenyan violence. *BBC News*: www.news.bbc.co.uk/2/hi/africa/8198171.stm

Prophets and Visionaries

- Deganawida. *Encyclopedia of World Biography*: www.bookrags.com/biography/deganawida/
- Ellsberg, Robert. (2002). *All Saints: Daily Reflections on Saints, Prophets, and Witnesses for Our Time.* The Crossroad Publishing Company
- Jamboree: www.jamboree.freedom-in-education.co.uk/real_history/hiawatha_deganawida.htm
- Wikipedia

Mohandas Gandhi

- Ellsberg, Robert. (2002). *All Saints: Daily Reflections on Saints, Prophets, and Witnesses for Our Time.* The Crossroad Publishing Company
- Fisher, Louis. (1962). *The Essential Gandhi.* Random House
- Sharp, Gene. (1973). *The Politics of Nonviolence.* Porter Sargent Publisher

Dorothy Day

- Buttry, Daniel L. *Interfaith Heroes 2.* Text adapted from the chapter on Dorothy Day. *ReadTheSpirit*
- Ellsberg, Robert. (2002). *All Saints: Daily Reflections on Saints, Prophets, and Witnesses for Our Time.* The Crossroad Publishing Company
- Forest, Jim. A Biography of Dorothy Day. *The Catholic Worker*: www.catholicworker.org/dorothyday/
- *Milwaukee Journal,* use under Creative Commons: www.flickr.com/photos/78953420@N00/2251717957
- Randall, Beth. Illuminating Lives: Dorothy Day
- Schreiber, Le Anne. (December 22, 1982). Review of Breaking Bread: The Catholic Worker and the Origin of Catholic Radicalism in America by Mel Piehl, *New York Times*
- *The Catholic Worker*: www.catholicworker.org
- Wikipedia
- Photo: Courtesy of the Marquette University Archives

Martin Luther King, Jr.

- Biography in Context (formerly Biography Resource Center). Black History Month, Gale Cengage Learning: www.gale.cengage.com/free_resources/bhm/bio/king_m.htm

- Branch, Taylor. (1988). *Parting the Waters: America in the King Years, 1954-63*. Simon & Schuster
- Dekar, Paul. (1993) *For the Healing of the Nations: Baptist Peacemakers*. Macon, Georgia: Smyth & Helwys Publishing
- Ellsberg, Robert. (2002). *All Saints: Daily Reflections on Saints, Prophets, and Witnesses for Our Time*. The Crossroad Publishing Company
- King, Martin Luther, Jr. (1964). *Why We Can't Wait*. Penguin Books
- King, Martin Luther, Jr. (1963). *Strength to Love*. Fortress Press
- Nobel Foundation: nobelprize.org/nobel_prizes/ peace/laureates/1964/king.html
- Washington, James M. (Ed.). (1986). *A Testament of Hope: The Essential Writings and Speeches of Martin Luther King, Jr.* HarperCollins

Masahisa Goi

- Byakko Shinko Kai: www.byakko.org/1_about/goi/ index.html
- Peace Pole Makers USA: www.peacepoles.com
- World Peace Prayer Society: www.worldpeace.org
- Peace Pole Image: Courtesy of The World Peace Prayer Society: www.worldpeace.org/gallery_pp_project. html#
- Photo: Courtesy of The World Peace Prayer Society: www.byakko.org/1_about/goi/index.html

Helen Caldicott

- Australian Broadcasting Corporation: www.abc.net. au/schoolstv/australians/caldicott.htm

- Hughes, Dennis. An Interview with Helen Caldicott, MD. *The Share Guide*: www.shareguide.com/Caldicott.html
- *Los Angeles City Beat*: www.lacitybeat.com/cms/story/detail/?id=5227&IssueNum=198
- Nobel Foundation: nobelprize.org/nobel_prizes/peace/laureates/1985/physicians.html
- Women's Action for New Directions: www.wand.org/about/brief-history-of-wand/
- Women's International Center: www.wic.org/bio/caldicot.htm
- www.helencaldicott.com

Dalai Lama

- Dalai Lama: www.dalailama.com
- Nobel Foundation: nobelprize.org/nobel_prizes/peace/laureates/1989/lama.html
- Universal Declaration of Nonviolence. Monastic Interreligious Dialogue website: www.monasticdialog.com/a.php?id=689
- Photo: www.buddhismus.at/service/serv6.htm, released into public domain by buddhismus.at

Desmond Tutu

- Allen, John. (2006). *Desmond Tutu: Rabble-Rouser for Peace*. Lawrence Hill Books
- Nobel Foundation: nobelprize.org/nobel_prizes/peace/laureates/1984/tutu.html
- Tutu, Desmond. (2007). *Believe: The Words and Inspiration of Desmond Tutu*. Blue Mountain Press
- Tutu, Desmond. (1999). *No Future Without Forgiveness*. Doubleday

Jim Wallis

- Boston Pledge of Resistance: Records, 1983-1990, Joseph P. Healey Library. University of Massachusetts, Boston: www.lib.umb.edu/node/1551
- *Sojourners*: www.sojo.net
- Wilson, John. (June 14, 1999). Mr. Wallis Goes to Washington: The Transformation of an Evangelical Activist. *Christianity Today*
- Photo: Courtesy of *Sojourners*: www.sojo.net

Litany of Martyrs

- Ellsberg, Robert. (2002). *All Saints: Daily Reflections on Saints, Prophets, and Witnesses for Our Time.* The Crossroad Publishing Company

Anne Frank

- Anne Frank Museum, Amsterdam: www.annefrank.org
- Ellsberg, Robert. (2002). *All Saints: Daily Reflections on Saints, Prophets, and Witnesses for Our Time.* The Crossroad Publishing Company
- Frank, Anne, *The Diary of Anne Frank*

Victor Jara

- Cantor, Paul. *Who Killed Victor Jara?*: www.counterpunch.org/cantor08282008.html
- Jara, Joan. *Three Chapters from Victor: An Unfinished Song*: www.historyisaweapon.com/defcon1/jaraunfinsong.html
- Wikipedia
- Photo: By Antonio Larrea, Brigadistas de la Memoria Popular, Wikipedia Commons

Stephen Biko

- Biko, Stephen. (1986). *I Write What I Like*. Harper and Row
- Boddy-Evans, Alistair. *Stephen Bantu (Steve) Biko: Founder and martyr of the Black Consciousness movement in South Africa*. About.com: African History: africanhistory.about.com/od/stevebiko/a/bio-Biko.htm
- Ellsberg, Robert. (2002). *All Saints: Daily Reflections on Saints, Prophets, and Witnesses for Our Time*. The Crossroad Publishing Company
- Kgokong, Mpotseng Jairus. Bantu Stephen Biko. *ChickenBones: A Journal*: www.nathanielturner.com/bantustephenbiko.htm
- South African History Online: www.sahistory.org.za/pages/people/bios/biko-s.htm
- Woods, Donald. (1987). *Biko*. Henry Holt
- Photo: www.voordorpvooruit.nl/straatnamen/strijders/Steve%20Biko/biko_steve.jpg

Rutulio Grande and Oscar Romero

- Brockman, James R. (1989). *Romero, A Life: The Essential Biography of a Modern Martyr and Christian Hero*. Orbis Books
- Ellsberg, Robert. (2002) *All Saints: Daily Reflections on Saints, Prophets, and Witnesses for Our Time*. The Crossroad Publishing Company
- Lamperti, John. *Father Rutilio Grande, Another Salvadoran 'Revolutionary'*. Article formerly on the web at: fssca.net/pastreports/rutilio/rutilio2007.html
- Lernoux, Penny. (1980). *Cry of the People*. Doubleday
- O'Malley, William J. S.J. (1980). *The Voice of Blood: Five Christian Martyrs of Our Time*. Orbis Books

- Photo of Oscar Romero: www.newmancentre.org

Jerzy Popiełuszko

- *BBC World News, On This Day*: news.bbc.co.uk/onthisday/hi/dates/stories/october/30/newsid_4111000/4111722.stm
- Theophilus, G.J.B. The Martyrdom of Fr. Jerzy Popiełuszko in *Martyrs in the History of Christianity*. Ed. Franklyn J. Balasundaram for Religion-Online: www.religion-online.org/showchapter.asp?title=1570&C=1479
- Wikipedia

Peace Theorists

- Ellsberg, Robert. (2002). *All Saints: Daily Reflections on Saints, Prophets, and Witnesses for Our Time*. The Crossroad Publishing Company
- Gorenberg, Gershom. (April 6, 2009). The Missing Mahatma: Searching for a Gandhi or a Martin Luther King in the West Bank. *The Weekly Standard*
- Pruitt, Dean G. (July 1986). Trends in the Scientific Study of Negotiation and Mediation. *Negotiation Journal, Vol. 2, No. 3*
- U.S. Institute of Peace: www.usip.org

Paolo Freire

- Critical Pedagogy on the Web: mingo.info-science.uiowa.edu/~stevens/critped/freire.htm
- INFED: www.infed.org/thinkers/et-freir.htm
- National-Louis University: www..nl.edu/academics/cas/ace/resources/paulofreire.cfm
- Paolo Freire Institute, UCLA: www.paulofreireinstitute.org/

- Photo: by Slobodan Dmitrov, under Wikipedia Commons

Gustavo Gutiérrez

- Answers.Com: www.answers.com/topic/ gustavo-guti-rrez
- Gutiérrez, Gustavo. (1973). *A Theology of Liberation: History, Politics and Salvation.* Orbis Books
- Hartnett, Daniel, S.J. Remembering the Poor: An Interview with Gustavo Gutiérrez. *America The National Catholic Weekly*: www.americamagazine.org/ content/article.cfm?article_id=2755
- Lernoux, Penny. (1980). *Cry of the People.* Doubleday

William Ury

- Fisher, Roger & Ury, William. (1981). *Getting to YES: Negotiating Agreement Without Giving In.* Penguin Books
- Program on Negotiation, Harvard University: www. pon.harvard.edu/about/
- Ury, William. (1999). *Getting to Peace: Transforming Conflict at Home, at Work, and in the World.* Viking Penguin
- William Ury: www.williamury.com/
- Photo: www.williamury.com/ by Carl Studna, used by permission

Gene Sharp

- Albert Einstein Institution: www.aeinstein.org
- Canadian Centers for Teaching Peace. *Gene Sharp: A Biographical Profile*: www.peace.ca/genesharp.htm
- Gene Sharp. (February 16, 2007). Master of Nonviolent Warfare. *Guerillas Without Guns*:

guerillas-without-guns.blogspot.com/2007/02/gene-sharp-master-of-nonviolent-warfare.html
- Pal, Amitabh. (March 2007). Gene Sharp Interview. *The Progressive*
- Shanahan, Noreen. The NI Interview: Gene Sharp. *The New Internationalist*: www.newint.org/issue296/interview.htm
- Stolberg, Sheryl Gay. (February 16, 2011). Shy U.S. Intellectual Created Playbook Used in a Revolution. *The New York Times*
- Wikipedia
- Author's personal conversations with Gene Sharp
- Photo: from Albert Einstein Institution: www.aeinstein.org

John Paul Lederach

- Johnston, Douglas & Sampson, Cynthia. (1994). *Religion: The Missing Dimension of Statecraft*. Oxford University Press
- Lederach, John Paul. (1999). *The Journey Toward Reconciliation*. Herald Press
- Lederach, John Paul. (1997). *Building Peace: Sustainable Reconciliation in Divided Societies*. U.S. Institute of Peace
- Lederach, John Paul. (1995). *Preparing for Peace: Conflict Transformation Across Cultures*. Syracuse University Press
- Wright, Walter A. *John Paul Lederach: A Peacebuilder Bibliography*. Mediate.com: www.mediate.com/articles/wrightW2.cfm
- Author's personal conversations with John Paul Lederach

- Photo: Matt Cashore, University of Notre Dame, used by permission

Advocates

- Americans Who Tell the Truth: www.americanswhotellthetruth.org
- Ellsberg, Robert. (2002). *All Saints: Daily Reflections on Saints, Prophets, and Witnesses for Our Time.* The Crossroad Publishing Company
- International Campaign to Ban Landmines: www.icbl.org

Frederick Douglass

- Americans Who Tell the Truth: www.americanswhotellthetruth.org
- Frederick Douglass. PBS: www.pbs.org/wgbh/aia/part4/4p1539.html
- *The Life of Frederick Douglass.* National Park Service: www.nps.gov/archive/frdo/fdlife.htm
- Thomas, Sandra. *A biography of the life of Frederick Douglass:* www.history.rochester.edu/class/douglass/home.html
- Photo: Public Domain: National Archives and Records Administration, # 558770

Jeannette Rankin

- Americans Who Tell the Truth: www.americanswhotellthetruth.org
- Jeannette Rankin Peace Center: www.jrpc.org/about_jrpc/jeannette_who.html
- Lewis, Jone Johnson. Jeannette Rankin. About.com, Women's History: womenshistory.about.com/od/congress/a/jeanette_rankin.htm

- Wikipedia

Peter Benenson

- Amnesty International: www.amnestyusa.org/about-us/peter-benenson-remembered/page.do?id=1101182
- Death of Amnesty International Founder. (February 26, 2005). Amnesty International Press Release
- Nobel Foundation: nobelprize.org/nobel_prizes/peace/laureates/1977/amnesty.html
- *Time*, Europe Edition: www.time.com/time/europe/hero2006/benenson.html
- Wikipedia
- Photo: www.britannica.com/EBchecked/topic-art/21127/

Alison Des Forges

- Alison Des Forges. (February 19, 2009). *The Economist*
- Chan, Sewell & Hevesi, Dennis. (February 14, 2009). Alison Des Forges, 66, Human Rights Advocate, Dies. *The New York Times*
- Ghosts of Rwanda. *Frontline* interview of Alison Des Forges: www.pbs.org/wgbh/pages/frontline/shows/ghosts/interviews
- Human Rights Watch: www.hrw.org/en/news/2009/02/13
- Photo: Human Rights Watch: www.fray.slate.com/id/2211384/

Shirin Ebadi

- Bergland, Nina. Peace Prize Winner in Oslo Spotlight. *Aftenposten,* English Web Desk: www.thewe.cc/

contents/more/archive/december2003/shirin_edabi_peace_prize_winner.htm

- Casey, Maura J. (February 7, 2007). Challenging the Mullahs, One Signature at a Time. *The New York Times*
- Nobel Foundation: nobelprize.org/nobel_prizes/peace/laureates/2003/ebadi.html
- Solholm, Rolleiv. (December 10, 2003). Shirin Ebadi to receive the Nobel Peace Prize Wednesday. *Norway Post*
- Wikipedia
- Photo: by Shahram Sharif, under Wikipedia Commons

Leymah Gbowee

- Center for American Progress: www.americanprogress.org/events/2008/11/inf/GboweeLeymah.html
- Gbowee, Leymah. Acceptance Speech. John F. Kennedy Library Foundation: www.jfklibrary.org/Education+and+Public+Programs/Profile+in+Courage+Award/Award+Recipients/Leymah+Gbowee+and+the+Women+of+Liberia/Acceptance+Speech+by+Leymah+Gbowee.htm
- Herbert, Bob. (January 31, 2009). A Crazy Dream. *New York Times*
- Hunt Alternatives Fund: www.huntalternatives.org/pages/7352_leymah_gbowee.cfm
- Pray the Devil Back to Hell. Fork Films, produced by Abigail E. Disney and Gini Reticker
- WIPSEN Africa: www.wipsen-africa.org
- Photo: Michael Angelo, www.praythedevilbacktohell.com/press/files/

Color_portrait_Leymah_Gbowee_2330x3495_credit_
Michael_Angelo_for_Wonderland.jpg

Trainers and Teachers

- Eiben, Vicky. The Folk School Tradition. The Driftless Folk School

Myles Horton

- Ball, Glen M. Highland Folk School. *The Tennessee Encyclopedia of History and Culture*: tennesseeencyclopedia.net/imagegaller. php?EntryID=H048
- Eiben, Vicky. The Folk School Tradition. The Driftless Folk School
- Highlander Research and Educational Center: www. highlandercenter.org/about.asp
- Seeger, Pete, & Reiser, Bob. (1989) *Everybody Says Freedom: A History of the Civil Rights Movement in Songs and Pictures*. W.W. Norton & Co.
- Wikipedia
- Photo by Cappy Coates: Courtesy of the Highlander Research and Education Center

James Lawson

- Halberstam, David. (1998). *The Children*. Random House,
- Swomley, John M. (2003). James Lawson, a Living Civil Rights Hero. Human Quest, July/August
- This Far by Faith. PBS: www.pbs.org/thisfarbyfaith/ witnesses/james_lawson.html
- *Vanderbilt's most famous expellee settles back on campus*. Vanderbilt University: www. vanderbilt.edu/news/releases/2006/10/25/

vanderbilts-most-famous-expellee-settles-back-on-campus-civil-rights-leader-james-lawson-teaching-and-writing-in-nashville.58847

- Author's personal conversations with James Lawson
- Photo: Joon Powell, Creative Commons Attribution: commons.wikimedia.org/wiki/File:Jameslawson.jpg

Hildegard Goss-Mayr and Jean Goss

- Deats, Richard. (2009). *Marked for Life: The Story of Hildegard Goss-Mayr*. New City Press
- Photo: Courtesy of Richard Deats and the Fellowship of Reconciliation USA Archives

George Lakey

- Bischoff, Michael. An Interview with George Lakey. Spirit in Conflict: www.clarityfacilitation.com/papers/george.html
- Training for Change website: www.trainingforchange.org
- Vesely-Flad, Ethan. *George Lakey: strategic campaigner & recipient of the 2008 Dr. King Peace Prize*. Blog of Fellowship of Reconciliation: www.forpeace.net/blog
- Author's personal conversations with George Lakey
- Photo: John Mayer, courtesy of George Lakey

Mubarak Awad

- A Victory within Ourselves: An Interview with Mubarak Awad. *Sojourners*, January 1989
- Gorenberg, Gershom. (April 6, 2009). The Missing Mahatma: Searching for a Gandhi or a Martin Luther King in the West Bank. *The Weekly Standard*

- Schiff, Ze'ev & Ya'ari, Ehud. (1989). *Intifada:The Palestinian Uprising-Israel's Third Front*. Touchstone Books
- *SourceWatch*: www.sourcewatch.org
- Wikipedia
- Photo: Courtesy of Mubarak Awad

Ouyporn Khuankaew

- A Fighting Chance. *The Bangkok Post*, August 26, 2008
- Khuankaew, Ouyporn. *Feminism and Buddhism: A Reflection through Personal Life & Working Experiences*: www.bpf.org/tsangha/ouyporn.html
- Khuankaew, Ouyporn. *Buddhism and Domestic Violence: Creative Responses to Karmic Fatalism*: www.bpf.org/tsangha/tsm03report/Karma%20Book/gender.html
- Outstanding Women in Buddhism Award, 2006 Award Recipients: www.owbaw.org/2006.htm
- Summers, Jeanne Matthews. Ouyporn Khuankaew, Women's Partnership for Peace and Justice in Thailand: www.warren-wilson.edu/~religion/thailand/ouyporn.shtml
- Photo: Courtesy of Ouyporn Khuankaew

Organizers

- Levy, Jacques E. (2007). *Cesar Chavez: Autobiography of La Causa*. University of Minnesota Press

Thomas Clarkson

- Carey, Brycchan: www.brycchancarey.com/abolition/clarkson.htm

- Hochschild, Adam. (2005). *Bury the Chains: Prophets and Rebels in the Fight to Free an Empire's Slaves.* Houghton Mifflin
- Painting by Carl Frederik von Breda at the National Portrait Gallery, public domain

Ella Baker

- Americans Who Tell the Truth: www.americanswhotellthetruth.org/pgs/portraits/Ella_Baker.php
- Olson, Lynne. (2001). *Freedom's Daughters: The Unsung Heroines of the Civil Rights Movement from 1830 to 1970.* Simon & Schuster
- The Ella Baker Center for Human Rights: www.ellabakercenter.org/page.php?pageid=19&contentid=9
- Wikipedia
- Photo: theatreforthefreepeople.files.wordpress.com/2009/02/ellabaker21.jpg

Bernard Lafayette

- Halberstam, David. (1998). *The Children.* Random House
- Gentile, Greg. Civil Rights reflections, lessons from Bernard Lafayette Jr. *The Good 5¢ Cigar*: media. www.ramcigar.com/media/storage/paper366/news/2008/11/14/News/Civil.Rights.Reflections.Lessons.From.Bernard.Lafayette.Jr.Available.On.Tape.Fo-3544703.shtml
- Middebury College: cfm40.middlebury.edu/node/497?PHPSESSID=8f2b31c7a9fbe8ddb51a15b59e727635
- True, Michael. *INTRODUCTION: Dr. Bernard Lafayette*: supportcom.com/PEP/www.pepeace.org/current_reprints/06/lafayette-bio.htm

- Author interview with Bernard Lafayette
- Photo: Courtesy of Bernard Lafayette: www.uri.edu/mcc/DiversityAwards/2005/image/lafay.png

César Chávez

- Ellsberg, Robert. (2002). *All Saints: Daily Reflections on Saints, Prophets, and Witnesses for Our Time.* The Crossroad Publishing Company
- Levy, Jacques E. (2007). *Cesar Chavez: Autobiography of La Causa.* University of Minnesota Press
- www.readthespirit.com/explore/2011/4/1/celebrating-cesar-chavez-with-his-prayer-for-workers.html
- Photo: en.wikipedia.org/wiki/File:Cesar_chavez_crop2.jpg, by Joel Levine under Wikipedia Commons

Adolfo Pérez Esquivel

- Adolfo Pérez Esquivel: *1931—: Artist, Activist Biography*: biography.jrank.org/pages/3971/P-rez-Esquivel-Adolfo-1931-Artist-Activist.html
- Esquivel, Adolfo Pérez. (1983). *Christ in a Poncho: Witnesses to the Nonviolent Struggles in Latin America.* Orbis Books
- McManus, Philip & Schlabach, Gerald (Co-ed.). (1991). *Relentless Persistence: Nonviolent Action in Latin America.* New Society Publishers
- Nobel Foundation: nobelprize.org/nobel_prizes/peace/laureates/1980/esquivel.html
- *SGI Quarterly*: www.sgiquarterly.org/global2008Oct-1.html
- Photo: Wikipedia Commons

Ken Sehested

- Baptist Peace Fellowship of North America: www. bpfna.org
- Global Baptist Peace Conference: www. globalbaptistpeace.org
- *Prayer & Politiks*: prayerandpolitiks.com/
- Author's personal conversations with Ken Sehested
- Photo: www.anderson.edu/chapel/sehested.html, used with permission

Lucius Walker

- Cuba Solidarity: www.cubasolidarity.net/pastors.html
- *Escambray*. Digital newspaper of Sancti Spiritus province, Cuba: www.escambray.cu/Eng/news/ Cpastorblockade0907281115.htm
- Interreligious Foundation for Community Organization/Pastors for Peace: www.ifconews.org
- *SourceWatch*: www.sourcewatch.org/index. php?title=Lucius_Walker._Jr.
- Author's personal conversations with Lucius Walker
- Photo: Courtesy of Pastors for Peace

Teresita "Ging" Quintos-Deles

- Center for Asia-Pacific Women in Politics: www. capwip.org/resources/leaders/phil.htm
- Garcia, Ed (Ed.). (1994). *Pilgrim Voices: Citizens as Peacemakers*. Ateneo de Manila University Press
- GasWikiPhilipinas: en.wikipilipinas.org/index. php?title=Teresita_Quintos-Deles
- *People Building Peace: 35 Inspiring Stories from Around the World*, European Center for Conflict Prevention, 1999: www.gppac.net/documents/pbp/2/4_contin.htm

- Sicam, Paulynn P. & Tripon, Olivia H. (2006). *Filipino Peace Women*. Anvil Publishing
- Photo: Dan Buttry

Mayerly Sánchez

- Carrillo, Pablo & Homer, Karen. (July 24, 1998). Peacemaking in Colombia: A Nobel Cause. *World Vision Today*
- Carter, L. Randolph and Shipler, Michael. (2005). And a Child Shall Lead: The Children's Movement for Peace and Return to Happiness in Colombia. *People Building Peace II: Successful Stories of Civil Society*, Paul van Tongeren, Malin Brenk, Marte Hellema, & Juliette Verhoevern (Ed.). European Centre for Conflict Prevention
- Colombian Youth for Peace: www.colombianyouthforpeace.org
- Pearl, Mariane. (June 2007). Global Diary: A Child of War, Building Peace. *Glamour*
- Sellers, Jeff M. (December 3, 2001). A Child Shall Lead Them. *Christianity Today*
- Photo: Colombian Youth for Peace: www.colombianyouthforpeace.org

Mediators

- Ellsberg, Robert. (2002). *All Saints: Daily Reflections on Saints, Prophets, and Witnesses for Our Time*. The Crossroad Publishing Company
- Kraft, Barbara. (1978). *Peace Ship: Henry Ford's Pacifist Adventure in the First World War*
- The Corrymeela Community website: www.corrymeela.org

- Wells, Ronald A. (1999). *People Behind the Peace: Community and Reconciliation in Northern Ireland.* Wm. B. Eerdmans Pub. Co.

Adam Curle

- Adam Curle Obituary. University of Bradford: www. bradac.uk
- Mitchels Barbara. Adam Curle 1916-2006: www. latinovac.org/skakljikas/?p=16
- Sampson, Cynthia. (1994). 'To Make Real the Bond Between Us All': Quaker Conciliation During the Nigerian Civil War. *Religion, the Missing Dimension of Statecraft.* Douglas Johnston & Cynthia Sampson, (Co-ed.). Oxford University Press
- Woodhouse, Tom. (October 4, 2006). Adam Curle: Quaker and pioneer of peace studies in Britain. *The Guardian*
- Photo: Bradford University: www.brad.ac.uk/acad/ peace/images/adam_curle_2001.jpg

Óscar Arias Sánchez

- Arias, Oscar. (July 9, 2009). The Perils of Latin America's Oversized Militaries. *The Washington Post*
- Missouri Southern State College: www.mssu.edu/ International/Latinam/arias.htm
- Nobel Foundation: nobelprize.org/nobel_prizes/ peace/laureates/1987/arias.html
- *The Boston Globe* Archive: www.boston.com/globe/ search/stories/nobel/1987/1987h.html
- Wikipedia

Carl Upchurch

- *Carl Upchurch, 1950-2003: In Memoriam.* www.carlupchurch.org
- Kelly, T. L. (2004). The Theme of Transformation in the Work of Carl Upchurch. *New Tomorrow: A Voice for Blacks and Latinos.* New York: Alberto O. Cappas, Publ. From a graduate paper, Portland State University, June 1999. Portland, OR: web.pdx.edu/~psu17799/upchurch.htm
- Upchurch, Carl, *Convicted in the Womb*, Bantam Books, 1996
- Urban Peace, Justice and Empowerment Summit 2008: urbanpeacejustice.com
- Author's personal conversations with Carl Upchurch
- Photo: Urban Peace, Justice and Empowerment Summit: urbanpeacejustice.com/home/?p=15

Jimmy Carter

- Carter, Jimmy. (1982). *Keeping Faith: Memoirs of a President.* Bantam Books
- Jimmy Carter Center: www.cartercenter.org
- Nobel Foundation: nobelprize.org/nobel_prizes/peace/laureates/2002/carter.html

Wati Aier

- Aier, Wati. Naga Reconciliation: A Journey of Common Hope. Unpublished speech
- Arriens, Jan. (September 19, 2008). Accompanying the Peacebuilders. *The Friend*
- The Morung Express: www.morungexpress.com
- Author's personal conversations with Wati Aier
- Photo: Dan Buttry

Hizkias Assefa

- Assefa, Hizkias. (March/April, 2003). Critical Perspectives on Peace Theories and Practice. *New Routes*
- Garcia, Ed. (Ed.) (1994). *Pilgrim Voices: Citizens as Peacemakers.* Ateneo de Manila University
- Heroes for a Culture of Peace: www.peacekids.net/heroes/pages-a/assefa-quotes.htm
- Peacebuilder program at Eastern Mennonite University, fall/winter 2008: issuu.com/easternmennoniteuniversity/docs/peacebuilder_fall_08/18
- www.zoominfo.com/people/Assefa_Hizkias_415808225.aspx
- *People Building Peace: 35 Inspiring Stories from Around the World*, European Center for Conflict Prevention, 1999
- Photo: Courtesy of Hizkias Assefa

Nonviolent Activists

- Americans Who Tell the Truth: www.americanswhotellthetruth.org
- Ellsberg, Robert. (2002). *All Saints: Daily Reflections on Saints, Prophets, and Witnesses for Our Time.* The Crossroad Publishing Company
- Nobel Foundation: nobelprize.org/nobel_prizes/peace/laureates/1960/lutuli.html

Abdul Ghaffar Khan

- Easwaran, Eknath. (1984). *A Man to Match His Mountains: Badshah Khan, Nonviolent Soldier of Islam.* Peteluma, California: Nilgiri Press

Diane Nash

- Dukes, Howard. The Daring of Nonviolence: Civil Rights Activist Diane Nash Is Sure It Has Power to Disarm Injustice. Common Dreams.org: www.commondreams.org/headlines05/0116-05.htm
- Halberstam, David, (1998). *The Children*. Random House
- Olson, Lynne. (2001). *Freedom's Daughters: The Unsung Heroines of the Civil Rights Movement from 1830 to 1970*. Simon & Schuster
- Author's conversations with James Lawson

John Lewis

- Halberstam, David. (1998). *The Children*. Random House
- Holmes, Marian Smith. (February, 2009). The Freedom Riders. *Smithsonian*
- Office of Congressman John Lewis: johnlewis.house.gov

Bolivian Women Hunger Strikers: Nellie Paniagua, Angélica Flores, Aurora Lee, Luzmila Pimentel

- Boots, Wilson T. (1991). Miracle in Bolivia: Four Women Confront a Nation. *Relentless Persistence: Nonviolent Action in Latin America*. Philip McManus & Gerald Schlabach, (Co-ed.). New Society Publishers
- Johansen, Ruthann Knechel. (July, 1978). Giving Birth to a New World. Speech at Manchester College: globalwomensproject.wordpress.com/giving-birth-to-a-new-world/

- Salina, Gloria Ardaya. (1994). Women and Politics: Gender Relations in Bolivian Political Organizations and Labor Unions. in *Women and Politics Worldwide.* Barbara J. Nelson & Najma Chowdhury, (Co-ed.) Yale University Press

Daniel Berrigan, Philip Berrigan

- Hedges, Chris. (May 20, 2008). Daniel Berrigan: Forty Years After Catonsville. *The Nation*
- Holy Outlaw: Lifelong Peace Activist Father Daniel Berrigan Turns 85. Democracy Now! The War and Peace Report, June 8, 2006
- Jonah House: www.jonahhouse.org/danProfile.htm
- Katzberg, Joyce. *Philip Berrigan – Presenté!* CommonDreams.org: www.commondreams.org/views02/1230-05.htm
- Religion: A Marriage of True Minds. *Time*, June 4, 1973
- Remembering Peace Veteran Phil Berrigan (1923-2002). Democracy Now! The War and Peace Report, May 26, 2003
- Wikipedia
- Photo: Courtesy of Jonah House: www.jonahhouse.org/pics67-73.htm

Mothers of the Plaza De Mayo

- Asociasión Madres de Plaza de Mayo: www.madres.org/
- Esquivel, Adolfo Pérez. (1983). *Christ in a Poncho: Witnesses to the Nonviolent Struggles in Latin America.* Orbis Books
- International Museum of Women: www.imow.org/wpp/stories/viewStory?storyId=1106

- McManus, Philip & Schlabach, Gerald. Co-ed. (1991). *Relentless Persistence: Nonviolent Action in Latin America.* New Society Publishers
- Omang, Joanne. (March 23, 2006). Looking for Answers in Argentina. *The Nation*
- Women in World History: www.womeninworldhistory. com/contemporary-07.html
- Photo: Courtesy of Raymond Ker, Cape Town, South Africa

Lech Wałęsa

- Ash, Timothy Garton. Lech Walesa: Poland's brash union organizer stood up to the Kremlin and dealt the Eastern bloc a fatal blow. *Time,* The Time 100: 205.188.238.181/time/time100/leaders/profile/walesa. html
- Kreis, Steve. Lech Walesa: www.historyguide.org/ europe/walesa.html
- Nobel Foundation: nobelprize.org/nobel_prizes/ peace/laureates/1983/walesa.html
- Photo: by Sławic, Wikipedia Commons

Maha Ghosananda

- Garcia, Ed (Ed.). (1994). *Pilgrim Voices: Citizens as Peacemakers.* Ateneo de Manila University Press
- Preah Maha Ghosananda, Gandhi of Cambodia: www. ghosananda.org/bio_book.html
- Website of the Proposed Buddha Statue and Mausoleum for Samdech Preah Maha Ghosananda Var Yav: www.mahaghosananda.com
- Wikipedia
- Photo: Wikipedia Commons

Women in Black

- Svirsky, Gila. *Women in Black: A Book.* Unpublished manuscript: www.gilasvirsky.com/wib_book.html
- Traubmann, Tamara. (March 18, 2008). Women in Black marks 20th year, but occupation continues. Ha Aretz: www.haaretz.com/hasen/spages/939707.html
- Wikipedia
- Women in Black: www.womeninblack.org
- Photo: www.flickr.com/photos/davidmasters/3077382294/ (Google Advanced Search as labeled for commercial reuse)

Artists

- Americans Who Tell the Truth: www.americanswhotellthetruth.org
- Dick Gregory: www.dickgregory.com
- Headlam, Bruce. (March 14, 2009). For Him, the Political Has Always Been Comical. *The New York Times*
- Playing for Change: www.playingforchange.com

Pete Seeger

- Americans Who Tell the Truth: www.americanswhotellthetruth.org/pgs/portraits/Pete_Seeger.php
- Pete Seeger: www.peteseeger.net/biograph.htm
- Rodgers, Jeffrey Pepper. (2002). How Can I Keep from Singing? Acoustic Guitar, July
- Seeger, Pete. How Waist Deep in the Big Muddy Finally Got on Network Television in 1968. From "Give Peace a Chance," a 1983 exhibit at the Peace Museum in Chicago

- Wilkinson, Alec. (April 17, 2006). The Protest Singer: Pete Seeger and American Folk Music. *The New Yorker*
- Author's correspondence with Pete Seeger
- Photo: Josef Schwartz, permission under Wikimedia Commons

Arnold Ap

- Black Paradise. *West Papua: Spirit of Mambesak.* CD booklet
- Budiardjo, Carmel (Oct-Dec, 2008). Arnold Ap and Theys Eluay: Political Assassinations Targeted West Papua's Culture and Political Identity. *Inside Indonesia, No. 94*: www.insideindonesia.org/content/view/1134/47/
- Kirksey, Eben. (April 2002). *Playing Up the Primitive.* New Internationalist: www.newint.org/issue344/playing.htm
- Rayfield, Alex. (April-June, 2004). Singing for Life. *Inside Indonesia, No. 78*: insideindonesia.org/content/view/234/29/
- Photo: Inside Indonesia: www.insideindonesia.org/content/view/1134/47/

Václav Havel

- Radio Prague: www.radio.cz/en/article/36022
- *ReasonOnline*: www.reason.com/news/show/28781.html
- Václav Havel: www.vaclavhavel.cz
- www.kirjasto.sci.fi/vhavel.htm

Vedran Smailović

- Chopra, Swat. The Cellist of Sarajevo. *Life Positive*: www.lifepositive.com/Mind/Positive_Chronicles/The_cellist_of_Sarajevo.asp
- Wikipedia
- Photo: Mikhail Evstafiev, Wikipedia Commons

Yuri Shevchuk

- DDT website: www.ddt.ru/
- Gaze, Novaya. (June 17, 2008). Patriotism is no fat yachts: en.novayagazeta.ru/data/2008/42/00.html
- Jackson, Patrick. (March 25, 2004). Russian Rock Band Keeps the Faith. *BBC World News*: news.bbc.co.uk/2/hi/entertainment/3568405.stm
- Russmus.net: www.russmus.net/band.jsp?band=Yuriy_Shevchuk
- Wikipedia
- Photo: Home English: www.homeenglish.ru/ArticlesShevchuk.htm

Zargana

- Arkar, Moe. (April 24, 2009). Imprisoned Zarganar in Failing Health. *The Irrawaddy*
- Harding, Andrew. (December 1, 2008). Burma: Zarganar Defies Junta. Unrepresented Nations and Peoples Organization
- Harding, Andrew. (September 25, 2006). Laughing in the Face of Danger. *BBC News*
- Jones, Clayton. (June 22, 1989). A Political Wit Stings a Dictator. *The Christian Science Monitor*
- Lintner, Bertil. (1989). *Outrage: Burma's Struggle for Democracy*. Review Publishing Company Limited

- Thi, Awzar. (June 5, 2008). *Cyclone Relief No Laughing Matter*. UPIASIA.com
- Stories from citizens of Myanmar told to the author
- Photo: www.irrawaddy.org/article.php?art_id=15530

Banksy

- Banksy. (2005). *Wall and Piece*. Century
- The Bristol graffiti artist with the international reputation. BBC: www.bbc.co.uk/bristol/content/articles/2008/04/04/banksy_feature.shtml
- Farag, Ines. (June 25, 2009). Nonviolent Action and Art. Nonviolence International newsletter
- Weburbanist.com: weburbanist.com/2008/09/07/banksy-art-and-graffiti-the-ultimate-guide/
- Wikipedia
- Photo: In the spirit of Banksy—who knows?

Bono

- @U2: www.atu2.com/band/bono/
- Cogan, Višnja. (2007). *U2: An Irish Phenomenon*. Pegasus Books
- The ONE Campaign: www.one.org
- Traub, James. (September 18, 2005). The Statesman. *The New York Times Magazine*
- U2. (2006). *U2 by U2*. Harper Collins
- U2 Website: www.u2.com
- White, Stella. (May 16, 2008). Rocking the Peace. *The Daily Mail*

Epilogue

- Krist, Jan. Hope: www.youtube.com/watch?v=dkJHxJteN6w
- Merton Thomas. *New Seeds of Contemplation*

- Wells, Ronald A. (1999). *People Behind the Peace: Community and Reconciliation in Northern Ireland.* Wm. B. Eerdmans Pub. Co.

Colophon

DAVID CRUMM MEDIA LLC produces ReadTheSpirit Books using innovative digital systems that serve the emerging wave of readers who want their books delivered in a wide range of formats—from traditional print to digital readers in many shapes and sizes. This book was produced using this entirely digital process that separates the core content of the book from details of final presentation, a process that increases the flexibility and accessibility of the book's text and images. At the same time, our system ensures a well-designed, easy-to-read experience on all reading platforms, built into the digital data file itself.

David Crumm Media has built a unique production workflow employing a number of XML (Extensible Markup Language) technologies. This workflow, designed by Publisher John Hile, allows us to create a single digital "book" data file that can be delivered quickly in all formats from traditionally bound print-on-paper to digital screens.

During production, we use Adobe InDesign®, <Oxygen/>® XML Editor and Microsoft Word® along with custom tools built in-house.

- The print edition is set in Minion Pro and Myriad Pro typefaces.
- Cover art and Design by Rick Nease: www.RickNease.com.
- Editing by David Crumm and Stephanie Fenton.
- Copy editing and XML styling by Celeste Dykas.
- Digital encoding and print layout by John Hile with design assistance from Brad Schreiber.

If you enjoyed this book, you might also enjoy

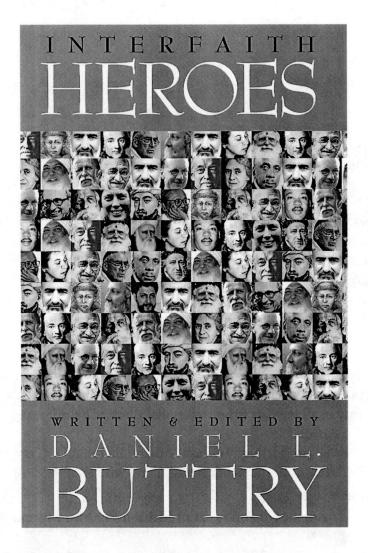

INTERFAITH HEROES

WRITTEN & EDITED BY

DANIEL L. BUTTRY

A Daily Reader of Inspirational Stories about Leaders Reaching Out to Spiritually Unite People and Build Stronger Communities.

http://www.ReadTheSpirit.com/Interfaith_Heroes/

ISBN: 978-1-934879-00-9

If you enjoyed this book, you might also enjoy

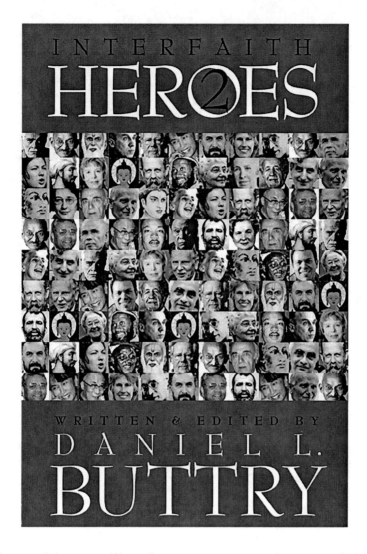

We need heroes like these now more than ever! Help us encourage people to reach out across boundaries of faith, ethnicity and race to build stronger communities.

http://www.ReadTheSpirit.com/Interfaith_Heroes/

ISBN: 978-1-934879-14-6

If you enjoyed this book, you might also enjoy

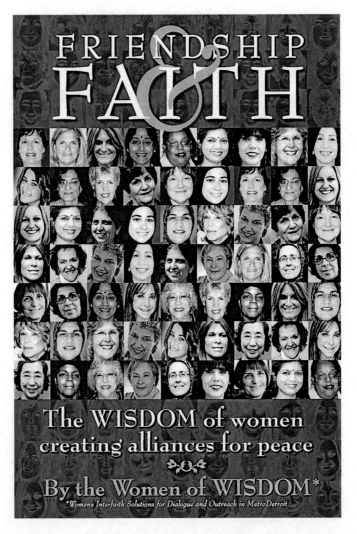

Finding a good friend is hard. Preserving a friendship across religious and cultural boundaries—a challenge we all face in our rapidly changing world—is even harder.

http://www.FriendshipAndFaith.com

ISBN: 978-1-934879-19-1

If you enjoyed this book, you might also enjoy

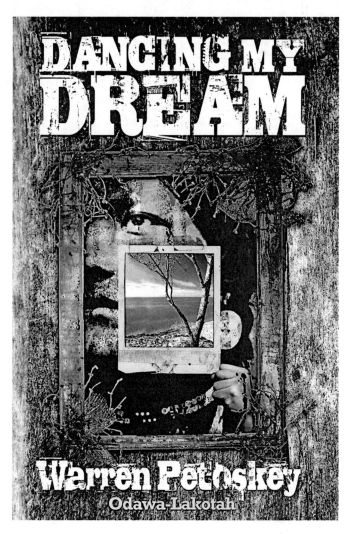

Dancing My Dream is my story of preserving Native American culture while living in three sometimes conflicting nations: Odawa (or Ottawa) and Lakotah—and as an American citizen as well.

http://www.DancingMyDream.info

ISBN: 978-1-934879-16-0